Toy Theory

Toy Theory

Technology and Imagination in Play

Seth Giddings

The MIT Press
Cambridge, Massachusetts
London, England

The MIT Press would like to thank the anonymous peer reviewers who provided comments on drafts of this book. The generous work of academic experts is essential for establishing the authority and quality of our publications. We acknowledge with gratitude the contributions of these otherwise uncredited readers.

This book was set in Stone Serif and Stone Sans by Westchester Publishing Services. Printed and bound in the United States of America.

Library of Congress Cataloging-in-Publication Data

Names: Giddings, Seth, author.
Title: Toy theory : technology and imagination in play / Seth Giddings.
Description: Cambridge, Massachusetts : The MIT Press, [2024] | Includes
    bibliographical references and index.
Identifiers: LCCN 2023054578 (print) | LCCN 2023054579 (ebook) |
    ISBN 9780262548212 (paperback) | ISBN 9780262379007 (epub) |
    ISBN 9780262379014 (pdf)
Subjects: LCSH: Toys. | Play. | Technology—Social aspects.
Classification: LCC GV1218.5 .G53 2024 (print) | LCC GV1218.5 (ebook) |
    DDC 790.1/33—dc23/eng/20240131
LC record available at https://lccn.loc.gov/2023054578
LC ebook record available at https://lccn.loc.gov/2023054579

10   9   8   7   6   5   4   3   2   1

Contents

Acknowledgments

The writing of this book was supported by my supportive and enthusiastic colleagues at Winchester School of Art, University of Southampton, including John Armitage, Dan Ashton, Miha Brebenel, Emma Reay, and Vanissa Wanick. Special thanks go to Megen de Bruin-Molé for her doll and transmedia expertise, Ryan Bishop for simulacral conversations, and Adam Procter for his endless creative and intellectual energy around play and technology. Students on the undergraduate Games Design and Art course have been a tolerant and gracious audience for my toy/game/intimate technology ramblings over a number of years, as have my recent PhD students, including Aybala Cakmakcioglu, Yijie Gao (Ink), Tianxiao Peng (Sky), and Samantha Schäfer. All have helped me keep in touch with recent developments and ideas in play, games and technology. I'm indebted to Jussi Parikka for his encouragement and feedback on the book planning and proposal. And many thanks to Dave Gibbons for his technical and aesthetic expertise in making many of the book's illustrations.

An early phase of the project included the preparation of a research network bid, which, although unsuccessful, involved a very productive workshop at WSA. I am deeply grateful to Paul Coulton, Andrew Manches, Jackie Marsh, Lydia Plowman, and Tara Woodyer, who contributed their time and expertise—our discussion significantly extended and shaped my approach to the book.

The chapter on "Construction Toys" was developed in part from a talk I gave in Cologne in 2018, many thanks to Hanns Christian Schmidt for both the invitation and our LEGO-related conversations. And to Andreas Lieberoth for the invitation to contribute to a PLAYTrack bootcamp on toy play and materiality at the Interacting Minds Centre at Aarhus University, also in 2018.

The "Cinema Toys" chapter is based on research conducted at the Bill Douglas Cinema Museum at the University of Exeter. The museum's curator, Dr. Phil Wickham, was an enthusiastic and deeply knowledgeable host. Tom Tyler has also been a generous and encouraging reader. Doug Sery at the MIT Press kickstarted the review process, and his successor, Noah Springer, has seen it through to publication with patience and sagacity.

Love and many thanks to Pen, whose contribution to this book has been an invaluable mix of research assistance, ideas, insights, memories—and patience with my lengthy musings over several years on the intricacies of doll mechanics and construction set semiotics.

Introduction

The End of Toys

If there is one factor above all others that epitomizes contemporary anxiety about a changing nature of childhood and children's play, it is technology. Free imaginative and outdoor play requires none of this technology, it is widely argued, and when indoors, children need only simple materials and objects with which to exercise their imaginations. Something very important is lost, it is assumed, when play—and, by extension, children's imaginative development—is mechanized and mediatized. Toy shop aisles are full of elaborately engineered devices and systems. Some might be recognizable to a time traveler from decades or centuries ago: dolls, vehicles, building blocks, balls, and hoops. For all their bright colors and specialized elements, the pieces in a *LEGO Dimensions* set would still be recognizable as toy building blocks. Although some of the specific imagery and storyworlds of contemporary LEGO media IP, including among many others *The Simpsons*, *Gremlins*, and *Star Wars*, would be novel even to the early LEGO players of the late 1950s (although not perhaps *Batman*, *Lord of the Rings*, and *Wizard of Oz*), there would be nothing fundamentally new or unfamiliar about the population of children's toys, games, and literature with fantastical and grotesque characters and dramas from popular culture and literature. In other ways, however, these boxes contain technologies undreamed of in the early to mid-twentieth century. The *LEGO Dimensions* player assembles a system from heterogeneous materials and devices: from actual plastic bricks, a videogame that virtualizes and animates these bricks and the characters and vehicles they construct, a backstory lending some coherence to the overall semiotic chaos, and RFID tags—radio frequency identification units recognized by a

USB "reader" connected to the player's videogame console. An RFID-enabled toy placed on the reader will trigger an event in the *LEGO Dimensions* videogame running on the console. Often, the character depicted by the toy itself will be doubled, an animated version appearing in the on-screen gameworld, manipulated now at one remove through the console controller rather than directly by the child's fingers.

Children's playful technoculture in the twenty-first century is popularly regarded as worrying: a world of solitary, addictive indoor games, awash with violent imagery or dangerous online threats. The transduction of the toy from tangible and manipulable object—whether through the open-ended and imaginative construction of LEGO microworlds or the toddler's intense connection to a favorite cuddly toy—to digitally constructed and animated characters on screen marks (it is assumed) a significant transformation of imaginative and physical play, one where the intensity of manufacturers' investment and marketing tactics is matched by prevailing fears about the future of play, even childhood itself.

When used in discussions about everyday life today, the term "technology" generally refers only to very recent devices and systems such as digital tablets, smartphones, videogame consoles, and software such as apps, social media platforms, and videogames. But games and play have always had their technologies and mechanisms. In the ancient world, Egyptian board game tokens and Roman knucklebones mechanized chance for ludic ends, externalizing mental operations of place holding and calculation in a play-driven prosthetics of memory and imagination. Today's commercial toy culture has its roots in eighteenth-century German artisanal manufacture, and the clockwork mechanisms and interactive paper engineering of Victorian toys and books are now seen as thoroughly charming rather than prescriptive and limiting to the imagination. Today, robots and balls, Barbies and LEGO, puzzles and game rules are all technical; all suggest particular games and modes of play and close off others. As I will argue throughout this book, however, the binary opposition between the "preferred" play, designed into toys and games by their manufacturers and marketers, and emergent or subversive play effected by children themselves should not be overstated. It underpins much of the critical study of toys and children's media culture but risks overlooking both the material and technical operations of play objects and the peculiar nature of children's play itself, in which ostensibly "conformist" play can prove on closer scrutiny to be much more complex. For example, a toy car, alongside its obvious use in the imaginative simulation of driving and racing, could be caught up in a narrative game, becoming an anthropomorphized character with a story and personality, or alternatively deployed as a missile in a playground game of destruction.[1] While no doubt most younger children do at times conjure up intense games with simple objects such as sticks, pebbles, and cardboard boxes, ethnographic studies suggest contemporary play is more often realized in a diverse range of imaginative, engineering, and experimental approaches to play with any and all materials to hand: domestic objects, "traditional" toys such as vehicles and dolls, media images and storybook characters, crayons and paper, videogame worlds and social networks.[2] Contemporary childhood in the developed world is thoroughly postdigital, with children respecting no hard and fast distinctions between actual environments and material toys, on the one hand, and virtual worlds and simulated objects, on the other. These are *all* technologies, not just the sophisticated media machines of mobile devices and game consoles.

Unbox: The Speed and Slowness of Lucy, Batman, Batman, Gandalf, and Dumbledore

—I'm going to build Dumbledore [sings:] Dumbledore, Dumbledore . . .

—Technically, you're building *Gandalf.*

[They rip open the small plastic bags containing LEGO pieces and minifigs]

—[In a gruff voice] I only use black and very very very dark gray . . . Why am I quoting Batman? Black and dark gray, black and dark gray.

—[Opens small card carton] His cape gets its own box! . . . cape gets its own box, it's *cape-able* of doing it!

—That's a bad joke . . .

—It's a cape-astrophe! [Sings] Dumbledore! Dumbledore!

—It's *not* Dumbledore . . .

—Dumbledore! Dumbledore! Dumbledore!

The two brothers, neighbors of mine, are sitting on the rug, setting up a *LEGO Dimensions* set, working with a printed book of instructions, opening bags of bricks, and clicking minifigs together (figure 0.1).

Figure 0.1
LEGO Dimensions (the LEGO Group 2015–).

The promise of hybrid toy–videogame systems such as *LEGO Dimensions* and broader developments in the Internet of Toys[3] is to collapse boundaries between the virtual spaces of videogames and digital networks and the actual environment and objects of everyday play, not least toys. Hybrid game systems produced by multinational toy and media companies, such as *LEGO Dimensions* and *Disney Infinity*, both acknowledge and exploit the tendency of children's imaginative play to grab, mix, and hybridize diverse fictional worlds and characters. The *LEGO Batman* films and *LEGO Movie* films themselves are a sustained joke about the mix and jumble of the modular toy itself, an analog and allegory of mixed-up sets and stories in everyday bedrooms.

—You just put it [shows a minifig, then places it on the RFID reader] here and
    it works!
—Gandalf does all the magic!
—[Singsong voice] Gandalf, magic, makes it all work . . .
—[Rummaging in the bricks] Where's whatshername? Lucy. Lucy.
—[The older boy stands up, moves away from the LEGO and picks up a 3DS
    console] I'm not as into LEGO as I was . . .
—[The younger, still rummaging and sorting bricks] I need some sort of tray!

After twenty minutes or so of construction, the structure illustrated on the box and in the instructions is still far from complete. It is supposed to form a tall hoop-like shape, a "portal" now familiar from SF and fantasy film and TV. While the actual LEGO play has proved absorbing, particularly for the younger child, the lure of the videogame and its promise to connect with and animate the minifigs and vehicles is overwhelming. With a little pragmatic testing, they determine that only the base of the portal is needed to connect the figures to the videogame. They work out quickly where and when the minifigs, on their RFID-enabled bases, needed to be placed on the platform to solve on-screen puzzles. This placing was done carelessly and quickly, eyes on the screen.

—Yay! We've done it!
—[With exaggerated American accent] Oh my gaad, so exc-iting!
[After the first puzzle is solved, the older boy guides the younger:]
—Press A
—Where's Batman? Let me try.
—It's working—it's working—it's working.
—Go through there . . .
—The speed!!

Observing this play over several hours, it became apparent that the navigation of space was less significant to the structure of the play than was the negotiation of time. The *LEGO Dimensions* game set both absolute and negotiable constraints on the temporal and attentional dimensions of play; for example, it mirrors the traditional construction of LEGO—the relative slowness and rhythm of checking printed instructions, rummaging for the required brick, clicking it into place—on the screen with a virtual booklet that can be flicked through at speed, the software automatically completing the virtual version of the model. The younger child's love of actual LEGO construction fought with the screen's insistent promise of animated action. Some cutscenes and tutorials can be skipped, others can't, an automated disciplining of attention. Rhythm and speed are impelled and constrained by machinic cape-abilities: scrutinizing diagrams, finding the necessary piece in actual play, by the coded rhythm of the videogame and the affordances of the avatars.

This particular moment of play, for all the novelty of the new game sets ("We're the first people to play this!" they whispered at one point), is also part of at once the longitudinal flows of both domestic media life and entertainment-industrial strategy. Immediate recognition of the Lucy/Wyldstyle character, the Batman joke about only working "in black, and sometimes very very dark gray," and the repeated refrains from the song "Everything Is Awesome" demonstrate the boys were very familiar with the *LEGO Movie* as well as the toys, and so they were cued in to its specific iterations of characters and mode of humor, as well as the diffuse and ubiquitous popular media universe it brings to bear (*Batman, Lord of the Rings, Harry Potter*). As Meredith Bak notes, LEGO has always been modular, and its distinctive studs and standardized minifigs easily dissolve proprietary IP into its recent fantastical products and "an infinitely compatible, sanctioned multiverse."[4] Thus, in the opening sequences of the game, the players encounter Batman rescuing Gandalf from the Balrog, but then two versions of Batman (one molded from light gray virtual thermoplastic, the other black) fight it out for authenticity.

The confusion by the younger boy of the Dumbledore and Gandalf characters hints at the limits of this semiotic strategy. Each wizard in its own cinematic representation is too closely constituted by popular generic signifiers of wizardness—long gray beards, robes, staffs, extravagant hats. For all their intended semiotic chaos, the *LEGO Dimensions* and *LEGO Movie* worlds are syncretic but not homogenous—IP edges are carefully fenced with ® and ™ symbols and elaborate industrial arrangements for licensing across Marvel, Disney, Warner Bros, and so on. Gandalf/Dumbledore represents a lapse in toyetic attention—a momentary industrial-transmedial failure.

[Black-clad Batman runs to and fro in a LEGO forest, collecting gold and silver studs. Even in the mini-Batmobile, he can't get past an aggressive tree blocking the path. Control is switched to Wyldstyle, but she is immediately overwhelmed by an attack from a troop of flying monkeys from *The Wizard of Oz*. Gandalf does not appear to be an option on this level.]

—[Quietly] There's no Dumbledore, we can't do it . . .

[. . .]

—Where's Dumbledore? Dumbledore is no more.

On the one hand, then, is the physicality of physical toys still important? What are the relationships between tactility and imagination, materiality and play? What would be lost if the infant's teddy bear were only ever touched via a capacitive smart device screen, dolls only ever posed, arranged, and talked to virtually in a simulated house, construction toys only ever assembled as intangible virtual structures? Does the design of new platforms such as *LEGO Dimensions*—hybrids of virtual gameworlds and actual toys—mark a rallying of "traditional" play with physical objects, materials, and environments or its death throes? And what else might be lost if touch and manipulation are flattened onto the screen or distanced through the keyboard and analog stick with its force feedback? On the other hand, what does it matter if "traditional" toys and games *are* mediatized and augmented: board games supplemented with video or digital media; playground equipment with interactive devices and game mechanics; dolls and cuddly toys with Wi-Fi-enabled cameras and microphones; the overengineering of simpler, more authentic objects—and hence their behavioral, imaginative possibilities?

Posed in this way, such questions assume their own pessimistic answers. They are driven by a set of cultural and philosophical assumptions about the relationships between technology and the mind, between human and nonhuman agency, between economic and historical change and structures of thought and behavior, the material and the immaterial. This book poses alternative questions—questions that address toys and play explicitly but which also draw out underlying conceptual concerns about the nature of the technical and the embodied, the artificial and the natural, technocultural continuity and change, cognition and imagination in an era of "lively machines."[5]

The significance of the toy will be pursued through two intertwined lines of enquiry. The first is a sustained interrogation of the ambiguous nature of the toy itself as a historical, cultural, economic, and technical object, and the second is a rethinking of the history and philosophy of technologies and media from the neglected perspective of play and play with objects. These two lines of enquiry will be linked by a sustained interest in the relationships between materiality (technologies, bodies, environments) and imagination. Toys are technologies uniquely mobilized by imaginative processes: from young children's animation of dolls or bricks in imaginative play to global imaginaries of popular cultural characters, narratives, and themes; from the exploratory and acquisitive dynamics of commercial transmedia systems such as *Pokémon* to the shifting relationships of engineering and narrative play that characterize products such as LEGO; and from the delegation or distribution of aspects of imaginative play to software-driven gameworlds to ideas and dreams of artificial life and intelligence in play with software toys, robots, and virtual pets. Although the intersecting domains of the virtual and the everyday are writ large in postdigital play culture, this interplay between mechanical devices and imaginaries of life, consciousness, and other intangible but real forces has been evident in toylike technologies such as the programmable "thinking" and "writing" automata of eighteenth-century Europe and the plethora of scientific and optical toys that shift between serious research and novel spectacle over centuries, resulting in—not least—cinema and other media technologies. As well as this strong connection over centuries in the toyetic reflection on, and speculative manufacture of, artificial consciousness and agency, this book's genealogies of various types of toys will suggest a more diffuse underpinning continuity: toys are unique among artifacts in their fundamental articulation of the aesthetic, semiotic, and imaginative with the mechanical and the operational.

Much scholarly work on modern toys approaches them as primarily a medium of communication, depicting or embodying adult behaviors or fantasy worlds for the purposes of cultural or ideological reproduction in childhood, not least the mechanisms of gender. Dollhouses, toy soldiers, dressing up in nurse or firefighter uniforms or in princess or knight costumes, weapons, vehicles, action figures, animals—all are messages of welcome, or a warning, from a beckoning world of grown-up activities and responsibilities, often manifested in hyperconsumerist delights and rigid gender dimorphism. Yet, they are also, necessarily, abstracted: scaled down and simplified for practical play with small hands and bodies; stylized in form by manufacturing economies and the material qualities of die-cast tin and blow-molded plastic; and rendered fantastical by the vivid aesthetics and outlandish worlds and genres of animation and other children's media. Crucially, toys are material-semiotic *machines*, any communicative operations fully bound up in their material capabilities and functions.[6] Toys are not interpreted, or "read," as we understand ornaments, books, or images as cultural texts; they are handled and manipulated, placed and juxtaposed, talked to and animated. They are models of phenomenal and symbolic worlds, but in the sense of the model as *simulacrum* not as faithful copy. They are simulacra in ways that bring together the contemporary sense of the term—of new hyperrealities of media images and networks—with the ancient and medieval fabrication of artifacts and automata—in poetry, philosophy, and engineering[7]—devices that model actual human and animal activity but which take on their own new artificial character.

These references to simulation, automata, robots, and so on suggest, then, that the postdigital refers not only to technocultural developments subsequent to the advent of computer media in the late twentieth century but also to the contemporary necessity of thinking postdigitally: we cannot but regard the long genealogy of technology (and play) through the lens of concepts of simulation, virtuality, and (nonhuman) animation. The current Internet of Toys and toys-to-life systems are fully part of this genealogy or media archaeology of technologies and technological imaginaries of the animation of playful objects—from children's play with dolls and toy animals as if alive to robots and automata, computer-animated game characters, and the persistent cinematic and literary fascination with animating toys.

I will suggest throughout this book that attention to toys and *toying* can challenge the dominant metatheory of technocultural development across the anthropology and philosophy of technology. I will question the assumption that objects fabricated or adapted by human hands have always served primarily the *instrumental* needs of human survival—from hand axes and fire to wheels, to clockwork, steam, and computers. What if sociotechnical development has always been driven not primarily by need but rather by *play*, by a toying with materials and environments, that objects from weapons and tools to ritual and ornamental artifacts were fashioned playfully *before* they were turned to practical use? What if the precultural, prehuman origins of technics were located not in the familiar image of the adult chimpanzee's use of a stick as a tool for extracting termites and grubs from tree bark, but rather in the juvenile chimpanzee's cradling the stick, making it a nest and laying it down to sleep?[8]

What, then, is the future of play with things? On the one hand, we have anxieties about children's digital media as an unfolding future of alienation and the limitation of imagination. On the other hand, of course, designers and producers of playful media project ideal futures of everyday fulfilment through their products and services. Digital media and the playful lie at the

heart of theoretical debates and practical initiatives in current design thinking and innovative business practices. With videogames at the vanguard,
the possibilities of play for economic gain and for social change have been
widely trumpeted. We are, it is claimed, seeing an emergent ludic culture
in which popular media is reshaped by agonistic and simulational forms of
communication and a social world in which experimentation with digital
and other technologies resonate with new forms of participatory culture.
Apps, gamification strategies, "serious games" initiatives, artist and activist
interventions, popular media, hybrid and smart toys, and newly augmented
and mixed realities all compete for attention in a rapidly transforming postdigital media ecology. The academic field of games studies has generated a
number of framings of, and predictions for, the significance of play in the
postindustrial world[9] and the "ludification" of twenty-first-century culture.[10]
Alongside these critical approaches, sensitive to the commercial, industrial,
and political interests in a putatively playful polity, are a wide range of more
enthusiastic and utopian imaginings of future cities and industries liberated
by play, games, and the imagination, from "playable cities" initiatives[11] and
alternate reality games[12] to the blurring of work and play by global corporations such as LEGO and Google,[13] a shifting to center stage of game forms
and play activities in popular and official culture, popular media from entertainment to news, business training, policymaking, and urban and economic
development.

Amid all this attention to play and games, however, the toy is rarely mentioned. And yet for millennia, this ambiguous, derided, and critically ignored
object has populated human lives from infancy. Play objects offer infants
their first tactile and manipulable engagement beyond their own and their
mothers' bodies. In some lines of thought, toys enculturate, educate, train,
and adapt growing bodies and minds to the physical, cognitive, and cultural
roles of adult life. To today's post-Romantic worldview, they symbolize the
apartness of childhood as a realm of innocence and vulnerability. A toy is
an ambiguous object, an often-overlooked link between ostensibly incom-
patible domains: they are the most loved and subjectively intense objects
but also the most ephemeral and throwaway. As transitional objects, they
mediate the emergence of the human subject in infancy,[14] while in a late
capitalist cultural economy, they epitomize the cynical accumulative strategies of commercial transmedia.[15] Toys represent and model the adult world

to the growing child. Yet, at the same time, they offer themselves to children as tools to invert and parody that world. They are material objects: designed and fashioned to be tangible, touched, and manipulated. Yet, they are also the least material of objects, tending in play to conjure and scaffold imaginary events and worlds and, in literary and cinematic fiction, to come to life in dreams and secret adventure. In a postdigital media landscape, the material and the immaterial dimensions of play are complicated and multiplied by their transductions across intangible virtual worlds and networked spaces of computer games. Like simple tools, toys are artifacts that are not restricted to the human—wild animals, including cats, primates, otters, and birds play with materials and objects. Yet, some of the most sophisticated technologies ever produced, from eighteenth-century automata to contemporary robots and artificial intelligence (AI), are toylike in their noninstrumentality, flexibility, novelty, and spectacle. Toys epitomize the poles of commodity culture: luxurious and indulgent or ephemeral and throwaway. Designers of educational toys from the late eighteenth century to contemporary edutainment apps regard the toy as integral to knowledge and reasoning, but toys are also policed by educators—there are bad toys too, distracting, addictive, trivial, and morally suspect.

Unbox: Repurposing *Battleships*

Clearing up after our children one day, we picked up a toy, a damaged apparatus comprised of a gray plastic tray and several dozen small white and red pegs. As designed, and before it was broken, it opened out from a small case to form two playing board areas separated by a vertical screen. A version of the pen and paper game *Battleships*, the pegs were intended to be deployed in short lines on each player's board, each line of two, three, or four pegs standing for a different class of warship. Each player attempts to uncover the other's schematic naval deployment through a guesswork of coordinates, firing imaginary missiles at A6, G1, and so on until a hit is made. The playing boards were flanked by colorful images depicting imaginary control panels with buttons, displays, and switches, dramatizing the game's mechanic of random selection as tactical technics. Paper inserts with a printed pattern of water sat under the transparent pegboards, reinforcing this simple simulation of maritime warfare. Only one board survives, as the case hinge was broken and the central screen lost (figure 0.2).

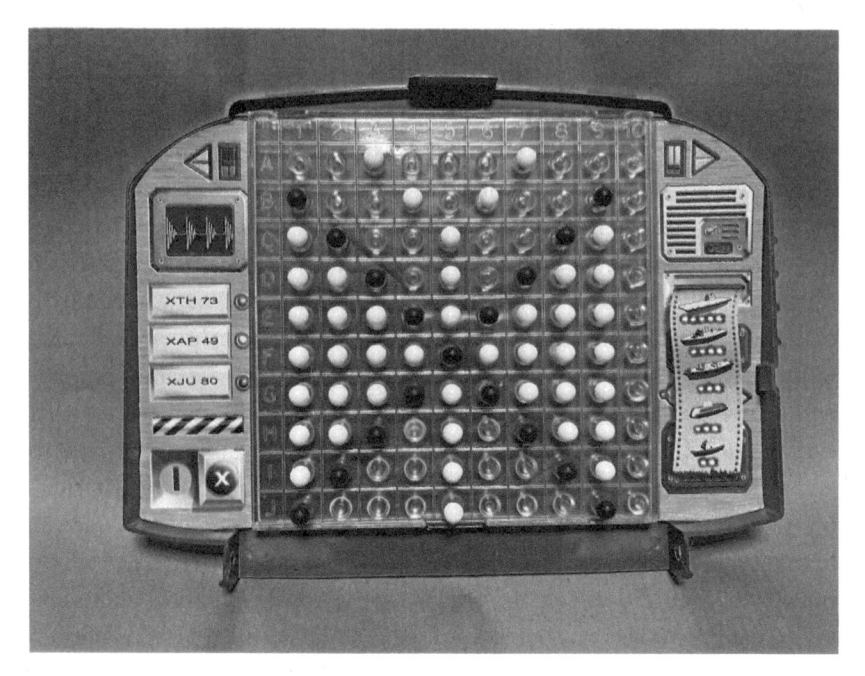

Figure 0.2
Broken plastic *Battleships* game, repurposed as a drawing tool. UK, circa 2005.

During the day's play, the child had ignored the graphics, theme, rule-set theme, and past experience of playing *Battleships* and had instead placed pegs into the board to form a pattern: a striking symmetrical butterfly with a white body, antennae, and wings edged in red. The game apparatus had been repurposed into a drawing tool, patterns and figures traced with its grid of colored pegs.

The repurposing of toys or other nonplay objects for imaginative play beyond their designed or intended use is a familiar feature of children's engagement with their material environments. On one level, it can be accounted for in the design language of affordance: the material and physical properties of artifacts lending themselves to alternative, unexpected uses. On another, though, it draws attention to some specific dimensions of body–technology relationships—dimensions that both shed light on the material nature of play and question some key assumptions in the philosophy of technology, epitomized by toys as play objects and toying as a mode of technocultural behavior.

What If?

> Although toys are now a striking cultural event, there is not even an embryonic theory of toy technology.[16]

This book toys with ideas: ideas about objects and materiality; about play and culture (and nature); about technologies, technics, and techniques; about imaginative and cognitive behavior in play with objects and environments—behavior that is not limited to or bounded by *human* players but rather distributed through the objects, subjects, and environments. Its opening gambit is to ask, "What if . . . ?" What if the history and development of technology were not driven by the invention of practical tools and their application to the pressing environmental demands of human survival such as making shelters, hunting and processing animals for food, and the manufacture of clothing? What if, instead, the first artifacts, the first technical objects—hand axes, spears, sewing needles—were produced not in a time of pressing need but rather in moments of respite from the immediate demands of sustenance, defense, and shelter? What if they were instead the products of a distracted manipulation of materials to hand—sticks, stones, animal bones, and skin? It seems unlikely that the first spear would have been *designed* in the contemporary sense of the term—that is, the product of a need identified in a Stone Age mind (such as "What extension or augmentation of my body can I devise to bring that animal within reach and hasten its death?"), pursued through the purposeful selection and whittling of a stick of appropriate weight and malleability to produce a weapon light enough to be thrown a good distance but heavy enough to provide the momentum needed to pierce hide and muscle. It seems unlikely that the need, and technical solution to that need, sprang fully formed. So, what if instead this process was, initially at least, one of noninstrumental *toying* with materials and objects? Imagine instead the playful balancing and throwing of sticks, of whittling smooth, of sharpening to a point—perfected through games of target practice perhaps before any animal was struck in reality. How would the Stone Age imagination know what the material qualities of weight, momentum, and air resistance were, the relationships between bodily movement and movement-space, without an abstract, playful toying with objects, a toying with the environment?

What if, then, the practical and instrumental possibilities of these first tools (and, by extension, the subsequent prehistory and history of all human-produced artifacts and systems) were epiphenomenal to, an *artifact* of, the fashioning of toys? What if technologies have always been at least as much toys as tools? And what if technocultures, from the paleolithic to the postdigital, have always developed, individuated, as much through noninstrumental motives of play, play with materials, machines, bodies, and ideas? This would question assumptions of the primacy of the human mind and imagination over the body and its environment, the hierarchy of—and significant separation between—cognition (and imagination) and embodied (and environmental) action. What if we were to rethink the anthropology of technoculture, and the philosophy of technology, as a nonteleological and noninstrumental development driven by play in and with environments and objects, by aesthetic and kinesthetic motives, not any immanent desire for larger control?

A *gambit*, in its original sense of the opening move in a game of chess, is in part an offering or acceptance of the invitation to play. It is a stepping out of the rational, the necessary, and the instrumental into a different spatial, temporal, and ethical dimension where different rules of behavior and causality apply. What if, the chess players implicitly ask as they make their first moves, we each accept that these sets of pieces of turned wood are opposing armies—copies of some lost feudal model—set to fight to the death of the king according to arbitrary but utterly rigid rules of movement and combat? The "what if" worlds of chess and the child's imaginative play are akin to the philosopher's seriously playful thought experiments. To ask "what if" is a primal and speculative move, at once simulacral and playful. It establishes an alternative reality within the everyday, sets up objects, subjects, and dynamics, part of yet parallel to the mundane and instrumental, and asks different questions of objects, bodies, and environments.

This book, then, takes toys as a particular category of artifacts and toy play as a particular mode of engagement with the world. But it also deploys the toy as a device and a thought experiment for rethinking the character and development of technology and technoculture at large. While this philosophical game may not overturn established histories and philosophies of technology, science, and culture, it has the potential at least to unsettle and decenter them—like play itself—to test the rules of order and convention, and to conjure up alternatives. But also, and again like play itself, this thought experiment is not mere whimsy: it is grounded in, and emerges from, attention to the realities of bodies, minds, machines, materials, and environments. This "what if" is not a question so much as a mode of thought or behavior, an attitude to the world and playful—toying—engagement within it.

Toys themselves barely register in the philosophy of technology, or in anthropology, and only intermittently in studies of culture, art, and media. With a handful of exceptions,[17] when they do feature, it is often at the very edge of critical attention: in the prehuman realm of childhood, the most despised base layer of consumer culture, as *other* to the noninstrumental but elevated objects of art and religion, or at best as playful novelties noticed only for their part in the progression of more serious or worthy practices. Scholarly critiques of toys in the context of children's media culture and everyday play often have a marked tendency to extrapolate theoretical and ideological models of the induction of children into adult life from the design and marketing of toys and games rather than studying the dynamics of actual toy play. While media studies in general concedes that popular texts might be read and repurposed by their audiences, the same imaginative and critical agency is not always granted to the child media consumer. With their narrative frames and transmedial reach, Disney, *Pokémon, Neopets, Masters of the Universe*, and so on all "limit the imagination" of the child as viewer.[18] Toys, in this pessimistic schema, are positioned as even worse than TV programs, movies, and advertisements, as they engrain pernicious patterns of thought and hypergendered body images not only through their stories and imagery but also behaviorally through the repetitious "training" of play itself.[19] The paucity of observational or ethnographic description of children's play across apposite academic fields of research is glaring.[20]

To foreground the toy in postdigital technoculture and in the philosophy of technology and media is not in itself a whimsical, domesticating, comforting move (although it might also suggest a rethinking of the technocultural significance of whimsy, the domestic, and the comforting). Contemporary toys are commodified and mediatized, disposable and wasteful, ideological and even surveillant. Myth, literature, art, cinema, and TV are haunted by scary toys and effigies that come to life. There is also a persistent sense of the toy as dissembling and deceitful, from mechanical and optical tricks, puzzles, and hidden chambers. Just as there is something toyetic in simulacra, from ancient automata to contemporary robotics, there is always something simulacral in the toy. As Gregory Bateson put it, the baby doll is not a baby, but it is not not a baby.[21] From the animism of infant love for their teddy bear to the fascination of the Surrealists and horror cinema with the erotics of dolls and mannequins, the line between the animate and the inanimate, the organic and inorganic, the everyday and the uncanny is at its weakest in the toyetic.

To play is to play with ideas about or impressions of the social environment as much as with material objects. A toy is at once a symbol and a part of its environment. Just as paleolithic children must have played with the material and ideas to hand—bones, mud, sticks, images of animals, and ritual symbols—so growing into a mediated, networked, virtualized environment requires play with concepts and symbolic relationships, to-hand devices, and distributed communication. Close attention to children's play today elicits complex, dream-like condensations and sublimations of technologies, interfaces, adult behaviors, and mediated dramas. This book asks, then, what are the implications of regarding technology as a whole as noninstrumental, nonteleological, open, and fundamentally mobilized by, and mobilizing, imaginative processes? How might critical attention to playful objects cast a new light on technology, opening up ideas about use and instrumentality, embodiment and excess, the machinic and the imaginative, the material and the semiotic, communication and nonsense?

A Note on Method

I draw on a range of methods and approaches in the research for this book. Histories of play objects, theories of play and technology, and accounts or studies of actual play have been sifted from across the humanities and social sciences, along with nonacademic books and articles, children's literature, and screen media. The field of game studies has over the past few decades gathered a rich collection of sources and concepts pertaining to play and games across psychology, science and technology studies, philosophy, media and film theory, and so on—although surprisingly little direct attention to toys. Some research was conducted in museum collections of toys, notably the Bill Douglas Cinema Museum at the University of Exeter, on which chapter 6 is largely based. Other collections I visited include the Musée de Poupées et Jouets in Josselin, Brittany, and Den Gamle By in Aarhus, Denmark.

I draw on my ethnographic and memory-work studies of children's embodied and imaginative engagement with videogames, toys, and other playful technologies, notably in the unboxes in the introduction, chapter 4, and chapter 5. These studies are characterized by small-scale participant observation of moments of play, ranging from ad hoc and opportunistic attention to playful events in my own family life to more formal and organized research such as the robot design workshop detailed in chapter 5's unbox. Such projects generally focus on children's play and imaginative activity, but I have also conducted memory work with adults on their own childhood experiences with LEGO (see chapter 4). While no universalizing claims about childhood or toy play can be made from such small studies, they do offer a necessary degree of focus on and description of the intimacies of human–technological relationships, the interplay of mechanics, hands, eyes, and imagination, and immediate material and semiotic environments without which any broader statements or assumptions about play are unreliable. Although informed by ethnographic practices and traditions, I tend to refer to this methodology as microethological in that the objects of the research are not the human participants per se but rather the interconnected behaviors, their coming together—in moments—with nonhuman participants, including technologies and their milieus.[22]

Where possible, I have handled the toys I describe and played the games. The importance of this hands-on technical and imaginative manipulation of play objects for analytical insights into their possible operations in play is explored in chapter 6. Throughout, I maintain that we should regard any assumptions of the imaginative and mechanical operations of toys in children's play either in history or today as tentative at best. While the representational or symbolic forms and imagery of toys are integral to their appeal and often shape or inflect the imaginative worlds of their playing, they should not be read off as determining this playing and these worlds. Empirical descriptions of actual play, my own and that of others I cite here, demonstrate that toys are repurposed, their ostensible meanings shifted, inverted, often even ignored altogether as other material and technical qualities, and imaginative resources, are brought to bear. Toys are not texts.

Rather, they are machines—some with textual components. I draw on theories and philosophies of technology and media in everyday life to open up and articulate these components in everyday use, but I note also the distinct characteristics of the playful machine over its instrumental cousins. The animated toys of children's literature, television, and cinema provide a wealth of imaginative resources for addressing the interplay of the material and the imaginative, the playful and the dramatic, in toy culture.[23] As such, the methods here are inflected by the speculative, the "as if," and the "what if," and they are informed by the fictional, but this speculation and these fictions are articulated with, where possible, material engagement and lived experience.

The Structure of This Book

This book begins with a chapter, "Toy-Being," that sets out in broad terms my concerns with the technological nature of toys and the toyetic nature of technology. Playing with Martin Heidegger's concept of tool-being, it addresses unresolved issues in the definition of the toy and of play with toys, and it sketches key theories of technology and culture that will inform the following discussion. Each of the subsequent chapters takes a particular type of toy as its focus, including dolls, soldiers, and construction toys. Some of these types are broader and looser in scope. Chapter 5, "Robots," addresses the toylike characteristics of the long history of automata from ancient Greece to contemporary robots and smart toys. Chapter 6, "Cinema Toys," rethinks cinema and television as subsidiary to toy culture rather than vice versa as generally assumed. The concluding chapter 7 addresses the fate of the physical play object in the contemporary cultural–industrial landscape of hybrid physical–digital toys and games and online play platforms. Each chapter contains one or two breakout boxes—unboxes—with case studies that take a particular play object or type of toy to open up key concepts and make thematic and genealogical connections that cut across the chapters. The unbox headings are a nod to the children's performative practices of making and sharing videos of the unboxing and reviewing of toys on YouTube (itself unboxed in "Unbox: Unboxing and the Mechanics of Surprise" in chapter 7).

Woven through all these chapters is a set of characteristics that I suggest are essential to grasping the technics, design, experience, and affects of toys. These are scale, tactility, and manipulability/operability. In addition, a set of broader concepts and frameworks have proved productive throughout in addressing the distinct nature of toy culture: historical/industrial synchrony and asynchrony, the imaginary and the imaginative, kinesthesia, synecdoche, simulacra, and the toyetic. These terms will be explained in more detail in chapters 1 and 7.

1 Toy-Being

The "technology" conceptualized by the philosophy of technology, and cognate fields such as science and technology studies (STS), cyberculture, anthropologies of technology, and media studies, is a contested and polyvalent object of enquiry. From the material infrastructure of a social economic order to systems of knowledge and their application, and from everyday relationships between humans and nonhumans to articulations of politics, ethics, and social organization, technology is configured across diverse disciplinary and discursive frameworks. Despite this heterogeneity, however, the prevailing assumption is that these objects of enquiry are human-made artifacts and systems designed and produced largely for *instrumental* purposes, for practical and material ends: agriculture, domestic labor, manufacture, mining, construction, power generation, health care, and so on. For instance, both Karl Marx and Martin Heidegger explained the relationships between individuals, societies, and the wider world through the productive operations of tools and machines, from the artisan's hand tools to the vast factories, power generation, and engineering projects of the Industrial Revolution.[1] Broadly speaking, the philosophy of technology assumes tools and technical systems to be one category of artifact, and the products of these tools and systems—commodities, for instance, or, more tangentially, art objects—to be another, demanding different sets of questions and concepts. Heidegger and Marx each assert a particular historical and technological periodization, with the revolutionary upheavals of the Industrial Revolution a moment of fundamental change in humans' relationships and agency with their material and social environment. For Heidegger, the shift from artisanal to industrial production is catastrophic, the industrial characterized by a rapacious instrumentalism in which the world is transformed to a "standing reserve," nothing but a supply of resources to be extracted and exploited. For Marx, industrialization was at once convulsive but necessary, a revolutionary step to a future in which technology affords the control of the environment by its operators for the social good. For each, and for philosophies of technology in general, the salient apparatus and techniques are those of *production*—the factory system for Marx, technologies from hand axes to hydroelectric plants for Heidegger. To understand the transformative power of industrialization and its implication for human society and agency, one must look in part to the machines, systems, techniques, and knowledge that drove factories, hydroelectric plants, and transport. Technologies here are objects and systems that *do* things, that are deployed to intervene, shape, process, transform, and distribute materials for purposeful ends. A toy, then, could only ever be a mere by-product of these technological and economic processes, its own technological or mechanical capacities of no consequence. It is clear that play and playful objects have no immediate relevance for these philosophies of industry and epochal historical change, although, as we'll see, key aspects of both thinkers can be brought to bear on less instrumental technics—from Marx's commodity fetishism to Heidegger's positing of the relationship between the hand and the tool as emblematic of phenomenological approaches to agency and being in the world.

There are whole classes of material artifacts studied in depth by philosophers, historians, archaeologists, anthropologists, and media scholars that are, by and large, not considered as technological in their application or significance. These would include art objects—paintings, prints, sculptures—objects approached through questions of aesthetics, symbolic regimes, ideology, and cultural reproduction, but rarely thought of in terms of technology, as functional or operational in the world. The modes and techniques of manufacture of crafted objects such as ceramics, textiles, and ornamental and practical domestic artifacts may fall within the purview of philosophies and anthropologies of technology—developments in ceramics or forging, weaving or enamel, for instance. However, like art objects, their significance in the study of culture and social organization tends to be placed firmly in the realms of the symbolic, the aesthetic, and the communicative. They often have practical, tool-like uses, for storing and serving food, clothing bodies, and so on, but these uses, and the material characteristics of the objects themselves, tend to be taken as self-evident and unworthy of sustained critical attention. The processes of manufacture, sourcing raw materials, and organizing production fall within the *technical*—the form, decoration, and color of the artifact—and the ritual or domestic uses to which it is put fall within the *cultural*—the aesthetic, the symbolic.

Another category of artifact, one that crosses that of art and craft objects, is that of objects designed and fabricated for ritual use. It is telling that of the two main examples of technologies that Heidegger discusses in "The Question Concerning Technology," one is not a tool at all but rather a silver chalice, a ritual object whose salient characteristics are aesthetic, cultural, luxurious even, but not "useful" as such. Of course, in the technological order of the industrial society that Heidegger is critiquing, both ritual/luxury objects and toys are instrumental in the sense that they are designed, produced, and marketed for particular users and for profit. These overlap the categories of art and craft artifacts, as they often facilitate a ritualized version of everyday more instrumental practices (the plates and cups of the Latin Mass, for instance). Like modern toys, ritual objects can be the product of extensive expertise and investment of time and resources, realized as highly symbolic in form and decoration. But also like toys, they can be little more than a momentary grabbing and enchanting of material objects to hand, sticks and earth, sand and feathers transubstantiated into humans and animals, animated in the imaginative and liminal space-time of ritual, from the consecration of everyday foodstuffs in formal religion to the transmutation of base matter into objects of desire or enmity in sympathetic magic.

But toys are technical objects. They often have moving parts and, as such, are machines in their own right—for example, twentieth-century electric train sets or the jointed dolls found in the graves of Roman children. Nonmechanical toys too have their functionality entwined with their material and technical characteristics: the cuddly toy with its soft surface and pliable substrate, designed for tactile and reassuring intimacy; the toy soldier that makes sense only as one of larger set, arranged and deployed in a playful strategy. Toys are functional; they are used to *do* things, just not things with immediate practical ends. They are symbolic, communicative objects, like paintings and ornaments, and play with toys has an abstract formalism and intensity that is redolent of ritual. But they are also handled, placed, animated, and combined in the imaginative and voluptuous "work" of children's play.

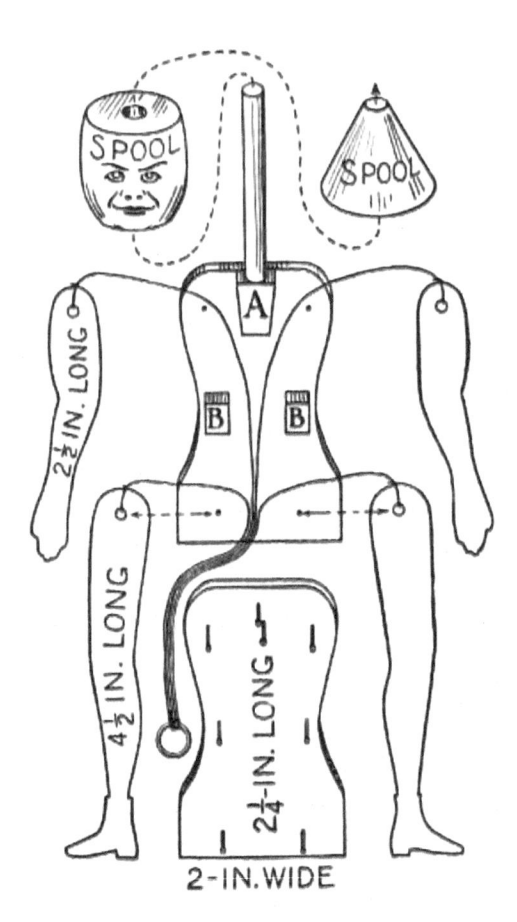

Figure 1.1
Instructions for home construction of a jumping jack puppet. A. Neely Hall, *Home-Made Toys for Girls and Boys*, 1915.

So, again, "what if" technology were always already playful, fundamentally toyetic? For my thought experiment to be sustained, evidence and interpretation is needed of the playful dimensions of technics as both archaic and immanent, evidence of a lusory attitude[2] in the creation of devices or a demonstrable flexibility and latitude in the uses to which devices might be put—from the paleolithic era to the current information age. This will be an underpinning theme to the book, but for now, we can take the wheeled objects described in "Unbox: Wheeled Toys" as a compelling example of the decoupling of mechanical invention from instrumental application.

Unbox: Wheeled Toys

An animal on wheels: a simple body cut from a thick sheet of wood, with two drilled holes—each holding a spindle with rough, thick discs at each end. The animal shape's simplicity suggests a speediness in manufacture rather than symbolic abstraction; one could imagine a busy adult quickly carving a number of these to keep children amused while they work. This said, the sketchy lines of the animal's body capture the curve of a horse's neck, head forward and back arched, an outline that suggests forward motion, speed, and action. This was carved by a hand well-versed in fashioning more sophisticated objects with animal form. It was made in Egypt, at least two thousand years ago, and ancient animals on wheels have also been found across Eurasia and in the Americas. In her *History of Toys*, Antonia Fraser includes illustrations of a wheeled porcupine and lion carved from limestone in Persia circa 1100 BCE.[3]

Figure 1.2
Wheeled horse. Akhmin, Egypt, Roman period.

What is striking now is how similar these toys are in scale, form, material, and mechanism to recent wheeled toys, particularly those made for younger children. The object tells us something else as well: the simple mechanics suggest a great deal about how the toy was played with. Figures of humans or nonwheeled animals can only hint at the possible stories and scenarios that were conjured up as children animated them in play, but mechanical toys demonstrate their *physical* possibilities at least. This horse, fashioned to fit the scale of a child's hand and the sweep of their arm, was pushed backward and forward, released to trundle down a slope, or in a longer continuous wheeled gallop, the child crouched, squatting-hopping along. Many ancient animals on wheels from across the world featured a hole drilled through their noses, some still with the string or cord with which a child would have pulled them along.

Wheeled animals are strong evidence in support of this book's opening thought experiment: that technology was toylike before it was practical and instrumental. We know that the invention of the wheel happened a long time ago, not least from the familiar themes of cartoons depicting cavemen carving heavy stone circles and axles in a multitude of jokes on primitive invention. The wheel has become an archetypal image of the emergence of human civilization and its efforts to overcome nature and amplify bodily strength. It is generally assumed that wheels were developed in a teleological line of descent in the augmented transportation of heavy materials: from sledges, sledges on rollers, then spindles or axles with freely rotating discs. This last innovation occurred in Mesopotamia around six thousand years ago, spreading to Europe soon after. However, the linear, necessity-driven model of technological and civilizational development is undermined by the observation that these first wheeled devices in Mesopotamia appear to have been used to carry religious statues in ritual processions rather than transport goods. Practical farm vehicles with wheels and axles do not seem to have been deployed for another two thousand years,[4] and the Middle Eastern cultures that introduced the wheel to Europe subsequently abandoned it as a primary mode of transportation in favor of the pack animal. George Basalla uses these examples to challenge the assumption that the invention and adoption of technologies is driven by necessity and basic biological need: "A necessity for one people, generation, or social class may have no utilitarian value or may be a superficial luxury for another people, generation, or social class . . . Far from fulfilling universal needs, they derive their importance within a specific cultural context or value system."[5] The wheeled toys of Mesoamerica, of Aztec Mexico, followed the same logic. They reverse the conventional timeline of invention: that practical machines are subsequently modeled and scaled down by an indulgent adult for children's play. They are, the archaeologist Gordon Ekholm argued, "best explained as a pure discovery or invention—the visualization of a mechanical device and the making of a model."[6] Produced from the third century CE to the European arrival in the sixteenth century, these clay figurines on wheels are toys proper, with no apparent ritual significance, and—crucially— they appear long *before* any practical use of wheeled transport in central America. Rollers and wheels were of no use in rough and mountainous terrain, and goods were transported by human carriers—so, these toys could not have evolved from them. A better explanation, Ekholm suggests, is that the spindle and its whorl (as used in textile production perhaps) suggested a playfully mobile mechanism and the "inventor" simply made a workable model in clay in the form of an animal.[7]

But these animals also stretch the notion of "model": they are recognizable as a depiction of a horse, say, but a strange dream-like horse, one with wheels instead of legs, a hybrid of nature and machine. As a kinesthetic machine,

Figure 1.3
Lupilu polar bear pull-along toy. Lidl, UK, 2022.

however, it makes perfect sense. The mechanical aspects of these toys challenge dominant notions of aesthetics and symbolism then. They clearly cannot denote actual animal bodies and locomotion, but neither are these wheels abstraction, ornament, or stylization in the ways that preindustrial nonnaturalistic art is generally interpreted. Aesthetics follows noninstrumental function, and a *sort of* animal looks back not to an actual referent but is a *model*, looking forward to its mechanical instantiation in play—a copy without original.

The relationship between the tool (or toy) and the hand is not only one of the extension of, or mediation between, the body and its cultural, economic, and physical environment. Heidegger extends the notion of tool to *equipment*—that is, the tool deployed, put to a task. It is "essentially 'something-in-order-to.'"[8] Paul Dourish notes that "equipment" for Heidegger denotes not a single object but rather sets or systems of functional technical objects: "equipment does not stand alone. Equipment is linked to other equipment in the way that it relies upon, works with, suggests, is similar or dissimilar to, or is otherwise related to other equipment."[9] Equipment in this sense highlights two important issues. First, it reminds us of the distinct status of the toy as a technical device that problematizes the notion of the "something-in-order-to" equipment that has no instrumental aim or closure, for which the (playful) process itself is the "end." Second, it draws attention away from the discrete object to the material and imaginary sets and environs of playful technics, whether the collectable series of modern commercial toy systems or the loose and heterogeneous universe of a child's bedroom, an environment of competing proprietary products (LEGO, Playmobil, *Bratz*), technological substance (thermoplastic, wood, pixels), and uses (solitary distraction, social play, educational applications). These cluttered microcosms are the product of and are nested within the circuits and drives of advertising and marketing, electronic broadcasting, digital networks, global cultural economies of commodities, transmedia franchises, and intellectual property.

Philosophies of technology have a tendency to see the technocultural past through a polarizing lens, filtering out ornament and ritual object from practical devices and systems, whereas preindustrial cosmologies did not make any such clear distinction. It is commonly understood that there was no concrete conceptual or institutional distinction between technology (including engineering, craft production, etc.) and art (painting, ornament, etc.) in Europe from antiquity to the Renaissance—techne covered both.[10] On the other hand, in late twentieth-century cultural theory and philosophy, it was a commonplace assumption that, with the post–World War II rise of consumerist and media cultures, the distinction between technics and aesthetics collapsed along with those between high culture/popular culture and politics/aesthetics.[11] Although toys are rarely mentioned, the *toylike* in a general sense permeates the zone in which this maligned reconvergence of the art and craft of techne is effected. If the technological and material character of the mass media and of commodification is downplayed in these debates, dissolving into the proliferation of signs and fashion, *play*, in broad terms, was a salient concept—the play of signifiers, of identity—presented as an emancipatory or progressive process in some accounts[12] or as the imminent loss of meaning and reality in others.[13]

Recent technological change, notably the popularization of digital technology and networks, and the concomitant pressure on people in their everyday lives to research, configure, network, and upgrade media devices and networks keeps the technical and operational characteristics of these devices firmly in view. Children's play with phones, tablets, and games consoles is now characterized as play with "technology," whereas the predigital technics of LEGO and Meccano (or dollhouses, jack-in-the-boxes, slinkies, kaleidoscopes, spinning tops, etc.) were rarely referred to as such. From this dual starting point, a paleolithic stick doll or pre-Columbian wheeled animal at one end and their contemporary analogs at the other—the Wi-Fi- and Internet of Toys–enabled Barbie or the *Grand Theft Auto* virtual vehicle—I argue that an alternative perspective of everyday technology is needed, one that foregrounds the noninstrumental dimensions of technics and techniques: the emergent, the kinesthetic, the imaginative and imaginary, and the simulacral. If a toy is a technological object but not a tool—or perhaps a tool for radically noninstrumental "uses" of play, sociality, and bodily and cognitive pleasure—then we need to reimagine the implicit categorization of manufactured objects, systems, and human–nonhuman relationships in philosophy and cultural theory. Toy play, from the grasping and imaginative transformation of natural objects such as sticks and feathers to touchscreen devices and digital game controllers, via several centuries of play with industrially

Figure 1.4
Toys-to-hand: action figures in play circa 2003. DUPLO World app on Android tablet, 2023.

and commercially produced toys, is manifested in the picking up, arranging, and manipulation of these objects. Echoing Heidegger's figuration of the relationship between human hands and tools and machines, I assert that the primary characteristic of a toy as an artifact is its capacity for manipulation by the hands. At the very least, play with toys appears to blur the distinction between Heidegger's "ready-to-hand" and the "present-at-hand." To toy with an object is to trace its contours, touch its surface, or test its latitude for movement or its pliability or "give" to pressure—this is the present-at-hand in its most immediate sense (figure 1.4). But the toy in a moment of imaginative or dynamic physical play can also vanish from the player's attention. In material terms, as a ready-to-hand tool, a toy deployed for sustained skillful techniques (a spinning top, Rubik's Cube, moving image projector) might slip below the horizon of conscious attention into muscle memory, the player's attention distracted or directed elsewhere. In imaginative play, toys and other objects and bodies "to hand" dissolve, transferring their properties of scale and resemblance to solitary or shared imaginary worlds and roles or metamorphosing into quite different objects and entities.

What Is a Toy?

There is no clear definition of "toy." The English word itself does not translate easily; in French, *jouet* or "plaything," in German, *spielzeug* or "play-stuff."[14] A "plaything" in English can function as a synonym for a child's toy, but it can also refer to something, or often *someone*, not usually considered a toy, that is picked up and played or toyed with by another. A plaything is often a "mere plaything," carrying the connotation of a person or object debased, of a power relationship exercised through a distracted or sadistic whim. The *-zeug* of *spielzeug*, Kevin Schut explains, can mean either "stuff" or "thing." "Stuff" here, as in English, can mean not only the trivial and low value but also a shapeless material with potential for shaping and fabrication, "something that has the potential for play."[15]

Looking around him at toys and toy culture in the United States in the early 1980s, Brian Sutton-Smith sketched a list of characteristics.[16] He suggests: (1) toys are miniatures; (2) toys are quite different from what they represent; (3) toys are part of children's play; and (4) their meanings and activation in play are very much determined by context. These factors capture something of the nature of the most familiar toys: toy animals, vehicles, dolls, buildings, and so on—objects mobilized and animated in children's play, bearing mimetic resemblance to the adult, nonplayful world of people, machines, and the built environment. These characteristics are by no means exhaustive, however, and significant exceptions can be found to at least the first three.

With regard to the first characteristic, miniature, many toys, if not most, are small-scale models, however abstracted, of actual world objects and entities. Miniature toys have their own distinct mechanical and phenomenological characteristics. Play with dollhouses, sets of toy animals, vehicles, train sets, toy soldiers, and so on is predicated on the animation of a microworld. The appeal of others, such as tiny facsimiles of consumer goods and food, seems to be rooted in their level of tiny detail or perhaps the unsettling delight of seeing and holding the familiar in such a transformed state. However, as we'll soon see, the miniature is not an essential feature of toys, and many toys are not miniature replicas as such, or their ratio of size to any nonplay referent is less significant. Rather, it is driven more by material, practical, and bodily properties than by imaginary or symbolic ones. A toy elephant is by necessity scaled down, whereas a toy mouse or puppy may be "life-size." Thus, questions of *scale* are central to the toy, but this is always scale in relation to the child's body and to their hands and fingers in particular, not to actual world objects and environments. Finally, the miniature is a historical aesthetic category in its own right, epitomized in toys and toylike artifacts but not exhausted by them. Miniature paintings, sculpture, hidden scenes, and characters in boxes and peep devices have their own aesthetic qualities and symbolic genealogies, some of which will be picked up later in relation to dollhouses, optical toys, and toy soldiers.[17]

In terms of the second characteristic, Sutton-Smith's insistence that toys are quite different from what they represent is an important one, and it is surprising how often this simple fact is underplayed in cultural and media critique of popular toys. Toys are differentiated from other objects in the everyday environment not only by their scale, as noted above, but also often in the abstraction and stylization of their design. Toys for infants and young children in particular tend to be characterized by simple forms and bright colors. There are resonances, he suggests, of the magical and ritual objects from which they seem to have developed: "Perhaps religious, magical or playful attitudes all share a perceptual sense that there is something different about miniature objects, which contrast so strangely with everyday life."[18] Sutton-Smith notes the schematic and mechanical abstractions of many toys. Toys can be abstract or near abstract. Building blocks resemble actual bricks in some toy sets, early LEGO for example, but less so in others, Froebel's didactic "Gifts," for instance (see chapter 4). Balls, spinning tops, kites, and optical toys such as kaleidoscopes may have representational images printed on them but, in form and function, do not copy any preexisting functional object or activity (see "Unbox: Unimaginative Toys" later in this chapter). In imaginative play, the articulation of the mimetic or symbolic aspects of toys with the mode of play itself is complex and ambiguous. It is a widespread assumption that children in play are rehearsing or training for adulthood, acting out adult roles and behavior, learning to use adults' tools. Media critics have studied toys as if they are straightforward representations (of war, cities, gender stereotypes) but miss the abstractions of the fabrication of toys in themselves and the maelstrom of imaginative play. Close ethnographic studies of children's play document much more surreal, metamorphic, and ironic worlds, with metalevel observation, parody, inversion, and violence. Even serious and educational toys, construction sets, for instance, model (or encourage the modeling of) buildings, cities, vehicles, and machines, but these are not *models* in the architectural or design senses of the word—the visions these objects display will never be realized (chapter 4). Thus, there is something fundamentally simulacral about the toy: in play, it is a copy without an original, or a model without a plan or future.

At first glance, the third aspect of the toy—being part of children's play—would seem to be common sense but, in fact, suggests a new set of questions and contradictions. The question of what we might mean by "play" itself is huge, and definitions of childhood and children are also notoriously elusive.[19] For now, I would interrogate the notion that play with objects is a behavior exclusive to childhood. I've already mentioned the notion of certain luxury products described as toys for adults, but what about more straightforward understandings of play? Adults participate in their children's imaginative play with toys; they play competitive games with balls and shuttlecocks, board games, and videogames. Some build LEGO[20] or Airfix kits, construct and manage model railways, or collect and photograph dolls.[21] Types and lines of toys are designed and marketed for a postpubescent demographic, from collectibles such as the Funko POP! series of stylized media characters (see "Unbox: The Material-Semiotics of Tea with Mrs. Nesbit" in chapter 2) to executive toys such as Newton's cradles, playful gadgets, and nostalgic reissues of objects such as Rubik's Cubes. Art, literature, and film for adults also feature animated toys, from the Surrealists' violently erotic dolls to the demonic Chucky of the *Child's Play* horror films (see chapter 2). Many adult toys—or adults' playful behavior with objects—test other limits to conventional definitions of toys. Luxury yachts and sports cars are referred to sardonically as toys, and they have certain toyetic dimensions. Although practical vehicles, they are machines used primarily for pleasure, status, and performance. They are not handleable or manipulable in the way a toy car or boat would be, but they are still mobile and controllable. Balls in sport or tokens in a board game are *play objects* but not generally regarded as toys in their own right. They are closer to *tools* in that their function and operation is subsumed into a wider more formalized purpose of rule-bound game play (see "Unbox: Unimaginative Toys"). While no doubt, like a shuttlecock or a *Monopoly* token, they could possibly be picked up and incorporated into an imaginative play event in which they took on unintended attributes and characters, their everyday and intimate contexts of use would tend to militate against this. Finally, the collection and display of toys is a long-established pastime, from antique dolls to contemporary collectibles. However, these objects are not played with and may never leave their original packaging (a cultural and moral dynamic dramatized in the film *Toy Story 2*). Their everyday existence is more as an ornament or as an item valued for its place with a set of like objects that are rare.

Sutton-Smith's approach to studying toys is anthropological and histori-cal rather than philosophical or taxonomical. The characteristics he suggests are not meant to be definitive, and he is careful to assert that toys and their meaning are very much determined by cultural and historical context. Con-cerned with children's lives and play in the late twentieth-century US, he sees toys as taking on a new and distinct role in response to fundamental changes in children's everyday lives after the Industrial Revolution. Sutton-Smith sees toys constituted in a nexus of economic environment, famil-ial care, responsibility, and ritual as a palliative to a childhood experience transformed over the course of the late nineteenth and twentieth centuries. With industrialization, universal education, and reduced child mortality, the well-off family of the developed world shrank and withdrew indoors.[22] Children no longer contributed to the family income. They had fewer sib-lings, and schools regulated their playtime and segregated them according to strict age bands. Their access to open space for play and sociality had been incrementally hemmed in by formal parks and playgrounds, back gardens, and bedrooms, not least because cars came to dominate urban and suburban space. This, coupled with the forces of middle-class propriety and aspiration directing their free time to educational, sporting, and cultural pursuits, has made childhood a more regulated, surveilled, solitary existence. With the removal of children from the workforce, the advent of universal education in the nineteenth and twentieth centuries, and the gradual spread of Victorian bourgeois family organization and values to lower middle- and working-class families—including strict divisions between public and private, the valori-zation of worthy and educational activities for children over free outdoor play—the child's life became increasingly solitary and domestic. Toys offered both new forms of home-based education and moral guidance[23] and solace for the socially and physically constrained child—"the toy as consolation": "The toy is a model of the kind of isolation that is essential to progress in the modern world. Just as it . . . is abstracted from the world about it, which it represents in some way, so must growing persons learn to abstract themselves from the world around."[24] For Sutton-Smith, then, the modern toy is largely a palliative for this impoverished experience, a set of artificial companions to populate the bedroom or tools for playful-instrumental advancement and "development." The toy abstracts the world for the child and, in so doing, he suggests, renders the child themself more abstract, perhaps more object-like, more toylike.

In another ironic epochal shift in children's culture, Sutton-Smith high-lights the significance of Christmas in children's material lives in the developed West. For the modern toy, and by extension modern childhood, the year revolves around Christmas the way that preindustrial agricultural societies revolved around harvest both materially and symbolically. Christmas triggers a huge movement of toys from manufacturers and retailers to children's homes and bedrooms through the gift-giving of parents and other close relatives (Sutton-Smith suggests 60 percent of toys bought were as Christmas presents). But as all anthropologists know, no gift is ever a simple act of generosity. It is always in recognition of a gift already given, a reciprocation, or it is imbued with the iron expectation itself of reciprocity, a future return gift. The toy here is nothing if not fully part of this potlatch economy—Christmas toy giving is far from being an act of generosity from generation to generation. Children and childhood have already given most of what they once had to adult society, and toys are the meager return. From this perspective, the salience of toys in the twentieth century is as the currency of a modern form of archaic gift exchange, with children obligated to respond to the annual deluge of toys with gratitude, thank-you messages, and with dedicated and demonstrative engagement with the gift itself.[25]

Toys, then, are ambiguous. The toys and play cultures Sutton-Smith is describing here are historically and culturally specific, born of the post–World War II period of mass production, media franchising, and—for some families in the Global North—affluence. However, they echo and accentuate a profound ambiguity in the material, moral, and affectual status of the toy at large. An emblem of childhood, the treasured toy is redolent of innocence and imagination and evoked in the depiction of children's suffering from news photographs of teddy bears or dolls in the rubble of war or the UK charity Children in Need's sick but smiling Pudsey Bear mascot. A toy can be the most intensely valuable object in a child's life, as any parent whose young child has lost their treasured teddy or rabbit will recognize, a relationship with an object that can be deeply felt, and integral to subject-formation[26] or one of companionship and play. Kept to hand, in bed and on journeys, plush surfaces gradually wearing down and losing color as a distinct smell accrues—the treasured toy of early childhood sustains an intimacy that is tactile and olfactory as well as imaginative and playful.

On the other hand, the toy and the plaything have long been a short-hand for the most trivial and inconsequential aspects of life and culture,

Figure 1.5
Toy luxury / toy trash. Above: giant branded teddy bear in a Burberry store, 2018.
Below: fly-tipping, Bristol, UK, 2020.

emblems again of childhood but mirroring the profound ambiguities that construct both childhood and play as concepts, the pleasurable and unproductive, the whimsical and the undeveloped. And in their recent industrial and postindustrial incarnations, toys epitomize the most despised, trivial, and throwaway characteristics of material, economic, and cultural environments: utterly commercialized, plastic landfill, cheap and nasty, a detritus of pocket money toys, Christmas stocking fillers, birthday party novelties, and transitory crazes (figure 1.5). The once-loved (or never-loved) toy is swept away into an affect-less moraine, in the corners of bedrooms, bagged up and dumped at charity shops or cable tied to the radiator grilles of trucks. The contemporary toy betrays its artisanal and affectual heritage, in terms of both its sheer multiplicity, devalued through mass production and availability, and its material constitution: plastics, with all the connotations of those derided synthetic substances.[27] And in the early twenty-first century, it seems even the relative solidity of plastic dissolves in the virtual and transmedial, the surreptitious colonization of domestic life by AI and networked surveillance effected by smart toys, videogame worlds, and mobile devices. These ambiguities and contradictions are significant and, I will argue, key to grasping both the character of toys as a distinct and important class of objects (and play, and toying, as significant modes of behavior and being in the world) and to opening up entrenched assumptions about technology and technoculture at large.

The contemporary toy, then, is a mass-produced item, a commodity par excellence, the product of a global industry dominated by media corporations such as Disney and Marvel, as well as toy companies such as LEGO, Hasbro, and Mattel. It is defined economically and industrially, found in dedicated toy shops or in the toy aisles of supermarkets and department stores. As such, it can be dated back to eighteenth-century Germany, where the production of toys as by-products of artisanal expertise and production in wood turning, metalwork, and so on turned into an industry in its own right. Contemporary commercially produced toys are integral to the recent "entertainment supersystems" or transmedia universes of media franchises and merchandising and to the new Internet-based platform media and economies (see chapter 7). If toys were once the by-products of the Industrial Revolution, they are now central to, and emblems of, a global entertainment and information economy. Mickey Mouse heralded this cultural economy in Disney's cinema-marketing-theme park synergy from the 1930s. Today, he is joined by *Pokémon*, *The Avengers*, *Minecraft*, and *Sonny Angel*.

Studying the current changes in toy production and play requires acknowledgment of this late capitalist ecology. However, again, toys pre-date capitalism and feudalism, they are a persistent feature of human culture across millennia. Although references to toys in archaeology and anthropology are rare and fleeting, they appear to be an integral part of the material culture of preindustrial and ancient societies. Animal- and human-shaped objects and balls and hoops—clearly designed as toys—have been unearthed in the archaeology of ancient Egypt, Rome, pre-Columbian South and Central America, and are found in paintings of children's play across Europe and Asia over centuries. Given that the manufacture of children's play objects in more recent centuries has often used soft or perishable materials such as wood, textiles, and feathers and, with some notable exceptions, were not valued as worthy of funerary preservation, we can assume that most prehistoric toys have moldered to nothing. In the moments where anthropology does notice children's play with toys, we can see another challenge from a prehistory of play: that toys were often objects designed and produced for other purposes but given to children as playthings temporarily or when no longer needed, either everyday items repurposed or discarded ritual objects. In *Tristes Tropiques*, Claude Lévi-Strauss recounted his observations of Caduveo women in Brazil making "little figures for the children with whatever came to hand: clay, or wax, or the dried pods of a large fruit which needed only minor additions or re-modellings."[28] In a passage that suggests toys have always been culturally and mimetically ambivalent, flickering between the sacred and the profane, he notes, "The children also had little wooden statuettes, often clothed with rags, which they used as dolls. Some little statuettes, seemingly very like the others, would be preserved with love and care by some of the older women and put away at the bottom of their baskets. Were these toys? Or likenesses of the gods? Or ancestor-figures? It was impossible to say, so contradictory were the uses to which they were put: and all the more so as one and the same statue would sometimes serve one purpose, now the other."[29] Toys, then, can be physical markers of processes of significant cultural change. Lévi-Strauss speculates that the giving of religious figures and objects to children as playthings could signal the beginnings of the decline of that religious system. Roger Caillois noted that games and play objects have often been generated by the entropy of religious cosmologies and ritualistic practices, the chalked game of hopscotch a profane echo of the medieval penitent tracing a symbolic labyrinth, the football once the embodiment of the Sun in a sacred game: "games and play are historically the residues of culture."[30] This is a tantalizing perspective and one that suggests contemporary toys could offer all sorts of diagnoses of contemporary cultural change (if not imminent collapse). However, Lévi-Strauss is not completely convinced by his own suggestion, and he posits instead a more persistent and less entropic dynamic in which the interplay of the sacred and the profane is always already fluid and open to question, "the opposition of the two is neither so absolute, nor so constant, as some philosophers have liked to suppose."[31] Toys pull in two directions, then: on the one hand, material traces of the gradual dissipation of the habitual and ritual in a culture over time and, on the other, cultural newness—the bringing of new objects and abstracted worlds into being. Today, toys are undergoing another transformation, with new forms and networks established by digital, networked, and transmedia environments, and so demand questions about the fundamental and enduring nature of play objects, and play with objects, of technologies and life with technology.

Toy Characteristics and Concepts

So, the toy is ambiguous and conceptually indistinct. Rather than establishing a clear definition of the toy, I ask instead what material and formal dimensions of objects picked up for play are salient, and in what ways are relationships, both physical and imaginary, articulated through this picking up and manipulation? In place of Sutton-Smith's features, I identify three such material dimensions and five overarching concepts of the toylike as it connects and articulates everyday children's play with technoculture at large. The three material dimensions—scale, tactility, and operability or manipulability—are discussed in turn below.

Scale

Relationships of scale between the toy and the human body—particularly the hands—are fundamental: most toys fit neatly in the hand, between fingers, or have parts that can be held or used to control the toy, such as a handle or a remote-control unit. The relationship of the size of a cuddly elephant or mouse to actual animals is more or less arbitrary; the relationship with playing hands is absolutely determined. To define toys as "objects that are *toyed with*" would appear tautological, but as a statement, it does some work. Any object has the potential to be a toy if it has the capacity to be picked up, handled, positioned, and manipulated in a playful manner. At one level, then, the toy is miniature simply because that is the only way a car, a person, or a building can be picked up and played with. Thus, the ratio of scale of a toy car and an actual car is large, whereas the reduction in size of handleable adult objects such as kitchen utensils or packaging to fit children's hands is much less marked. Pretty much any small, moveable object can be recruited as a toy, whereas few objects significantly larger than the child's body can, unless light and flexible, such as a large cardboard box. Then there are toys that are not miniature because they don't model an actual world original: physical and kinesthetic toys such as spinning tops, Hula-Hoops, fidget spinners, or Frisbees (see "Unbox: Unimaginative Toys" in this chapter). The toylike is predicated less in mimesis or representation and more in manipulability and ergonomics. Whether ancient animals on wheels should be regarded as miniature representations of actual animals or as a new kind of machinic hybrid is an irrelevant question. A toy might depict or figure a nonactual entity—in play, a clockwork toy robot might summon a human-sized android from 1950s science fiction, or it might just stand for itself, a tiny automaton at large on the bedroom floor. Scale and representation get further muddled in the toyetic dimensions of videogame environments and entities. For instance, in moments of play, the characters in *LEGO Dimensions*—Batman, say, or Gandalf—flicker between popular cinematic characters, animated LEGO minifigs, and operational software agents with capacities to solve particular virtual-mechanical and navigational puzzles (see "Unbox: The Speed and Slowness of Lucy, Batman, Batman, Gandalf, and Dumbledore" in the Introduction).

Tactility

Tactility, texture, and malleability inflect the relationships between touch, grasping, affordance, and imaginative possibilities, from the pliable softness of the teddy bear to the smooth yet resistant surfaces of plastic and metal vehicles, dolls, and construction toys.

Manipulability/Operability

The manipulability and operability of play objects is key too. Toys always have a technical dimension, and many are handheld machines: from the rolling wheels of the wooden horse to the buttons and touch screens of contemporary digital games, and via the myriad mechanisms of joints, clockwork, axles, flaps, motors, and so on. So, toys are worked (they are squeezed, arranged, animated, set into motion, fiddled with, constructed), and they are nearly always worked by the hands in conjunction with the imagination. As such, the mechanical and technical dimensions of the child's hands and sensorimotor capabilities are as much in play, and being played with, as the toy object.

Throughout this book, these three characteristics will inform the descriptions and analyses of toys as objects with distinct material and imaginary properties in play. To pursue my second assertion—that we might rethink technology from the perspective of the toy—a set of five concepts will be applied to explore the relationships between toys and their prevailing technocultural milieus: historical/industrial synchrony and asynchrony, the imaginary and the imaginative, synecdoche, simulacra/simulation, and toying and the toyetic. These are discussed in turn below.

Historical/Industrial Synchrony and Asynchrony

In the following chapters, genealogies of playful objects will be traced backward and forward from prehistory and antiquity to the present day. In so doing, the interplay of continuity in the form of some toys over millennia will need to be articulated with the epochal transformations of industrial modes and social and economic organization through which they are produced and played with. There are remarkable resonances through ancient, medieval, early-modern, and contemporary play objects, and many types of toy have developed independently on different continents, as we have seen with wheeled animals. This is not to say that toys are ahistorical. Rather, it is to draw attention to persistent technical aspects of toys, play, and children's bodies, with their prevalent technological-economic paradigms and imaginaries. The sheer difference in scale, nature, and import of Heidegger's axe and hydroelectric plant as archetypes of human–artifactual relationships before and after industrialization is a vivid motif of epochal change in the domain of technical production. In the toyetic realm, it is echoed in the shift, say, from the wooden animal carved in the German workshop of the eighteenth century to the vast, commercialized virtual world of *Neopets* of the early twenty-first century. Symbolic and mimetic relationships between the toy and its moment are similarly disjunctive. At times, the toy and toylike object seem to express synchrony—the animal carved from an animal bone for example, or a modern industrial product such as Meccano—and encapsulate contemporaneous cultural priorities and imaginaries through their respective dominant technical modes and materials. At other times, the toy slips out of step—for example, the asynchrony of the twentieth-century clockwork toy, set into motion by a mechanism that epitomized the cosmology and biology of the eighteenth century but now supplanted by industrial steam power, the internal combustion engine, and electricity.

The Imaginary and the Imaginative

The notion of the technological imaginary is bound up with this historical and industrial synchrony. At times, the toy is central to the expression of the imaginary of dominant technological paradigms. Again, clockwork in the early-modern era serves as an example. From the motion of planets in space to the movement and behavior of human and nonhuman animals, all were understood in terms of clockwork, and clockwork drove the toylike automata that at once modeled and instantiated this mechanical cosmos.

Synecdoche

It is important to recognize, I would argue, that technological imaginaries are neither illusory nor merely metaphorical. This book makes a rhetorical shift—one with significant ontological implications: toys are not *metaphors* for their wider industrial and technological milieus but rather *synecdoches*—a part of the world for which they stand, not apart from it. This synecdochical relationship is direct both materially (formed from the same industrial processes and materials—ivory, the gears and springs of clockwork, the mass-produced and modular steel of Meccano) and immaterially (shaping, and shaped by, prevailing technological imaginaries).

Simulacra and Simulation

As I have alluded to on several occasions already, there is something fundamentally simulacral about the toy, and as such, these concepts need some further explanation and application here. The terms "simulacra" and "simulation" have fixed definitions only within quite discrete bodies of knowledge from philosophy and art history to computer science. This book makes no attempt to establish overarching definitions. Rather, it highlights and sets to work the diverse and often contradictory complex of ideas, concepts, examples, and mechanisms that the terms bring to bear. In very general terms, the toyetic and the simulacral link together a constellation of cultural, philosophical, and everyday concepts and objects, including the substitute and the copy, the fake and the model, illusion and secrecy, legerdemain and trompe l'oeil, spectacle and artifice. Simulation carries connotations of trickery and dissimulation, of hyperreality and virtuality, but also of serious computer-generated models of actual-world systems. Whereas the objects that these concepts apply to are generally regarded in cultural theory as detrimental to, or at best peripheral to, the truthful, the authentic, the natural, and the original, I will argue that, through the prism of the toy, they constitute something fundamental in human culture as technoculture.

Simulacra speak to both ancient Greek art, particularly highly naturalistic depictions of the human body in painting and sculpture, but also overlap as a category with imaginary and actual automata from Greece to contemporary digital agents and entities. As such, they can be complicated machines, their effects deriving from the interplay of between their mimetic surface or elements—for example, the little whistling mechanical birds, *parerga*, that decorated early automata and the extensive pneumatic and hydraulic machines that animated them. In recent decades, this notion of the artificial *as* artificial, in which our attention is drawn to its synthetic or fabricated nature and often to a sense of the illusory, the deceitful, or dissimulation has been highly influential in cultural and media theory and their examination of postwar consumer and media culture. The work of Jean Baudrillard has been hugely influential here, although often poorly understood and applied. Baudrillard uses the terms "simulation" and "simulacra" more or less interchangeably, which doesn't help with the confusion, nor does his very general concept of simulation not as any particular device or system but rather as the now universal technocultural condition, synonymous with the "hyperreal." Baudrillard's simulation is famously "a copy without an original," a dynamic that, as we'll see, is played out in countless toys and games. The notion of the "fake" is never far from such discussions, and the canonic examples of a simulacral world—one in which established distinctions between the authentic and the synthetic, between a real world and representations of that world, have disappeared, eradicating both the authentic and the real as they are commonly understood—are, inevitably I would argue, very often toylike. Robots, virtual reality (VR), the play of signifiers in consumer culture and advertising, videogames, theme parks, and movie special effects all have distinctly playful dimensions. Toys have always prompted play with and reflection on the nature of models and copies, of replicas and substitutes, and a technological imaginary of the coming to life of artifacts that runs from the myth of Galatea and Pygmalion to Pinocchio and from the Golem to Buzz Lightyear. Toys are the very origins of the simulacra and underpin all since—and all simulations have the tendency toward the toylike.

For now, I will make the point that by shifting our attention to the toyetic and playful dimensions of simulacra, we can recast them not as a substitute for a vanished reality or as straightforwardly deceitful representations but rather as machines with a playful dimension, devices that play with the tensions between mimesis, mechanism, and emergent or virtual entities (figure 1.6). They may begin as some kind of depiction or copy of a figure, animal, activity, or environment—and carry a residue of this representation—but they circulate in the world as real artifacts with their own capabilities and potentials. They don't so much mask a (lost) reality as invent their own new ones—both in their technological materiality and in the diverse and contingent moments in which they are deployed and played with.[32]

Toys, then, are often, although by no means always, models of other things—animals, people, vehicles, buildings, and so on. As such they have a communicative dimension and are often studied as such. But what kind of communication technology is a toy? Toys' relationships to the vehicles, buildings, and human or animal figures that they ostensibly duplicate, are often interpreted as ideological, imbuing the child with dominant adult values or, as technologies, implicated in the *training* of the child for adult roles and expectations.[33] However, familiar notions of toys, and other children's material and media culture, as straightforward representations of the phenomenal world, or didactic instructions for it, are inadequate. There are several reasons for this, but for now, I would point out the mediating and transformational force of children's imaginative play that precedes and supersedes toys themselves, a force that is as likely to invert any toy's apparent meaning as to play with it "straight." Again, a toy is a technical object, at least as much a machine as a text.

Figure 1.6
Peace and Love Barbie (Mattel, 2000) and Roller-Skate Ken (Mattel, 1995). Doll and
Toy Museum, Josselin, France.

Unbox: The Hobbyhorse

The art historian Ernst Gombrich used the hobbyhorse as an object to think
through aesthetics of mimesis and abstraction, making connections between
preindustrial art and modernist abstraction—both of which he categorizes
as "conceptual art,"[34] sidestepping "the few islands of illusionistic styles, of
Greece, of China, and of the Renaissance, from the vast ocean of 'conceptual'

Figure 1.7
Hobbyhorse in *Children's Games* (detail). Pieter Bruegel the Elder, 1560. © KHM-Museumsverband, Austria.

art" In "conceptual" and ritual-based art, the naturalistic representation of bodies, animals, nature, and so on is always secondary to the object's function as a *substitute*.

The hobbyhorse itself is a surprisingly long-established and persistent toy. Horace mentions it, and there is an account of Socrates playing with one with his children.[35] It was particularly popular in medieval Europe and features in many depictions of childhood and street life, from the borders of manuscripts and illustrations in books from at least the end of the twelfth century to Bruegel the Elder's famous painting of children's street play in 1560 (figure 1.7). Wheeled hobbyhorses were sold in the streets of sixteenth-century cities. In what ways, though, does it gallop away from any significant representational or mimetic workings? Gombrich suggests that two conditions are needed "to turn a stick into our hobby horse: first, that its form made it just possible to ride on it; secondly—and perhaps decisively—that riding mattered."[36] I would qualify this second condition thus: it is not *riding* that mattered but *playing-at-riding*—and young children's play matters a great deal to them. To adapt this analysis to the terminology and concerns of this book, the hobby-horse is a simulacrum in a number of overlapping senses. Gombrich is clear that it is not an image or a representation—its head may look something like a horse (although many had very rudimentary approximations of the form of a horse's head), but no horse that ever existed looked like this spindly and limbless body, "satisfied with its broomstick body and its crudely carved head which just marks the upper end and serves as holder for the reins."[37] As such, then, it is at once a copy without an original and a substitute—but a substitute for *nothing*: the child is not replacing actual horse riding in their play. And it is functional, a play tool—a stick that can be held and charged around with, sometimes with wheels to facilitate its gallop, in a simulation of jousting or hunting: "The stick is neither a sign signifying the concept horse nor is it a portrait of an individual horse. By its capacity to serve as a 'substitute' the stick becomes a horse in its own right."[38] This substitutional character of functional objects is not, he asserts, limited to human artifacts. A cat will chase a ball as if it were a mouse. It doesn't matter that the ball bears no visual resemblance to the mouse. What matters is that it is chaseable. Play objects are "counterfeit coins which make the machine work when dropped into the slot,"[39] with the implication that simulation evolved long before human mimesis.

I would argue that the choice of a toy to open up these questions of the nature of art as substitute is far from random, and along the way, Gombrich references other toyetic forms and artifacts that we'll encounter later in this book: the infant's blanket (as transitional object), funerary objects, the myth of Pygmalion and Galatea, waxworks, wax poppets, and other magical effigies. The substitute, the conceptual, and the toyetic are bound up together in the obstinate materiality and operability of the artifice here: simulacra in that they are, at first glance, copies, but in their existence, affects, and operations, they are real in and of themselves.

Toying and the Toyetic

Critical attention to toys demonstrates that the instrumental nature of machines and systems is less stable than generally assumed. And it shifts ontological questions from the essences of particular types of object to the ways in which objects are used and their effects—that is, rather than cat-egorizing toys as distinct from other classes of artifact and technology, it suggests addressing modes of their "use" and play. Sticks, ritual figures, card-board boxes, and computers *become* toys in the moment of their play and sometimes only during that moment. The salient term here then is not "toy" but "toying": the engagement with the natural and artifactual environment characterized not by teleological and instrumental purpose but rather the material-semiotic, playful, and open-ended manipulation of stuff and ideas to hand. As a verb, the term can allude to relationships of power and agency: we can be "toyed with" by others—human and nonhuman.

I have appropriated the term "toyetic" from the language of recent commercial and mediatized toy production, where it refers to the visual characteristics of a character or other entity in a media franchise that are optimized for transmedia platforms and merchandising. The stylizations of cartoon animals and superheroes lend themselves to easy reproduction and recognition on crowded toyshop shelves or Internet media, and to easy identification of intellectual property in a cluttered media economy of copies and piracy. For instance, the characters Timon and Pumbaa in Disney's *The Lion King* are toyetic in their anthropomorphism and cartoon-animation aesthetic. However, the lions themselves were drawn more naturalistically, allowing other companies to produce sets of toy lions that cashed in on the movie's success without violating copyright. My adaptation of the toyetic draws on and includes this sense, but I use it more generally to denote the toylike, to refer to the material, mechanical, and semiotic characteristics of toys themselves that make them toys but which can also be found in other related technical objects and systems—objects and systems that might have the potential to become toys in certain circumstances or which relate to toys in interesting ways. As such, it allows us to use the toy to think about the playful, noninstrumental, and simulacral dimensions of technology at large. It suggests aspects and potentials of material (scale, touch, operability) and aesthetics that toys have and *do* and which characterize in varying ways many or most objects and systems. I use toyetic and not toylike, as the latter suggests a comparative or metaphoric relationship between technologies and toys rather than a synecdochical relationship in which the toy and the nontoy might share key capacities, mechanical, experiential, and imaginary. The toyetic allows us to track cultural, material, and experiential connections across objects and their use such as ritual objects, ornaments, automata, educational artifacts, popular media, and playful environments.

Unbox: Unimaginative Toys

There is a broad category of toys and play objects that have no mimetic aspect and are not models or replicas of other objects. Antonia Fraser's encyclopedic

A History of Toys details their invention, material and mechanical constitution, and cultural distribution.[40] Toys such as kites, tops, hoops, rattles, and balls can be found in the archaeology and depictions of childhood throughout history and across the world and are still manufactured and played with today. The baby's rattle appears to be a virtually universal toy, in their preindustrial form often made from gourds or nuts, the "most unchanging of all toys."[41] Balls have been made from fabric and reeds or glazed composition (Egypt circa 1400 BCE), from deer hide (North America), and skin stuffed with wool (Greece). Tops are generally turned wood, but stone or composition have also been used, and they are often brightly decorated, no doubt due to the optical effects and colorful patterns produced when spun rapidly. Greek tops were wound with string to start their spinning, whereas the whip technique (popular in modern Europe and North America) was a Chinese or Japanese invention. Fraser suggests that toys such as tops, balls, and rattles appeared in cultures all over the world at different times spontaneously rather than by the diffusion of an original invention.[42] Kites are a Chinese invention, and hoops were very popular in Greece, often featuring on vases depicting sporting activities.

The distinction between toys and sports equipment is far from clear and is often contingent on the immediate conventional or institutional contexts of play. A colorful plastic football kicked and thrown by a child in more openended and spontaneous play is a toy, whereas a leather ball in a rule-bound match feels like something more instrumental and tool like, albeit in the rulebound abstraction of the game. Play with each, though, relies largely on their distinct physical properties of scale, aerodynamics, and elasticity. Each is engineered for the "techniques of the body"[43] demanded by their respective modes of play: light flexibility in the plastic and weighty specialization in the leather. Objects such as Hula-Hoops, pogo sticks (figure 1.8), kites, spinning tops and even fidget spinners occupy a similar space, usually toys but with the capacity to be deployed in more competitive games. Like balls, their physical properties and kinesthetic ratio to the moving body are paramount—and this is why these toys can't be "miniature": their scalar ratio to the dimensions and movement of the human body, limbs, and hands is essential. The diameter of the Hula-Hoop and the dimensions of movement in the torso are tightly linked, and balls are scaled according to specific games and environments—from table tennis to the beach ball.

Playground equipment such as slides and swings work in concert with the child's bodily momentum. Long before cuddly animals, babies have been given rattles and corals with which to explore their emerging sensorimotor and audiovisual capacities.[44] Sex toys suggest a different take on the border between the toy and the tool, but they bear similarities in that they too are designed to serve

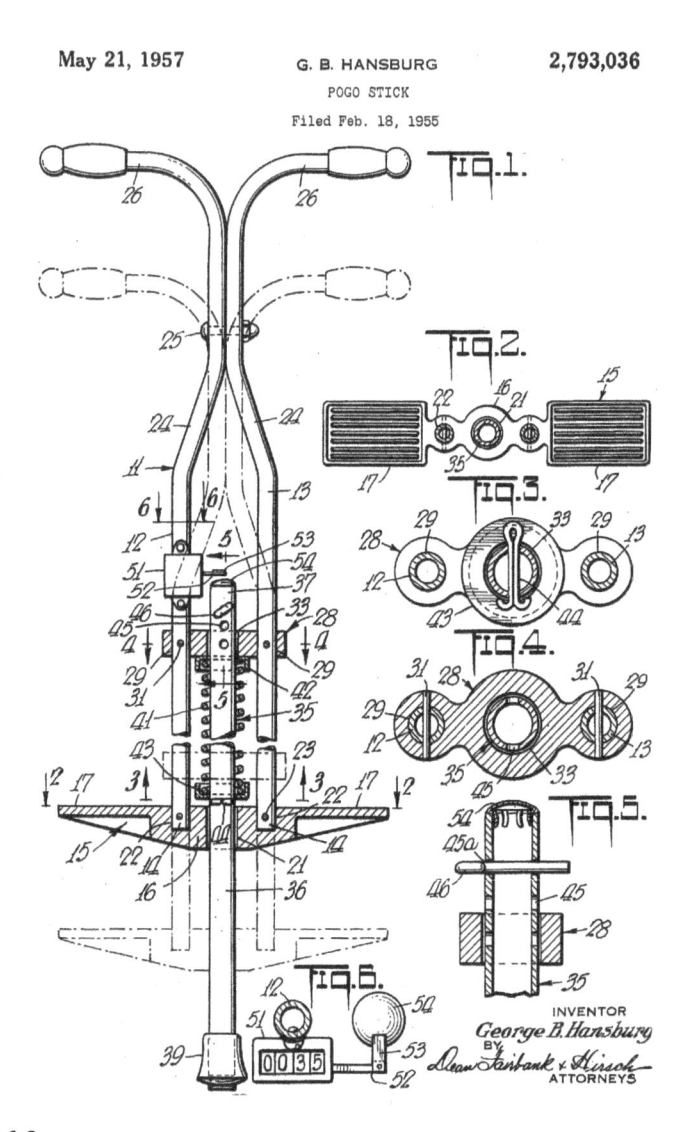

Figure 1.8
Patent for pogo stick mechanism. 1957. https://patents.google.com/patent/US279
3036A/en.

a function that is closely calibrated to the scale and possibilities of the body. They are tools for kinesthetic and sensorially pleasurable activity rather than productive or practical ends. My point here is that not only does play persist in adult and work behaviors, so too does play's embodied and technological instantiations: the toyetic.

To this nexus of object and dexterous hand or moving body in the operations of unimaginative toy play I would add the environment: the toy not so much as artifice, as model or substitute for the world, but rather as a part of the world, concentrated, rendered down into a manipulable form. Kites and windmills mediate air currents with running bodies. Balls bring gravity into playful collusion with hands and feet. Tops mechanize momentum and centrifugal forces. Rattles extend exploratory limb movements out into space and sound. From this perspective, it is less remarkable that such toys appear everywhere always: with the mechanics and axes of the child's body (and that body's predisposition to play), the materials to hand and fabrication techniques in preindustrial societies, and universal physical forces, these objects *must* be invented.

The title for this unbox is provocative and not entirely accurate (but I could not find or come up with a better one), as most of the toys given as examples here will be repurposed and reimagined as a different object or character in moments of imaginative play—or their "intended" use. Miguel Sicart makes a useful distinction between the "intrinsic" character of play with mimetic toys such as dolls and construction toys, in which play emanates from the toy itself, and the "extrinsic" appropriation of space effected by play with balls, Frisbees, and bicycles.[45] I would emphasize the kinesthetic, embodied dimension of this appropriation of space, the extension and mobilization of the body within the Hula-Hoop or across the park on roller skates. The "unimaginative" highlights, on the one hand, tool-like dimensions and "nonproductive" activity but, on the other, the centrality of the body and its sensorimotor capacities in play—a dimension that is crucial to all toy play. Indeed, we can look to Roger Caillois's notion of play as vertigo, embodied and sometimes disorientating, as a frame for this "unimaginative" play, in particular his examples of children playing with gravity as they jump or roll down hills. Then, the child's body itself is the technical object in play, the toy.[46]

The toy, then, is a boundary object between these broad categories of things: the instrumental tool, on the one hand, and ritual objects, art and craft objects, commodities, and media systems and objects, on the other. While this book will center on toys, this instability and its implications for technoculture at large will be key as well—with the argument that characteristics of toys as objects and toy play as a material-imaginary activity offer new ways of thinking about all these related objects and practices. As contemporary Internet of Toys and toys-to-life devices and systems make claims for the novelty of playful articulations of the concrete and the intangible, this open ontology and archaeology is needed to capture dynamics of technocultural change in popular media economies and everyday behavior. At a time when the existence of toys as physical objects appears to be under threat, genealogies of noninstrumental objects and environments offer ways of thinking about play in virtual, networked, and hybrid gameworlds. From the perspective of the archaic and the nonhuman, we can trace the persistent interrelationship of the material and the imaginary in play with objects—from chimps' stick dolls to contemporary hybrid virtual/actual systems. While looking back from this postdigital and transmedia moment, we cannot forget or unthink the simulated play-spaces of videogames in the past few decades: imaginative play and its media have (now) always been virtual realities. Toys offer intriguing, if enigmatic, answers to the broad questions of the nature of objects, materiality, the body, the mind, and their co-constitutions in networked and postdigital culture.

Toys mediate ideas and practices of the real, functional, and the everyday with the imaginary, magical, and phantasmagorical. They mechanize ideas and imaginaries in their design and production. So, the closest I can get to a definition of the toy for now is: "Toys are more or less mechanical objects (actual or virtual) that work on and with the body and imagination in broadly noninstrumental—and specifically playful—ways." Again, though, my aim is not to establish firm definitions and boundaries around classes of play objects and technologies. Rather, it is to suggest and analyze salient factors that characterize objects that can uncontroversially be described as toys and to track these factors out through other objects, environments, systems, and behaviors—not to separate toys out from the world but rather to look out from toys to rethink the world on their terms.

2 Dolls

Touching and seeing, the growing soul comes to an understanding with the world around it, and then with that which exercises the greatest influence upon it—man. For this reason, the doll takes the highest place in the imaginative play world of the child. The child who does not possess a doll will very soon make a substitute out of rags, a broom, sticks, bottles, pillows, which the realizing power of its imagination will endow with life. The moment of illusion, the autosuggestion, the self-deception—whatever it may be called—is so powerful that the child looks upon the doll of its choice as a living part of itself.[1]

Among the oldest and most persistent types of toy (or cultural artifact as a whole for that matter), the doll is culturally, geographically, and historically ubiquitous. The range of types, materials, types of play, and specific cultural significance is vast. This chapter can only touch on this variety in its exploration of the genealogy, manufacture, and symbolic and playful operationalization of the doll. It is not a history or comprehensive study of dolls but rather a genealogy of intersections between materials, manufacture, and mechanics and their imaginary and affective dimensions and operations. I take the doll as more or less human in shape and detail, although this is far from definitive. There are other anthropomorphic play objects that are generally not considered dolls as such—for example, miniature toy soldiers or LEGO minifigs. Many animal-shaped toys closely resemble dolls in their scale, materials, and modes of play and use—for example, *Sylvanian Families*. And in young children's play, nonanthropomorphic toys such as vehicles are often animated with personalities and social dramas. From this perspective, we could regard dolls as anthropomorphic in general body schema but often more chimerical in detail. As we'll see, the distinction between the doll as the plaything of children (and, at times, adults) and other anthropomorphic artifacts is far from clear, with religious figurines, effigies, and funerary and ornamental figures often closely related to dolls, or in some cases shifting between sacred ritual and profane status in their own career.

As Max von Boehn suggests in this chapter's epigraph, the doll is a paradigmatic artifact for the child, and it is one that has, around the world and over millennia, epitomized and modeled cultures and belief systems of, and as figured in, the human form. On the one hand, along with animal figures, it is among the oldest symbolic objects. However, on the other, it is often the most contingent: culturally and historically specific in its style, mechanics, symbolism, costume, and mode of manufacture (see, e.g., figure 1.9). It is a boundary object mediating ritual, magic, art, craft, and play. It teaches love, figures sex, and animates symbolic violence. It—in recent centuries at least—is a tool for the teaching of adult roles and a vector for intergenerational care. From antiquity, myth and literature have toyed with the imaginary of *animation*, the child's "endowing with life" of the doll in play refracted in stories of statues and figurines threatening or promising to come to life (see chapter 5). From archaic to industrial cultures, the making and use of humanoid figures has been integral to the negotiation of death and life after death (see "Unbox: Poppets"). The commercial manufacture and consumption of toys in the nineteenth century inspired poetic and philosophical reflection on the doll as simulacrum—a likeness of, or substitute for, the human being. And in the late twentieth and early twenty-first centuries, the gendered doll—particularly Barbie, with her own late-modern paradigmatic plasticity—has emblematized and allegorized gendered cultural politics and theory. The prevalence of the evil animated doll in TV and cinema horror epitomizes both the ancient feeling of immanent animation and the uncanny and a contemporary horror at the fakeries and deceit of late-modern culture, while from ancient myth to the contemporary sex industry, dolls and human-shaped artifacts (specifically female) have promised (men) erotic encounters with the artificial.

All dolls, however simple in form, have a mimetic dimension. They figure the human or the animal in varying degrees of detail, from the most primitive, being little more than an object longer than it is wide, to the ingenious verisimilitude of the Victorian crafting of porcelain faces and hands. As such, they are part of the culture of their makers and embody assumptions, values, and ideologies of body form, clothing, gender difference, and activities—and often broader cosmological figurations of the relationship between the human, the world, and the sacred. At moments in history, these representational aspects seem particularly apposite and vivid, saying something significant about prevailing social structures and values. Take, for instance the English carved wooden Puritan doll—the severity of the nonconformist worldview etched in the style of dress and the crude forbidding angles of body and face.[2] Or the contemporary Barbie doll—widely regarded as the epitome, or nadir, of hypergendered consumerism and fakery. At other moments, the relationship between doll form and dress and prevailing cultural values is less direct, the simplicity of form abstracted for easy manufacture or assumption of a child's desire for bright colors and simple shapes. However, the material and mechanical constitution of the doll—from ancient, jointed clay figures to the digital figurines of videogames—is as important as its representational aspects in its playful and symbolic operation.

At moments in cultural history and prehistory, then, the doll encapsulates something fundamental, cosmological even, about the relationship between the human body and its technological and symbolic milieus. At other times, often long periods of time, the doll recedes from significance, falling back into the everyday and unrecorded world of childhood. From everyday play to ancient myth, though, the doll remains a toy, with all the ambiguity of status and significance of the toyetic. As von Boehn noted, although he struggled to find precise terminology, play with dolls occurs in a "moment of illusion" through "autosuggestion" or "self-deception" or "whatever it may be called."[3] The doll has always been a simulacrum, mechanically and illusionistically. And, as Marquard Smith argues, the doll—perhaps uniquely—epitomizes aspects of all three instantiations of the "fetish," Western cultural theory's problematic concept of substitutional and animated objects. These are the anthropological fetish (a catch-all term for preindustrial and/or non-Western ritual objects), the Freudian fetish (eroticized objects substituting for the human body), and the Marxist commodity fetish (goods and resources taking magical life in capitalist markets).[4] At the end of this chapter, I'll address some implications of the doll for rethinking commodity fetishism in particular.

While it is likely that children have always played with everyday objects and materials that approximate the human figure,[5] the first manufactured anthropomorphic toys appear to have been religious artifacts—often ancestor images or funerary objects—handed to children once their ritual function was completed. This shifting of the artifact between ritual and play was

Figure 2.1
Sunshine Family dolls. Mattel, 1973. Photo: Dave Gibbons.

evident in archaic Mediterranean societies, recently observed in native cultures in the Americas, and in early-modern Europe when, during the Reformation, figures plundered from Catholic churches were given to children as playthings.[6] The earliest figures known to have been made specifically for children are found in ancient Egypt and Greece. As well as modeling the human form, they were often constructed with moveable limbs and designed to be dressed up or adorned with wax jewelry. They were usually made from baked clay, but there are linen Egyptian dolls from 1900 BCE, stuffed with strips of papyrus, with embroidered faces and hair made of thread.[7] Greek dolls fashioned from burnt clay had articulated limbs attached by hooks or cords.[8] However, even these toys proper appear to have retained ritual dimensions. Doll figures are found in the temples of Greek and Roman goddesses, suggesting their use in girls' rituals, discarded as tokens of childhood in rites of passage into adulthood and marriage. Greek and Roman records and literature document girls dedicating their dolls and dolls' furniture before marriage: "at Terracina a doll's miniature furniture was found as an offering to Venus of Anxur. It consisted of tables, a chair, candelabra, dishes and kitchen utensils all of lead."[9]

Simulacra and Substitutes

Three overlapping dimensions of the simulacral are encapsulated in the doll and doll-like figures: the copy or substitute (illusory, dissembling, profane, inauthentic), the animated artifact (automata, simulations), and the *new* (the artificial, the synthetic, the copy without original). With the advent of digital games and virtual worlds with anthropomorphic avatars and bots, we can add simulation in the recent computer-modeling sense as well. While all types of toys are characterized by, on the one hand, a core ambivalence between preciousness and abjection and, on the other, by their tendencies toward substitution, illusion, and deceit, dolls in their fictional depictions and in everyday play, collection, and display most persistently epitomize these dimensions. The simulacral runs through its etymology as well as its manufacture. The word may be derived from the Greek *eidōlon*, meaning "image" or "idol"[10] or, in the British Isles, as a diminutive of Dorothy (with "doroty" continuing as a word for a doll or puppet in Scots). It has been used historically to refer to both female pets and mistresses, hence its current connotations of feminine beauty tinged with vanity and the cosmetic, which appears to date back at least to the late Middle Ages.[11] Here, "doll" is also a verb, as one dolls oneself up. It is telling that the first mammal produced by cloning was named Dolly. The etymologies of "doll" and "toy" share a sense of the diminutive and often the inferior: not only a copy of an existing object, person, or creature but also a copy that is smaller, slighter. An alternative German term for "doll" is *Tocke*, referring to the blocks of wood from which early dolls were carved. Like "doll," *Tocke* came to carry gendered connotations of beauty and vanity.[12] In a religious text of the eighth or ninth century, rag dolls were referred as *simulacra de pannis* ("cloth simulacra"), a term that suggests suspicion of the pagan connotations of profane models of the human body.[13] The distinction between dolls and puppets is not clearly drawn in either etymology or history. Ventriloquists' dummies are also referred to as dolls, and magic dolls in England were called "poppets" (see "Unbox: Poppets"). In French, the doll is a *poupée*, in German also *Puppe*, from the Latin *pupus* or *pupa*, meaning "newborn child."[14] As Marquard Smith explains, *pupa* can also mean "little girl," as does *kore*, the Greek word for "doll." Both *pupa* and *kore* have connotations of "virgin."[15] "Poppet" is still used as a term of endearment, generally for young girls. We might extrapolate from this web of definitions the implication that the child itself is a kind of copy, diminutive, less formed, of the adult subject—doubly so for girls. So, unlike the toy in general, the doll is distinctly gendered in both form and etymology. Prehistoric figures and statuettes found around the Mediterranean and across Europe up until the Iron Age are almost exclusively female in form: "The features may be neglected, the limbs may be treated carelessly, but the sexual features of women are accentuated and brought into undue prominence."[16] Male figurines were rare before the Iron Age,[17] when they appeared in the form of warriors with armor and weapons, an early indication of the toy's symbolic relationship to changing social organization and technological paradigms. In modern times, the puppet has been widely used as a metaphorical and satirical image, figuring relationships of political control and dominance between toy and puppet master. For example, the *pantin* or jumping jack or, in German, *Hampelmann*.[18]

Dolls and doll-like figures have stood in for or substituted for the human in diverse ways, from the panoply of ritual figures categorized by Western anthropologists as idols and fetishes, to ancient mythical and actual automata, to the modern child's intimate companion and the avatars of digital games. Funerary figures, for instance, are a characteristic of many societies across time and continents. Shabti figures played a central role in Egyptian ritual and cosmological negotiation of the passage between life and death. Mass-produced in clay or wood, relatively crudely formed, they were dormant servants in large numbers, ready to awake and perform mundane tasks for their master or mistress once they had all passed to the afterlife. Shabtis are not toys, but neither do they fit materially or symbolically into the categories of art or ornament as many of the other sculptures entombed with them do. And when seen arranged in rows in museum vitrines, these little figures are strikingly reminiscent of displays of modern mass-produced toys. Economical in their mode of manufacture, originally little more than sticks, the molded clay figurines had none of the elaborate ornamentation or craftsmanship of other funerary objects.[19] Although particularly well represented in the archaeological record in Egypt, equivalent figures are a feature of cultures of Greece, Rome, China, Japan, and medieval Europe.[20] In one sense, then, these figures could be regarded as a genealogical and imaginary forebear of the automaton and robot—the artifactual self-moving figure often constructed to perform human tasks. In another sense, they are closer to *tokens* of the human being than representations of it; such funerary figurines are placeholders, signs, pointing beyond their own material or aesthetic value and existence to a virtual, lively presence in the next world. There are suggestions that, in some cases, funerary objects arose as replacements for actual human sacrifice. They are *substitutes for* rather than just *images of* human beings. Along with other primarily nonrepresentational or formalized modes of mediation—such as sympathetic magic (see "Unbox: Poppets") and animation (see next section), this ambiguous signification runs through the history of, and play with, dolls as toys.

Animation

The doll imaginary is, and has always been, one of substitution of the human being by an anthropomorphic artifact. But as well as the body, dolls take on the delegation of the soul—they promise a coming-to-life, like the shabtis, to realize their potential for work, play, companionship, love, and sacrifice. Many cultures' origin stories tell of creation through the animation of human-shaped artifacts or dead matter, not least the Eurasian myths of Pandora and Adam and Eve. There is a persistent fascination in adult literary, artistic, and philosophical attention, from ancient Greece to contemporary science fiction, of the doll and doll-like as objects with which to explore the transitions between the inanimate and the animate, between death and life. As such, a genealogy of dolls has much to offer in the study of the historical conceptualization of the human body and mind in the physical and imaginary universe. Chapter 5 will address this phenomenon in more detail, particularly in relation to intelligence, consciousness, and agency in automata—self-moving figures. For now, we will address the doll as animated only in the imagination and in direct play.

Unbox: Poppets

The figure combines a delicate attention to detail with a certain crudeness of form. The torso and head are well proportioned, but the arms are bulky and the legs tubular and sausage-like. The World War II–era uniform is neatly tightened at the waist, its buttons, insignia, and braid painstakingly stitched in gold thread over the brown knitted uniform. Hair and boots are knitted from the same black yarn, and the face is featureless apart from an economically embroidered splash of red lipstick. The head is at a sharp angle, as the ligature around the neck denotes the unfortunate figure's death by hanging.

Figure 2.2
Poppet craft. Left: Auxiliary Territorial Service sergeant. Right: Nurse. Both England,
1940s. Museum of Witchcraft and Magic, Boscastle, Cornwall, UK.

A card, typed in block capitals, accompanies this figure in its glass case and
informs visitors that it is an effigy of an ATS sergeant. It doesn't explain that
this means an officer in the Auxiliary Territorial Service, the women's branch
of the British Army in the 1940s. The card is written in the teasing and dis-
tinctly nonscientific language characteristic of the labels in this museum, the
Museum of Witchcraft and Magic in Boscastle, Cornwall:
A.T.S SERGEANT, ONE GATHERS THAT SHE WAS A GRADE A BITCH, A TRIFLE
HARD ON THE YOUNGSTERS IN HER PLATOON. SO TO EVEN THE SCORE,
THEY WOVE OR RATHER KNITTED A SPELL SO THE THAT THE SERGEANT
WOULD REALLY GET KNOTTED. THE FULL CHAPTER AND VERSE OF THIS
UNIQUE CASE IS LONG AND QUITE FASCINATING. DID THE SERGEANT
GET KNOTTED? WELL, YES, SHE DID, POOR SOUL. SHE SUFFERED A FATE
WORSE THAN DEATH, OR SO THEY SAY

The use of effigies of the human body in sympathetic magic is widespread, with crudely fashioned wood or wax figures found across Europe and across centuries. Known in the British Isles as poppets, there are clear affinities with other roughly human-shaped and doll-scaled magical objects such as corn dollies. The popular framing of these figures as "voodoo dolls" is largely inaccurate, the product of mid-twentieth century American popular media not Haitian vodou,[21] but is now embedded in a popular cultural shorthand of distanced and personalized magic, even featuring as a popular line of small toys.

Imitative and image magic appears to be universal in preindustrial cultures, and von Boehn lists numerous examples of toylike magic figures from Africa, Australasia, and Europe. Some appear to be talismanic—magic fertility items, for instance, carried by girls of marriageable age until they are married or have their first child. In Egypt, in the time of Ramses III, wax figures were molded and then damaged to cause harm to enemies, and in medieval Europe, wax figures were baptized and then melted as love spells.[22] The rough fabrication of wax, wood, paper, and clay dolls—and their immediate burning, melting, or piercing with needles and nails—transcends continents and epochs. The burning of effigies persists in contemporary festivals—for instance, Guy Fawkes Night in Britain—and is a common feature of performative political protest.[23]

The Boscastle museum contains other modern examples alongside pinned wax and clay poppets and votive body parts,[24] including a doll in the form of a nurse—again fabric based and from 1940s England but impaled with a large floor nail. Its information card suggests this was to trigger an abortion remotely. Whether this was an autoinflicted procedure or a malevolent act against a pregnant enemy is not clear.[25] The anthropologist of magic J. G. Frazer divided sympathetic magic into two broad types: "similarity" and contact or "contagion."[26] Traditionally, poppets work their magic through a willed connection to their victim rather than any detailed visual similarity, but they could be rendered more powerful through the incorporation of personal items, hair, or nail clippings from the target. Whether through contact with actual parts of the victim, through an ever-tightening connection established in the manufacture of the doll (modeling or stitching), or just through the magical ontology, the poppet is more synecdochical than mimetic, a part of its referent not just an image of it.

The persistence of this vindictive vernacular ritual—and the magical dimensions of the toylike—in industrial society is intriguing, suggesting, on the one hand, a deeply compelling impulse to inflict pain and revenge by the powerless but, on the other hand, there is surely something playful at work. We see toyetic crafting in the attention to detail, the distinctly toylike character of the knitted doll—and the museum card hints that this is a collective effort, a subversive coven of disgruntled privates filling the boredom of barracks life with a mischievous and subversive magical game. Traditional poppets are often quickly and roughly fashioned, as the wax and clay examples in the same museum case demonstrate, but surely the care and craft of the production of the ATS sergeant's effigy is part of the playful spell? The many hours of knitting and stitching, whether solitary or collective, added potency to the magic, channeling and *materializing* the resentment of the knitters, every stitch imbued with revenge. We might imagine that this playful witchcraft was not driven by any actual belief that the spell would "work"—that is, directly lead to the sergeant's death (by suicide). Rather, it was catharsis expressed through a residue of magical thinking, at most a wishful and superstitious feeling that this expression of resentment might lead at least to bad luck.

Industry and the Imaginary

Although an underlying toyetic imaginary of the animate human-shaped artifact appears historically and geoculturally universal, it evidently shifts its modes and moral registers according to historical, cultural, and technological milieus. Today, in postindustrial and consumer culture, the prevalent doll imaginary, for adults at least, is an anxious one. From the porcelain and lace of the Victorian doll to Surrealist art, and from Barbie to the promises—or threats—of sex robots, the doll is rendered as suspicious, uncanny, deceitful, manipulative, horrific—but often also erotic. For Freud, the doll channeled an archaic terror: not only the sense that the inanimate artifact might come to life, but also the obverse—a reminder that every human body will ultimately be rendered inanimate, a corpse. Interestingly, though, both Freud and Ernst Jentsch, whose work strongly influenced Freud's notion of the uncanny, use as examples mainly the life-size dolls, or automata, of E. T. A. Hoffmann's stories, particularly the Sandman (see chapter 5). In different ways, each psychologist implies that the toyetic dimensions of the uncanny are an adult issue, with the *child's* attitude to the animation of dolls in play largely free from such concerns. Freud suggests that children themselves have no fear of their toys coming to life, and for Jentsch, as Hannah Field notes, children's toys escape the uncanny because of "their scale and familiarity." She quotes him thus: "A doll which closes and opens its eyes by itself, or a small mechanical toy, will cause no notable sensation [of the uncanny], while on the other hand, for example, the lifesize automata that perform complicated tasks, blow trumpets, dance, and so forth, very easily give one a feeling of unease."[27]

Surrealist artists from the 1920s imbued the doll, the shop display mannequin, and other artifactual proxies for the human body and body parts such as artists' lay figures, tailors' dummies, and gloves, with a libidinal, paraphiliac charge.[28] And not only does the doll, as Freud would have it, threaten or promise the vivification of dead matter, it, in its own mute way, suggests that we humans may be less than alive, more object than subject. This anxiety is only heightened in consumer culture, where, as Smith suggests, "in anthropomorphizing things, in making them more humanlike, we in turn make ourselves more thing-like."[29] The Surrealists found their figures in the new commercial environs of the department store window and the fashion industry, along with their consumerist obverse—the discarded and out-of-fashion junk of the Parisian flea market. The flea market was a persistent subject for Surrealist and Surrealist-influenced photography in the 1920s and '30s, very often with mannequins, statues, and artificial body parts a central image.[30]

Some seventy years before the Surrealists, but still in Paris, capital of the new consumer society, the poet Charles Baudelaire offered a child's-eye perspective on new social, industrial, and material conditions through a world of toys. In an essay of 1853, "A Philosophy of Toys," he recalled a childhood experience in which he was offered a toy of his choice by an acquaintance of his mother, figured in this memory as "the Fairy Queen of Toys." The child was ushered into a room stuffed with a huge variety of toys, such that they "hung down [from the ceiling] like wonderful stalactites." They constituted a range "from the costliest to the most trifling, from the simplest to the most complicated,"[31] from which the child was invited to choose one to keep. This fairy-tale-like image of luxurious excess echoes the displays in the new department stores (and toy shops) and their promise of indulgence—but it was undercut by his mother's moralistic injunction to set aside his first choice of the "newest, the most beautiful, the most expensive, the most garish, the most original toy in sight" in favor of the "most mediocre."[32] This cornucopia was the product of a historical moment: a transition from the artisanal production of goods to the new materials and mechanical complexities and luxuries afforded by specialized and factory production, global trade, and new markets for fashionable and novel commodities, of which toys were exemplary. Baudelaire's prose poem "Le joujou du pauvre" ("The Poor Boy's Toy") of 1862 similarly allegorizes economic differentiation in accounts of children and toys. Setting out on a walk, the poet fills his pockets with cheap mechanical toys bought from street vendors to hand to any poor children he may meet. Instead, he comes across a tableau in which extremes of wealth—and notions of the animate and inanimate—are figured across types of toy and children themselves. A rich child clutching an elaborately dressed doll, "varnished and gilded all over, dressed in a scarlet tunic and decked with feathers and beads," is gazing enviously through the bars of his château gate at a dirty street child carrying his own toy: a live rat in a wire cage. The parallel between the gate and the cage is clear, but the poem figures the rich boy more as an analog of his own doll than of the caged animal. Like the doll but not the lively rat, he is restricted in his movement by his "stylish outfit of 'country' clothes." Like other "children of the rich," he is nurtured by wealth and, like the new luxury goods that surround him, "made of different stuff" from the child in the street.[33]

Across these two short pieces is sketched a rough schema of types of play object at the beginning of the industrial era and, conversely, of industrial and consumer relations as refracted through types of toy. Class is figured in the toys, most obviously in the juxtaposition of the lumpenproletariat youth's lively rat and the exquisite haut-bourgeois doll, but also, allegorically, through the variegated commodity phantasmagoria of the Queen of Toys' dream-like room. The rich child is doll-like in his exquisite appearance and restricted movement. Vivacity in this Parisian street belongs to the poor child unburdened by any such artifacts or commodities. However, the toys the poet buys at the start of his walk are particularly intriguing objects in this material-cultural microcosm of early consumer capitalism. These cheap "little contraptions"—in the original French, *petites inventions à sol*—are all mechanical in construction and attraction, including "a cardboard Punch and Judy which is worked by a string, or a couple of blacksmiths hammering on an anvil, or a rider whose horse's tail is a tin whistle."[34] Trifles but at the same time ingenious machines in a morphology of playful objects, they fall somewhere between the rat and the doll in their mechanical liveliness.

Unbox: The Material-Semiotics of Tea with Mrs. Nesbitt

In *Toy Story* (Pixar 1995), a physically and emotionally damaged Buzz Lightyear is found by Hannah, the (human) neighbor, younger sister of the malevolent

Figure 2.3
Buzz Lightyear / Mrs. Nesbitt. Funko Pop! vinyl figure, 2019.

toy bricoleur Sid. Buzz, a science fiction–themed action figure, is incorporated into a dolls' tea party, arranged around a toy table with a teddy bear and two dolls, one plastic and one rag. All the guests apart from Buzz have been decapitated by Sid, with their heads repurposed for his monstrous assemblages encountered elsewhere in the film. Buzz is adorned with a woman's hat decorated with a daisy, and a pink frilled pinny. For the tea party game, Hannah has renamed him Mrs. Nesbitt.

This moment in the film serves to emphasize Buzz's disillusionment as he realizes he is not actually a space hero but merely a mass-produced toy. It also dramatizes key characteristics of the technics and semiotics of the toyetic. That Buzz can be adapted into Hannah's game, repurposed as a guest at a genteel tea party, demonstrates the potential of objects to be rendered symbolically malleable in the physical and performative operations of imaginative play. The salient characteristics of the object here are not its visual and aural cues and design—Buzz, for instance, is emphatically gendered as male, technological in his flying space suit and helmet (these are integral to his molded plastic construction, his material being not a costume or accessories to swap or adapt), and uttering heroic catchphrases when his buttons are pressed. All of this dissolves in Hannah's imaginary domestic world. What matters are the material aspects of (rough) body schema, scale, and mechanism. Buzz becomes Mrs. Nesbitt because he is roughly the same size as the other toys and because his jointed body means he can be posed to sit at the toy table. Even better than the other toys, he is mechanically sophisticated enough to hold a toy teacup and teapot in his articulated hands. Indeed, some visual humor is derived from the use of his dismembered arm by Hannah to pour the tea. In a mechanical sense, then, he is *more* Mrs. Nesbitt than are the other guests (two of which are clearly gendered female). It helps that he is just about the right scale to be dressed in the doll's hat and pinny, although these are ridiculously small on him, the hat balanced on the dome of his space helmet, the apron stretched around his barrel chest. But this is for the film's comedic effect—in play terms, and for Hannah, the scale is close enough. The headless guests lend a macabre air to the proceedings, but they can still take their place round the little table and so function adequately. Although inert throughout most of the scene, like all toys in the *Toy Story* world these dolls are alive, and as Woody drags Buzz away, they wave goodbye to him. The split-second editing stops the viewer reflecting on the pathos of their mutilated but sentient existence, one of many mise-en-abyme moments in the *Toy Story* series.

The Animate Doll in Play

On one level, the uncanny doll imaginary supports this book's notion of the toyetic, material, imaginary, and philosophical figurations of prevailing technocultural regimes. Dolls would appear to be the paradigmatic toyetic object, mediating and articulating ideas and technical practices of human being and body, historical change, and cultural dynamics. Yet, here too, the doll has its deceitful aspects. The doll imaginary of death, sex, and deceit as I have briefly sketched it here is very much an adult one—at best, a loose and imprecise set of assumptions built from childhood memories, observations, and assumptions about children and play and, at worst, a dematerialized and illusory image of the affectual and mechanical character of noninstrumental object relations. In actual play with dolls, children conjure up imaginary scenarios and characters that address the animation of artifacts in quite different ways. Sex, life, death, and deceit *are* immanent to the child–doll relationship but in quite different ways to the fevered and gothic adult imagination in the modern era. Dolls in children's play may articulate deep-seated anxieties, desires, or fascinations, but they also channel the fleeting articulation of images, words, songs, and actions from the world around them, both lived and mediated—and it can be impossible to tell which when observing.[35] Modern dolls, Helen S. Schwartz argues, are artifacts that "remain stubbornly mute" about their play histories. Addressing G. I. Joe and Barbie, she questions the degree to which manufacturers' designs and parental guidance actually shape children's toy play: "We know from personal experience and anecdotal evidence that girls dressed Barbie dolls up and sent them out shopping, but we also know that other girls (or even the same girls at different moments) pretended that their Barbies were prostitutes, daring spies, or suicidal icons of the order of Marilyn Monroe, to be buried in the back yard."[36] Further evidence can be found in the accounts of adult respondents to Erica Rand's research on childhood memories of Barbie, as they informed her of "how much they had loved or hated Barbie and about what they had done with and to her—how they had turned her punk, set her on fire, made her fuck Midge or Ken or G. I. Joe."[37]

As the symbolic and play status of dolls has shifted in recent centuries between baby, companion, and playmate—as we'll see—so within the course of any particular event of play a doll can be cared for or collaborated with and can shift identity and character between offspring and playmate, and also parental and authority figures—often with a power dynamic of punishment and resistance. Play with dolls, by girls and boys, can be markedly violent or sexual in tone. Lois Kuznets suggests that the doll is "beyond all other playthings—teddy bears, toy tigers, or toy soldiers not excepted—the most capable of arousing a child's violent longing or loathing." Doll play is marked by not only "intense absorption" but also the "abusive acting out of negative emotions on its body."[38] This reminds us that, while not downplaying the adult messages about sexuality, violence, and consumerism that bedeck recent dolls, play has its own imaginative and embodied dynamics that can invert, mutate, or simply ignore them. Young children's play deals with sex, violence, and bodily functions in an often-gleeful manner. Indeed, the very notion of the "transgressive" in play is misleading: the flowering of images, jokes, songs, and scenarios driven by the taboo and the corporeal, the sexual, and the excretory seems a universal trait in young children's imaginative play, mischievous to some extent, cathartic maybe for maltreated children, but also a natural impulse in the exploration of bodily existence and growth,[39] one that does not disappear with adulthood but feeds into the diffuse cultural forms and activities of the carnivalesque. As I noted in the introduction, toy play is always already simulacral, abstracted from actual world objects and relationships; no less so in the ostensible hyperconformity of acting out the prescriptions of manufacturers and advertisers. As Schwartz puts it, we need "to supplement our study of toys as material culture with a history of the rich but often contradictory sense in which each particular toy came to life."[40]

So, any cultural politics of contemporary dolls as mediatized objects must attend to the peculiarities—and protopolitics—of children's imaginative play and to their material and mechanical configuration. I will address this latter aspect soon, but first I would note that all these aspects of dolls as technocultural phenomena—from the mimetic to the mechanical and from the philosophical to the everyday—can be linked together and articulated by the concept of *artifice* and within a more precise notion of simulacrum. Sticking with Barbie as our paradigm, we can see how both her line of descent from the earliest toy human figures and her current transmedia and popular cultural circulation are bound up in the artificial as a historical and cultural ur-form, one that encompasses ideas and philosophies, aesthetics and symbolism, technical innovation, cultural politics, and play.[41] As we have seen, the etymology and ancient mythology of dolls in Europe is bound up in a gendered complex of the secondary, the cosmetically beautiful as artifice and as animation—and hence always illusory and deceitful. Barbie is imagined to be the new artificial ideal of the human body, although an ideal that is distorted, sexualized, racialized, and dangerous. In academic and journalistic criticism, her stylized form and proportions are persistently scaled up in a game in which we are invited to imagine how she would look and move like if an actual person. From this perspective, she is a simulacrum in one of its earliest senses: a paradoxical artifact whose verisimilitude is so convincing that it must be read as illusory, so close in appearance to its referent as to be deceitful. The precision of Barbie's molded vinyl figure, the detail in her realistic face, and the real-world references of modern outfits and accessories for work and leisure dissimulate in their naturalism. No rag doll would be read in this way, imagined scaled up as a living woman, with proportions of limbs and head measured, and critiqued as an unachievable ideal.

Figure 2.4
Barbies, 1959–. Doll and Toy Museum, Josselin, France.

The doll, then, is an object that actualizes and animates moments of play, but neither directs nor determines it. And within the flow of play, the doll's material and technical characteristics are at least as important as its representational and symbolic dimensions. Of these characteristics, three have proved remarkably persistent over history, and remain significant today: clothing, scale, and materials and mechanisms.

Clothing

> Sitting on Kathy's upper bunk bed, we invented lives and situations for our Barbies. We did not focus on her glamorous body shape. What we cared about was that Barbie could get dressed up and go some place. Kathy could draw, design, and sew, and she made elaborate outfits for our Barbies, as we could not afford the regular Mattel-issue Barbie clothes. When we decided what we wanted our Barbies to be, and to do, and where they were to go, Kathy would lay out the appropriate wardrobes for their independent lives.[42]

A characteristic that appears throughout doll history and prehistory is the capacity to be dressed. While the cultural connotations of the extensive wardrobes of Barbie, Sindy, G. I. Joe / Action Man, and the Bratz cannot be separated from late twentieth-century fashion culture (and the *collection* dynamic of modern toy systems), the making of clothes and the dressing of the dolls is among the oldest forms of play, an everyday craft of making, sewing, and designing. It is evident too in the virtual dress design mechanics in digital playgrounds and videogames, from Barbie websites to *The Sims* and *Animal Crossing*.[43] The manufacture of miniature costumes was an important part of the eighteenth-century doll industry. There appears to be a transition, over many centuries, from naked religious figurine or icon with distinctly marked breasts and vulva to dolls whose carved or molded form incorporates clothing. Ancient jointed dolls were often molded as clothed to the knee, to allow articulated lower legs,[44] but naked figures were common again by the fifth century BCE—naked because they were intended to be dressed in miniature costumes.[45] Although evidence of a craft-based play that continues today, early dolls' clothing can also signal the ambiguity of ritual and play, as "doll clothes were also playthings to be dedicated before marriage."[46] Between votive offerings and *L.O.L. Surprise!* dolls lie millennia of folk and craft production of tiny costumes by children themselves, but also the product or by-product of adult expertise in textile art repurposed for the entertainment of children—just as were the techniques of wood carving and ceramics that produced unadorned figures.

The eighteenth and nineteenth centuries saw the commercial manufacture of toy clothing, along with the new industries of doll production. In the second half of the twentieth century, toy lines such as Barbie and Sindy— and, to a lesser extent, Action Man and G. I. Joe—included an extended and ever-changing set of costumes, vehicles, and accessories. Costume became as important as the toy itself, suggesting to young consumers play practices that include the pleasures of collecting, dressing up, and the imaginative engagement in play with the work and leisure roles suggested by the costumes, from bikinis to combat fatigues. Into the late twentieth century, the design and production of stitched or knitted garments by children and adult family members was a familiar craft and gift practice. It was common to see a favorite doll or teddy bear dressed in home-made clothing, either roughly stitched by the child owner or expertly knitted by an adult relative. The ways in which these loving acts of dressing shaped subsequent imaginative play or settled into their own pleasures of adornment and change are unrecorded but no doubt extensive.

Even the fashion doll has a longer genealogy, as the royal courts of Europe in the fourteenth century communicated the latest hair and clothing styles across the continent through the exchange of elaborately dressed dolls. Fashion dolls, or "pandoras," were mass-produced from the end of the eighteenth century.[47] At the same time, in Britain, paper dolls were sold, with sets of clothes to be cut from sheets of printed paper, a type of toy that persisted in children's comics and magazines into the late twentieth century and has been revived through online sites and participatory media.[48] Multimedia applications and videogames in the 1980s and 1990s picked up on and adapted fashion-doll design and craft. Players of the popular *Barbie: Fashion Designer* (1996) printed out their own designs onto fabric, colored and assembled into clothes scaled for their dolls. Barbie herself was modeled on the paper doll in both her dressing-up mechanic and her depiction as a young adult.[49] Fashion dolls, then, are models in various senses of the word: models *of* actual women and models *for* the clothing—evoking both catwalk models and store mannequins.

The act of "dressing up" in itself covers a range of playful activities and attitudes, including the collection, communication, and display of costumes, the making and giving of tiny clothes, the preparation of a doll for a particular play scenario (Barbie donning her vet outfit or a party dress, for instance) can be an imaginative and lively enacting of choice, dressing and accessorizing, and children dress up themselves with improvised or proprietary outfits, substituting themselves for the doll or action figure as they don princess or superhero costumes.

Scale

At the most primitive level, the doll is a scaled-down model of the human figure. A stick, perhaps with a bulbous end suggesting a head, will suffice. Most dolls and playful figurines over the centuries seem to have fallen within a range of 15–30 cm (with Barbie and G. I. Joe at the top of this range), figures that can be carried easily and manipulated by small hands. Miniature figures have been produced in recent centuries for dollhouses, and today, mass-produced systems of tiny figures and environments such as *Polly Pocket* and LEGO minifigs are popular. Figures larger than 30 cm, including animal toys, have tended to be made from fabric so they are lighter and more pliable, to be hugged perhaps rather than articulated in imaginative games. Not only is the issue of scale pertinent to the embodied and ergonomic aspects of doll play, it has also interacted with symbolic significance through a recurrent ambiguity of whether the doll represents an adult (generally, but not universally, a woman) or a baby. Until Barbie, most nineteenth- and twentieth-century lifelike dolls for children were modeled as babies or infants and sold with sets of baby clothes and accessories such as bottles and cribs. This design suggests to the child games of feeding, clothing, putting down to sleep, and of disciplining and admonition. As such, the baby doll embodies and mechanizes the long-held notion of play as a mode of education or training for children in their future, rigorously gendered, adult roles—here, for girls, the instillation of the values and rehearsal of the practices of motherhood. As always, though, we should not assume that imaginative play automatically follows pre-scripted intentions. Kuznets, for instance, questions assumptions that girls are socialized through mainly "protomaternal" doll play. She cites Naomi Lewis's assertion that the child is not the parent of the doll, "unless this happens to be the play of the moment."[50] The explicitly baby-shaped doll is itself a recent invention, appearing around the start of the nineteenth century. Eighteenth-century dolls, cheaply produced and sold in the street and at fairs across Europe and North America by traveling "toy-men," were advertised as "babies." But although simple in form, their features and body schema alluded to adult women, with more precise social and gender characteristics expressed mainly through their clothing.[51] Paintings and prints from the late-medieval to early-modern period in Europe and North America depict children clutching dolls shaped and dressed like adult women—although much smaller than, and carried by, the child, the dolls seem more a companion or confidante with whom to share stories and adventures than an infant to be cared for. In figure 2.5, from around 1460, the child holds both a doll and a toy cot or cradle, with the doll a near-identical miniature of her owner, including her elaborate long dress and bonnet. The cradle itself appears too small to contain the grown-up looking toy.

In part, this ambiguity may have been the result of a general lack of adult concern for the symbolic and didactic operations of toys in the early-modern period. The advent of unambiguously infant-like dolls at the end of the eighteenth century cross-fertilized with new ideas about childhood and education, and a new professional attention to children's instruction and play—from the inculcation of approved adult roles (motherhood for girls, martial values in boys) to more directed and ideological design and instruction.[52] Thus, from the eighteenth century, the pedagogical or disciplinary

Figure 2.5
Child with doll. Europe, 1460. From Max von Boehn, *Dolls and Puppets*, 2010 [1932].

role of dolls "prescribing appropriate femininity to girls" in particular was well established. However, Ariane Fennetaux is clear that girls in the eighteenth century were not necessarily "docile objects" of attempts by moralists, teachers, and toy manufacturers to instill symbolic and behavioral discipline. Rather, it was that play with dolls was a site of conflict and contestation through which girls could "resist and challenge adult prescriptions, and, through play, reappropriate the meanings of dolls."[53]

Materials and Mechanisms

As well as providing material aspects of the doll that inflect the toy's emotional and play potential, clothing and relationships of scale have been important factors in the pursuance of technological and illusionistic novelty in doll design and manufacture over time. They are each part of two key broader trajectories: the aesthetic/tactile and the mechanical. The doll is an affective and imaginative machine, its technical capacities bound up with its symbolic and aesthetic attributes. The form of dolls has often been determined by a material playoff between verisimilitude in form and detail, on the one hand, and lifelike or comforting feel, on the other. Materials such as carved and painted wood, modeled and molded clay, "composition" (a mix of materials that might include sawdust, glue, flour, resin, etc.), and porcelain allow the naturalistic shaping of hands, heads, and facial features but are hard objects without the soft and pliable touch of fabric dolls. Although early examples are unlikely to survive, rag dolls have been a widely produced, and given the material characteristics of fabric, stitching, and stuffing, they tend toward a simpler or more abstract silhouette, torso, limbs, and head, all of a stuffed piece. Character is picked out through the details of costume and embroidered or patched faces.[54] Even china dolls' bodies were generally made from stuffed fabric, partly for economic reasons (with the expensive materials and details reserved for the unclothed and visible parts of the body) and partly perhaps to retain something of the cuddly reassuring object. In recent centuries, dolls' faces have often been made from materials different from their bodies: wax, porcelain, rubber, and vinyl in a zoning of the artificial body into the simulacral (head, hands, sometimes limbs) and the tactile (pliable torso). The doll's body returned to homogeneity with the industrial development of soft but moldable materials: first rubber, then vinyl.

Until the emergence of mercantile capitalism in the early-modern period, doll manufacture was determined by the interplay of processes and materials to hand in everyday manufacture, economies of folk and artisanal production working with the immediate environment of natural resources and manufacture. These included wood, ivory, and bone carving; clay modeling and firing; and sewing, knitting, and bricolage with decorative elements. Ancient dolls were made from "wood, terracotta, bone, ivory, marble and alabaster," perhaps too "wax, leather and even linen."[55] Sticks or leftover products from woodworking suggested a primitive body schema, the doll emerging through decoration and costume not body shape—for example, the exquisite beaded effigies of Native North Americans. Leftover objects and materials were recycled, such as the adaptation of turned wooden pestles or champing trees into dolls in late eighteenth-century England[56] or the twentieth-century repurposing of wooden clothes pegs into simple figures with a tiny wrap of fabric and a little decoration.

The inclusion of hair has shifted back and forth over time between carved or molded as part the head to the attachment or implantation of actual hair (human, animal, later synthetic). Some Egyptian dolls had real hair attached with wooden pegs, along with inlaid eyes and jointed limbs,[57] and the molded head of Action Man was supplanted by his distinctive flock crew cut in 1970. For some dolls, the care and presentation of hair takes over from costume and dressing up as the primary play scheme, notably Barbie hairdressing sets, from playsets modeling hair salons to iterations of the doll focused on hairdressing (*Barbie Fantasy Hair Doll*) to the various large-scale heads for actual hairdressing. Hair play is not restricted to human-shaped toys; the animals in the popular *My Little Pony* line feature long manes designed for brushing and styling along with the imaginative play suggested by their media storyworld.

Many dolls, even some of the earliest, have working parts and so can be considered little machines. An articulated, poseable doll is likely to bring into being different imaginative behaviors than those of the rag doll or a set of tiny dollhouse figures. Scale, material, and mechanical movement do not determine the worlds and dramas brought into being in play, but they suggest, support, and delimit them. At a fundamental level, and at the very least, scale and material suggest whether the relationship between child and doll is likely to be, say, one of nurture and companionship (the soft rag doll, the baby doll) or of arrangement and social simulation (sets of tiny figures) or presentation and display (expensive and delicate dressable dolls and their costumes). The rag doll's loose and unbalanced body offers physical intimacy and portability and hence its animation as a companion and confidante, to be carried and hugged rather than positioned or displayed. Here, then, we see a mechanics of affect, with the rag doll not challenged in this role until the cuddly animal toy in the early nineteenth century. As Lois Kuznets suggests, "nurturing instincts can be more comfortably fostered by cuddly stuffed figures than they can by human or animal creatures made of metal, clay, ceramic, or even wood."[58]

In the late nineteenth and early twentieth centuries, numerous attempts were made to harness industrial materials and mechanical developments for the exploitation of novelty in toy production in the United States.[59] The "lifelike" became a key factor in attracting attention in a crowded market, with patents filed for elaborate mechanisms for eye movement, walking, talking, growing hair, digestion and excretion, dynamic limb movement, and so on. Eyes, and later voices, were the focus of particularly intense invention and innovation, with realistically modeled eyes that close when the baby is laid down invented in the early twentieth century and still in common use today. Carroll Pursell gives the example of a patent of 1901, an invention that "improved the construction of a doll, which is preferably made out of sheet metal, whereby it is rendered more durable and improved in various details," including mechanisms for opening and closing the eyes and supporting the teeth.[60] Dolls and action figures for boys in the 1970s incorporated a more active and surveillant gaze, such as the "eagle eyes" of Action Man that glanced from side to side when operated with a lever in the back of the doll's head and the "bionic eye" of Steve Austin, the hero of the 1970s TV series *The Six Million Dollar Man*, simply a tiny lens through which the child peeps again through the back of the head. Mechanisms for simulating speech or playing recorded speech have an even longer history. Baby dolls from the 1970s reveled in simulated bodily functions that demanded a maternal and caring play dynamic, including weeping and urination and hence diaper changing.

One of the most persistent and significant mechanical aspects of the doll is the joint. Contemporary action figures are articulated with a variety of types of connections and joints, from the simple swiveling arms and marching legs of the *Star Wars* figures in the late 1970s to the complicated engineering of more recent action figures. Articulated and naturalistically modeled baby dolls such as *Tiny Tears* could be posed as crawling, sitting up, walking, and lying flat, opening up actions and scenarios for the playing child. From the late 1950s and early 1960s, both Barbie and Action Man / G. I. Joe were engineered with a flexibility befitting the activities their designers anticipated for them. Action Man was particularly lithe, with ball-and-socket joints, augmented later with adaptations such as "gripping hands." His articulation lends itself to dynamic poses and elaborate interactions with accessories, environments, and other Action Man dolls. Barbie, however, initially at least, was only jointed at the shoulders, hips, and neck, although she has been incrementally redesigned to increase her flexibility, starting with bendable knees in 1965.[61] Barbie has been widely criticized for the ideological implications of her exaggerated body schema, but much less so for the mechanical and hence behavioral limitations of her engineering, which appeared to prioritize the wearing of costumes over dynamic physical action (figure 2.6).

Figure 2.6
Articulation of gender: Action Man / G. I. Joe (Palitoy/Hasbro) and Barbie (Mattel).
Photo: Dave Gibbons.

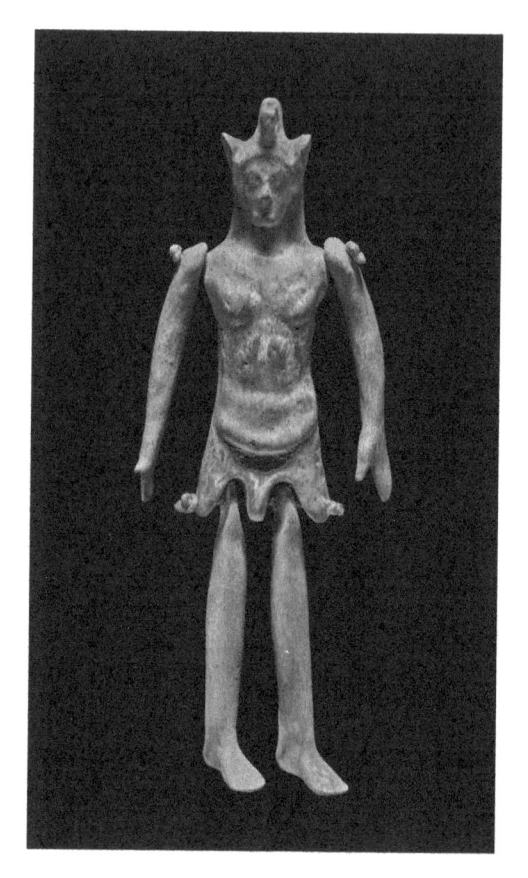

Figure 2.7
Terracotta jointed doll. Corinth, circa 450 BCE. © Trustees of the British Museum.

The jointed doll offers a simple mechanical dimension to play, one that allows the figure to sit without toppling over, perhaps to stand, to afford certain poses suggesting dynamic movement in the imaginative moment. For archaeologists, jointed limbs are a strong indication of the paradigmatic shift of archaic figurines from ritual object to actual toy. In the 1920s, Kate Elderkin argued that ancient Greek figurines with joints—although found in temples and hence still part of rituals of passage—were the first true manufactured toys. Jointed dolls have been found in temples of Apollo, suggesting boys' playthings, as well as similar female figures in the temples of Artemia, Aphrodite, Athena, and Demeter.[62] Pottery and wood female figures with moveable arms with joints at the shoulder dating back to 3000 BCE have been found in Egypt (figure 2.7).[63]

Figure 2.8
Action figures: Spiderman (Marvel). Photo: Dave Gibbons.

For the eighteenth-century toy-men, the jointed mechanisms of their "babies" (along with clothing and materials) were clearly a selling point, as they were advertised as having such features as "Undrest and dress'd, jointed, wax and common babies."[64] The late nineteenth and early twentieth centuries saw an explosion of new inventions and patents for all manner of doll mechanics, not least the engineering of joints. For instance, an advertisement, in 1904 by the Metal Doll Co. of Pleasantville, New Jersey, promoted a "JOINTED 'ALL STEEL' DOLL" with moveable eyes and removable wigs." The doll had joints at the ankle, knee, hip, wrist, shoulder, and elbow.[65]

The popular "action figure" type of doll is a recent innovation, its current form originating in the marketing of the first *Star Wars* film in 1977. From the start, then, it has been bound up in the merchandising of children's cinema and television, quickly becoming integral to new media business models in the 1980s (see figure 2.8 and chapter 6). As with Barbie and G. I. Joe, the distinctions between dolls and action figures are at once semiotic, material, and gendered. Scale again is pertinent: *Star Wars* figures were based around a standard 3¾", so bigger than traditional toy soldiers but significantly smaller than standard dolls. Though a little bigger than the long-established dollhouse figures and the roughly contemporaneous Playmobil system and LEGO minifigs, they lend themselves to modes of play comparable in material terms: they are designed to be collected and played with as *sets* of characters not as individuals, and their smaller size facilitates the construction (or purchase) of environments as storyworld stages for imaginative play.[66] The *Star Wars* action figures featured simple mechanics, molded plastic with swivel joints at the hips, shoulders, and neck. Costumes were mainly molded into the toy's body, but some featured additional fabric clothing such as capes. Like Playmobil and LEGO, the *Star Wars* figures' hands were molded to a standard sized grip to hold weapons, tools, and other accessories within their respective systems of interconnecting objects.[67]

Toy Fetish

Although the long history of costume, jointed bodies, and craft practices demonstrates a remarkable continuity in the materiality and technics of doll play, it by no means transcends social, economic, industrial, and cultural change, whether local or epochal. Materials, media, and fabrication processes, markets, and trade, and shifting ideas of—and messages to—childhood, inflect its images, forms, availability, and operations. Contemporary doll culture is bound up in new cultural, media, technological, and manufacturing milieus. Barbie has been joined by other 12" scale dolls—the cartoon-stylized fashion dolls *Bratz*, for instance, or Blythe (a revival of an early 1970s doll), with adult photoplay[68] and East Asian collecting, and global hobbyist and cosplay cultures.[69] Barbie has both pioneered children's transmedia and online media and, as a transmedial character herself, has entered complex and shifting popular cultural activities, in which the terms by which she is so often criticized—the "fake" and the "plastic"—become the site and material of performative and participatory culture in, for example, the career of the Trinidadian singer and rapper Nicky Minaj.[70] In her study of Minaj's Barbie personae, Jennifer Dawn Whitney draws on Simone de Beauvoir and Judith

Butler in their insistence on the inessentiality of femininity, of gendered bodies as simulacra, as "imitation without an origin."[71] Kim Toffoletti links Barbie to Donna Haraway's sexually disruptive cyborg, invoking a "hyperfeminine exaggeration . . . circulating in the ambivalent space between the image and its referent, between illusion and the real." If identity can be mutable and unfixed, the plastic body calls the "very notion of "real" into question."[72]

Along with videogames, Barbie websites from the early 2000s prefigured the current hybrid and networked commercial play environment in which toy and toylike figures take virtual as well as actual form.[73] Old marketing tactics of collectible objects and surprise mechanics have been mobilized to drive the business models of transmedia universes such as *L.O.L. Surprise!* dolls and LEGO.

These intertwined dynamics will be explored in more detail later in the book, but I'll end this chapter with one more dimension of the simulacrum, one with historical, philosophical, and material ambiguities that mirror that of the doll itself, and one that ties up with the notion of the uncanny doll with which this chapter started: the fetish. The doll encapsulates—and simultaneously undermines—all three main senses of the "fetish" as they have been used in critical theory.[74] Like the images of occult furniture that dance through the opening chapters of *Das Kapital*, toys are artifacts and technologies that take on imaginary life, and in consumer capitalism from the mid-nineteenth century, they present themselves as an intense concentration of all the attributes late twentieth-century cultural critique bemoaned in the commodity: fashion, glamour, novelty, depthlessness, meaninglessness, and distraction from the mundane realities of work and social power in parallel or miniature worlds of color, magic, and useless technological ingenuity. If Walter Benjamin saw in the new shopping arcades and department stores of the nineteenth-century dreamlike and toylike visions of the past and the future as an ideal realm free of the iniquities and power relations of modern capitalism,[75] then how much more vivid were the toy shops? As Baudelaire extolled, "There is in a great toystore an extraordinary gaiety. . . . Is not the whole of life to found there in miniature, and forms far more colourful, pristine and polished than the real thing? There you may find gardens, theatres, beautiful costumes, eyes as clear as diamonds, cheeks kindled with rouge, charming lace-work, carriages, stables, drunkards, charlatans, bankers, actors, punchinellos like fireworks, kitchens, and of course entire armies, in perfect discipline, complete with cavalry and artillery."[76]

Toys haven't always been commodities, but the economic and historical circumstances of their production have always shaped them materially and symbolically. So, what if, in acknowledging the precapitalist existence of their pseudofetishistic aspects—the dreamlike, the miniature, the magical, the substitutional, the abstracted—we rethink the historical novelty of commodity fetishism? From the perspective of the long history of the toy, core cultural dimensions of the commodity fetish appear more as particular instantiations of the always-already animate toyetic artifact, not a phenomenon exclusive to capitalist organization. Myth and literature are full of such automata, from the (adult) living statues and robots of ancient Greece to the specifically toy protagonists of children's literature and cinema, such as Pinocchio, the Velveteen Rabbit, Noddy, and Buzz Lightyear. Dolls are rarely free of the sense of immanent or uncanny life; they are emblems of gender identity and norms, of the interplay of the fake and the authentic, the artificial and the natural, the illusory and the real. What, then, if the fetish were flipped? If the commodity is toylike in its animation, its opening up of imaginary space and time within the economic and the material relations of the everyday, then the fetish ceases to be exclusively an imaginary substitute for a preceding object (a god, an other's body, or and unalienated social relationship), and reveals its simulacral potential: like the copy without original, a fetish without a disavowed object—but a real object, a functioning mechanism. The doll, then, is a privileged vector of what I'm calling the toyetic.

Conclusion

For all its apparent persistence and continuity over the course of human prehistory and history as a human-shaped artifact, the doll is marked by shifting roles, uses, and ratios of significance. Even its status as a child's plaything is not stable, as can be seen in the relatively recent phenomenon of adult collectors of dolls, from Victorian porcelain to the Barbie universe. It appears that dolls—and dolls' clothes and accessories—have been fashioned by children themselves for as long as they have played. However, across the broad sweep of the prehistory and history of children's play, it would be safe to assume that most humanoid play objects have been produced by adults for children. From the quick and rough fashioning of figures from the materials and with the techniques of the adult's primary instrumental craft—carved from wood or bone, stitched from leather or fabric, modeled from clay, or cast as ceramic—to the mass production and commercialization of the eighteenth century to the mediatized and virtualized systems of the late twentieth century to the present day, dolls have, through the materials and techniques of adult industry, directly or indirectly embodied adult notions of the body and the subject and their place in prevailing cosmologies, hegemonies, and libidinal economies.

But in their slight shifts in modes of manufacture and in style and costume across cultures and over time, dolls' fabricated faces may say little specific about their value to children or their animation in play. A key lesson from dolls that will inform the rest of this book is that neither the machinic nor the symbolic have any guarantee of determining any particular moment of toy play. Younger children in particular may move toys with their hands, or arrange them, with little or no engagement with the toy as a representation. Even less than props, they can at times seem to be little more than tokens to assist the imagination in articulating and following a line of fantastical thought. Or toys can be repurposed to fit the imaginative demands of the moment. In play itself, the toy goes beyond simple representation or signifier, and not merely through the imaginative slipperiness mentioned above. But dolls have also been a vector of care, like toys in general, gifts from parents and other older relatives. Brian Sutton-Smith's rather bleak view of the late-modern toy as palliative has truth, but the toy is also integral to a largely undocumented familial gift economy.

The doll tells us that toys are not so much representations as models, not metaphors but synecdoches: they are a part of the world they depict and render, through scale, material, and mechanics—manipulable both physically and imaginatively. This synecdochicality is overdetermined too: an expensive doll from the late nineteenth century is a by-product of industrial processes and innovations in materials, of international and global economic forces and trade, as well as a message to the little girl from the adult world about its values, priorities, and plans for her—a representation of the adult world but also a part of it, a device for instilling values, patterns, and behaviors. An Internet of Things–enabled doll today is explicitly and vividly connected to, and hence a node within, the networks of Wi-Fi, the Cloud, mobile data, social media, data mining, venture capital, media franchising, and transnational entertainment and media corporations. As a tangible object, the networked doll is a hand-sized artifact, but one that is far from disconnected and de-cathected from the gendered consumerist, connected, and surveillant world it domesticates and renders manipulable.

3 Toy Soldiers

The One and the Many

Doll-like figures for a long time appear to have been the only anthropomorphic toy. The next distinct category of human-shaped play objects did not emerge until the Iron Age. Wooden and clay soldier figures have been found in early Egyptian tombs, and little bronze warriors modeled in Phoenician style with tall helmets, shields, and swords have been unearthed in Sardinia and Italy, dating from around 1000 BCE, models of the Sardinian mercenaries who served in Egyptian battalions.[1] Other metal and clay miniature soldiers have been found around the Mediterranean, Europe, and Africa, with Roman war figures found in Spain, Germany, Britain, and Ethiopia.[2] Dolls and toy soldiers overlap at times over the millennia, but in general, they constitute very different types of toy and play. As well as the obvious sexual differentiation, the toy soldiers mark a paradigmatic shift from the realms of the ritual and mythic to those of the historical and geopolitical: these figures had a military vocation and concomitant accessories—weaponry, armor, and mechanical and animal transport. As play objects, they suggest different kinds of material interaction and hence different kinds of imaginative play from those of the doll figure. Toy soldiers set in play an alternative genealogy of the anthropomorphic toy, one that is more upfront in its technical aspects, and a broad mode of play that could be termed *simulational* as distinct from the simulacral doll. This chapter will explore the technological, ludic, and imaginative development of toy soldiers and wargames, touching on the implications of dolls and toy soldiers as didactic and ideological tools and exploring the toyetic centrality of war play to modern models and practices of strategy and organization—in war and beyond—from eighteenth-century military planning and enlightenment rationality through to contemporary virtual warfare, both playful and actual.

As we saw in the previous chapter, the doll is often a singular object, treasured, held close, and confided in, or posed and animated in conversational and imaginative play, perhaps with one or two others. It is a proxy for or duplicate of the child and is charged with the spirit of the animate artifact, in play it is *as if* it is alive. The toy soldier, however, is rarely singular; it is nearly always part of a set. A child may have enough dolls for a tea party (say, three or four) or a family-sized set of small figures for the dollhouse (say, five or six), but they can never have enough toy soldiers, as the more soldiers, the more elaborate and extensive the war. And as with dolls and doll play, the factors of scale, materials, mechanisms, and, to a lesser extent, clothing are pertinent to the material-imaginary operations of toy soldiers. As multiple objects, like the Egyptian shabtis, toy soldiers have generally been made from cheap materials, roughly molded from clay, carved or cut from sheets of wood, or cast in metal—initially bronze and later lead (and, in rare cases of armies forged for the children of royalty, silver), where the relative expense of the material balanced with the economies of mass manufacture. From the mid-eighteenth century, German and French manufacturers produced printed and cutout paper armies, which gained particular popularity during the Napoleonic Wars.[3] Casting in metal and printing on paper allow for a degree of detail in costume and accessories that is too fiddly or expensive in molding and carving. But any such detail on the toy soldier functions quite differently from the individuating outfits of dolls. Instead, it serves to identify and distinguish classes of figures rather than individuals, depending on the historical period and degree of sophistication of manufacture: foot soldier from officer, cavalry from artillery, regiment from regiment, and so on. To the modern wargamer, detail signifies historical accuracy not personality. Importantly, as we will see, there is no clear distinction between the toy soldier as a model of an individual warrior and as a more abstract token in board games, tabletop games, and digital games (and actual military planning equipment). In many such serious or playful simulations, one figure on the board can stand for a collective in the referent theater of war: an armored unit, a squad, a battalion, and so on. Even in the earliest toy soldier figures, we can see mounted soldiers carved as one with their horses. In the genealogy of war-themed play objects, the soldier toy shifts between figure and token, and play itself between imaginative worlds and the rule-bound game.

Toy soldiers, then, are *miniature* in a way most dolls aren't. Their scale establishes a quite different relationship between player and figure. In literature, this ratio has played out in dramas of power and pathos. Lois Kuznets recounts a number of children's stories featuring toy soldiers, each of which is driven by the soldiers' vulnerability in both their scale and warlike circumstances, "these miniature beings . . . may move the beholder by their apparent weakness and the bravery with which they endure it."[4] Scale, narrative, and imagination work together. She cites G. K. Chesterton:

> When an adult or child picks up a toy soldier, which is typically two or four inches tall, and holds it in the palm of his or her hand . . . the holder imagines its feelings of powerlessness, its dependence even as a combatant not only upon its imagined commander but upon the god that holds it and creates its character and story. Miniature soldiers thus arouse feelings of affinity, as well as of power and control, especially when the models are of creatures that in real life are proportionately bigger, sometimes *much* bigger and more powerful than the person holding them.[5]

With hobbyist wargaming in the twentieth century and its fantastical offspring, the tabletop role-playing game, the *miniature* figure became a distinct commodity in its own right, named as such, and generative of extraludic hobby activities such as collecting, painting, and physical modification (see "Unbox: Miniature War").

Perhaps the most generative toys in literary culture are the twelve small wooden soldiers given to Branwell Brontë by his father, which he shared with his sisters. Incorporated into the children's extensive storyworlds in the late 1820s and 1830s, the soldiers were given names and status in their plays, poems, and stories. Initially at least, the figures had clear martial and historical references (the Duke of Wellington, Napoleon), but they took on more allegorical form—fantastical giants that ruled over the expansive paracosms of Glassland and Angria.[6] The toys were "the seed-bed of juvenile fantasies, and the flowers from these seeds were . . . sometimes very surprising."[7]

While poetry, literature, and memoirs offer glimpses into the imaginative play worlds of childhood, they tend to be driven, formally and aesthetically, by individual protagonists and small group relationships, so that toy soldiers in such stories are animated with a degree of subjective motivation and pathos that may be fleeting in the imaginative flow of an actual play battle and completely absent from the tabletop or digital simulation of warfare. It may be that some children have carried a singular toy soldier as if it were a tiny companion or set up and enacted social dramas with a small handful of them, like the Brontës, but in the main, these tiny figures are designed to be looked down on from on high, positioned, organized, and moved in tactical arrangements—*deployed* as much as animated. The player is not a companion to the toys but rather a demiurge: a general or a god. Toy soldiers, then, muster existential reflections different from those of the doll. Often, they invite contemplation not on what it means to be alive but rather on what it means to die—or to be part of a scenario or theater of death. Where toy soldiers are used as symbols in broader culture beyond play, it tends to be as allegories of the morality of war and power. Their sheer multiplicity alludes to the disdain of their commanders and leaders for the lives of individuals.[8]

Military Training

> The toy soldier and the doll symbolize most clearly the division society makes between girls and boys at play—as well as the gender separation assigned to nurturing and aggressive instincts. Toys thus become ideal tools for societal gender modeling.[9]

As noted, most children's toys until recently have not been clearly distinguished as objects for boys or girls, but the long history of dolls and toy soldiers does signal a marked dimorphism in material form, expectations of the play of boys and girls, and an analogous differentiation of the adult roles projected for those boys and girls. But to what extent does this logic carry on into *play* with toys and games? Presumably, ancient toy soldiers at least celebrated a possible martial career for Greek and Egyptian boys, and in later historical moments (notably eighteenth-century Prussia, as we'll see), this is focused and developed as actual training in strategy and logistics that might have instrumental effects in a child's predisposition toward, and progress in, a future military career. At other points in the modern era, toy soldiers appear less didactic and more akin to dolls, employed as much to amuse and occupy children as to instruct them directly. Toy soldiers here, at most, instill a general positive disposition toward the military and toward battle and war as appropriate means of addressing nation-state interests and tensions.[10]

Toy play as training has its anxious flip side, though, as social attitudes to warfare shifted, particularly in the twentieth century. Concerns about the influence of war toys and media on children's attitudes to violence have been prevalent since the 1960s in Europe and North America, with toy guns and soldier costumes coming under criticism, along with violence-themed film, TV, and videogames. Recent decades have seen a move away from the direct historical references to World War II that characterized many boys' toys in the second half of the twentieth century toward fantasy and science fiction–themed warriors and conflicts.[11] There are earlier examples too—for example, war toys were banned in Germany after World War I as a condition of the Treaty of Versailles.[12] Recent moral panics over the effects on players of the depiction of violence in videogames highlight a particular toyetic and simulational register: toys and games are even worse than comics and movies, it is asserted, because, with them, the child enacts, performs, and "learns" violent behavior.[13] Tellingly, this criticism is always leveled at games that model hand-to-hand combat or gunfights at close quarters (*Mortal Kombat*, *Call of Duty*, etc.) and not the real-time strategy games that are the most direct descendants of miniature toy soldiers.

Again, though, we should not assume that because a toy is designed to encourage a particular imaginative and behavioral repertoire that it will necessarily be successful. As demonstrated by the Brontë children, toy soldier play has the same fantastical potential as doll play, albeit expressed in varying ratios of scale and subject–object relations. The symbolic form of toys does not determine imaginative worlds of play, and hence their effectiveness as didactic tools is unsteady at best. In everyday life, gender dimorphism can blur as, for instance, when brothers and sisters play together and share toys. But this is not to argue that aesthetic and mechanical characteristics are redundant. Imaginative play is inherently a flow of signs and operations, pre-scribed characters and emergent, spontaneous worlds. After all, even if we accepted the "training" thesis had some purchase on the growing child's cognitive development and ideological interpellation, playing with toy soldiers as a material practice does not position young boys in relation to war or combat in the same way that play with toy ovens or prams might position the practice and behaviors of domestic work in the embodied imagination of young girls. For this, we'd have to look to a different kind of toy scaled to the boy's body. There have been masculine and military-themed dolls over the past century or so that could animate individual adventure and hand-to-hand combat, most famously G. I. Joe / Action Man, but they have been much less prevalent than the miniature soldier sets. For the performance of subjective and bodily acts of combat, boys have used dressing-up costumes of knights or soldiers, handheld shields and weapons, mechanical guns (popguns, cap guns, water pistols, Nerf guns), and working bows and arrows or slingshots. We can counter this enactment of bodily combat with the child playing with a wooden or lead army: they are not on the front line, not cannon fodder, but rather the strategist—the general or monarch. As with doll play, it seems likely that toy soldier play offers the child a mechanism for playing out the power they are subject to in their everyday lives—by parents, teachers, older siblings—over smaller entities. Like the digital simulation games to come, we see here an ambiguous subject position for the player—but not an unlimited one, within the figures of authority who have some kind of purchase on the dynamics of the gameworld—the deployment of troops, the determination of outcomes of battles or skirmishes. This is illustrated in a telling passage in Winston Churchill's *My Early Life*, in which the future British Prime Minister and war leader was seen by his father in his nursery playing "a really impressive game of soldiers" and was asked if he would like to join the Army. "I thought it would be splendid to command an army, so I said 'Yes' at once; and immediately was taken at my word . . . the toy soldiers turned the current of my life."[14] The child immediately took "joining the army" to mean "commanding" it, an ambition prompted perhaps by the mechanics of miniature war play as well as the assumptions instilled by his upper-class privilege and education.

War Economy

As with so many toys, there is a direct relationship between toy soldiers' form—and hence their operations within play—and the economics of their materials and manufacture. Like other multiple token-like objects, notably shabtis, early warriors were molded from clay or cut from wood. Small tin figures of knights on horseback were produced for children in the thirteenth century, and these were sold alongside the similar pilgrims' tokens in stalls on Parisian bridges.[15] The grand armies given to royal children in the seventeenth century were cast in metal, generally lead but with some particularly ostentatious sets in gold and silver. Like the elaborate dollhouses that would soon join them in the nursery, these were displays of wealth and status.[16] As Dauphin, Louis XIII was given an army of three hundred silver soldiers by his mother. They were around 7 cm tall and were molded with pegs at their base rather than stands, and they were fitted into battle formations on a board. Louis XIV inherited and reinforced the army in 1650. It was then passed to his eldest son and further extended with troops, artillery, and buildings. By now, the model army was regarded not only as a toy but also as an integral part of a future monarch's military training. It was also evidence of the emergence of an international toy industry, with many of the units commissioned from manufacturers in Nuremberg and Ausberg.[17] To give an indication of the value of this silver army, it appears that it was later melted down to help pay for Louis XIV's actual military campaigns and replaced with a cardboard set.[18] Commercially produced soldiers for a wider market were flat, lead figures manufactured in Nuremberg in the mid-eighteenth century, with fully rounded models produced in France by the end of the century. These remained expensive and, up until the late nineteenth century, demanded a significant investment. So, they tended to be the preserve of wealthier families and adult hobbyists. The "toy soldier revolution," as the collector Norman Joplin terms it, began in 1893 with the British toy manufacturer William Britain's innovations in hollow casting.[19] Molten lead was swirled around the cast, coating it inside, with the excess draining out, meaning that the amount of metal needed for a solid figure could now produce three hollow ones.[20] This economical technique posed the first serious challenge to German dominance in toy manufacture.[21] Plastic figures were introduced in the late 1940s, partly as a response to postwar restrictions on the supply of metal. The British firm Airfix and the American company Beton used injection molding to mass produce very cheap 2⅜" or 60 mm figures, self-colored and in the form of US infantry, followed by other soldiers, "Cowboys and Indians,"[22] ancient Greek warriors, Arthurian knights, and so on (figure 3.1). The same materials and manufacturing processes were subsequently used to produce cheap farm and zoo sets.

Packs of these figures were often sold in general stores rather than specialized toy shops: in the UK, in Woolworths or newsagents, and in the US, in five-and-dime stores—from which they adopted their popular name, dime-store soldiers. Immortalized in the first *Toy Story* film (1995), a squad of "Army men" was animated with visual jokes about their material qualities and construction: the tags and seams produced by the cheap molding process carefully rendered in this early CGI, movement determined by feet fixed firmly to integral stands.[23] In the early 1950s, Kellogg's began commissioning toy manufacturers to produce injection-molded plastic figures for inclusion as free gifts in their cereal packets.[24] This mode of production facilitated the introduction by Britains in 1958 of a simple mechanical dimension

Figure 3.1
Toy soldiers / army men. Plastic, 5 cm scale. 1950s–. Photo: Dave Gibbons.

to 60 mm plastic figures. Torsos, heads, limbs, and weapons could be just as easily molded as separate units, and hence the bodies of their *Swoppets* range could be dismembered and reconstructed, and they had a certain degree of animation and poseability—heads could swivel on the neck, for instance.

All these dimensions of quantity, economics of production, relationality, and scale affect the mechanical operations and behavioral possibilities of toy soldier play. First, it is important to note that the toy soldier "machine" is the army not the individual. *Swoppets* and some artillery weapons in more recent toy lines notwithstanding, miniature soldier figures are rarely mechanical, tending to be carved or molded as solid or flat figures. They have no moving parts but become moving parts within the larger assemblage of the toy army. In their staging and deployment as tactical formations, supply lines, resources, and their operational effects on the opposing army,[25] their scale is salient (allowing for the extensive arrangement and manipulation of units) as is their economy (simply, cheap soldiers mean plenty of units for deployment). In children's play, they are animated by imaginative and action-driven activity; in adult wargaming, the imagination is regulated and augmented by the spatialization and randomization mechanics and algorithms of measuring devices and dice. And—predicated on this token-like, rule-bound, and combinatory mechanism of miniature soldiers—their battlefield world is a zone where the *toy*, the *game*, and the *simulation* most closely overlap.

Models of War

> The representational features of the wargame—such as the individual pieces standing in for whole military units, the scaled reduction of physical space to the dimensions of the game board or miniature terrain-analogy, the formulas for calculating conflict outcomes and losses, the representation of uncertainty and unanticipated factors by means of dice throws—all these served the purpose of what subsequently became known as "modelling" in the service of simulation.[26]

As we have seen, if paid serious adult attention at all by adults, toy soldiers for children have in earlier centuries been generally regarded as serving a more or less didactic function, instilling military and patriotic values in the ambient imaginative environment of the boy's emerging worldview—and in this, they were the counterpart of the girl's doll. But like the doll, at particular cultural-historical moments, they were brought to the fore, celebrated or denigrated, with significant toyetic claims made for their ideological operations in play. One such moment for playing war came at the end of the eighteenth century. In the late seventeenth century, Gottfried Wilhelm Leibniz had proposed reworking chess to make a more accurate model for actual war, but in 1780, Johann Christian Ludwig Hellwig took this idea further and devised a game that was to establish a technical and ludic model for the simulation of war that continues today.[27] He expanded the chess board's sixty-four squares to 1,666 squares, differentiated with five kinds of terrain, including mountains, forests, and bodies of water. This terrain affected the movement rates of the 104 pieces per side, with these units having their own movement rates according to their type: infantry, cannons, cavalry, and so on.[28] The board wasn't fixed but could be reconfigured by players to model recent or historical battle-fields or—as we'll see—imaginary ones. Hellwig's game was influential, and others, including his son, built on it in an ongoing attempt to simulate the complexities and environmental determinants of contemporaneous warfare more accurately (figure 3.2). Georg Venturini incorporated actual maps in the early nineteenth century, introducing "proper scale and reference to the real

Figure 3.2
Reconstruction of Hellwig's *Kriegsspiel*, 1780 (detail). HBK Braunschweig / Prof. Dr. Rolf F. Nohr. Photo: Ralf Wegemann. http://www.strategiespielen.de/johann-christian -ludwig-hellwig.

world."[29] *Kriegsspiel* was more substantially developed by another Prussian, Lieutenant von Reisswitz. Reisswitz's wargame was also turn based but developed, as Patrick Crogan explains, "complex rules which set out procedures for determining the outcome of individual conflicts between pieces in different circumstances such as relative unit strengths, terrain occupied, and so forth."[30] It had an umpire to arbitrate the rules, dice to introduce an element of chance in a battle, and at the end of the game, the number of casualties was calculated using loss tables.[31] For Reisswitz, the key weakness in *Kriegsspiel* was the topological abstraction of the grid—for instance, only one unit could occupy a single square on the map, and all units were of equal size. He introduced a sand table in which open terrain could be modeled and replaced lead or silver miniatures with wooden blocks that would more accurately depict the dimensions of actual troop formations.[32] The game also attempted a more fine-grained temporal frame, with turns reduced from *Kriegsspiel*'s day to a single minute.

In its systematization and ludification of war planning, *Kriegsspiel* combined the abstract strategic form of chess and Go with the expanded and flexible mobilization of the extensive toy army, and with ideals of rationality and social engineering. In so doing, it produced a seriously playful system from which derives one of the main contemporary notions of simulation: the modeling of complex systems for planning and prediction. For Jon Peterson, if chess was the "birth of simulation," *Kriegsspiel* was its coming of age, a realization of the Enlightenment dream that all sciences "could be reduced to systems with the clarity and consistency of Newtonian mechanics. If only sufficient data could be gathered and properly organized, then the outcomes of war could be determined."[33] For Crogan, modern wargaming is inseparable from the Enlightenment rationalist project and its influence on political, economic, and philosophical transformation in Western Europe from the eighteenth century.[34] Napoleon's victory over and occupation of Prussia in 1806 added a pressing practical impetus in Prussia to apply modern thinking to the perceived failures of government and military strategy. To extrapolate, wargaming at once instantiated, miniaturized, allegorized, and synecdochicalized Enlightenment philosophies, practices, and plans. Like the construction sets explored in the next chapter, the wargame is a model in two key senses: a miniature replica (here, dynamic and interactive unlike the static architectural model of the construction toy) and an operational plan, a testing or rehearsal with actual world ramifications and effects, both directly in the planning of specific conflicts and indirectly in the rehearsal of the logic of new rational and economic values and systems. A clear genealogical line can be drawn, then, from chess and the early wargame via extensive innovations in the mechanisms of tabletop war simulation in the nineteenth and twentieth centuries; cybernetics and game theory in World War II and the Cold War, to contemporary computer simulation and modeling of immediate and future theaters of warfare.

I would add to this picture, however, an insistence that the ludic and toyetic dimensions of simulation are not mere residual aspects of some primitive or childlike evolutionary stage of development but rather embedded deep in its genotype. From this perspective, recent descendants of wargames, from tabletop games such as *Warhammer 40,000*, role-playing games such as *Dungeons & Dragons* (*D&D*), and many videogames (and not only those with explicit war themes), are much more closely related to instrumental scientific and military simulation and planning than it might first appear. I will demonstrate this first through the tracing of a persistent genealogical interweaving of serious and play applications and game mechanics of toy soldiers and war play since *Kriegsspiel*, and second through the assertion that the simulation, as a flexible and responsive machine for experimentation, speculation, and prediction, has by necessity an unstable playful core. Each of these assertions requires an account of the development of wargames as material and ideational systems.

Wargames

At first glance, wargames would seem to epitomize the realist or mimetic ambitions of simulation design and application. That is, the more nuanced and responsive the system of figures, dice, calculations, resources, and terrain, the more accurately it appears to model actual military preparations and war. This logic applies as much to contemporary computer simulation as it did to Hellwig's table. But if we pay attention to the simulation's material and mechanical reality and to its ludic DNA, then the relationships between model and source look less straightforward. To my mind, any simulation—as a modeling or predictive system—is inherently unstable due to a simple paradox: the more a simulation models the complexity of its actual or imaginary source, the more mechanically elaborate, and hence divergent from it in material reality, it becomes. And the more a model attempts to simulate one dimension of a source system accurately (the dynamics of combat for instance), the more it tends to abstract others (supply lines, perhaps) and, again, the more obvious the mechanism becomes. Toyetic ergonomics is a simple but key factor here: the physical demands of miniaturizing an army to fit on a tabletop such that it can be quickly arranged and rearranged by the reach of an arm and hand. *Kriegsspiel* adopted the turn-based play and geometric board terrain of chess—conventions that move both games *toward* the source system of actual battle through the facilitation of a coherent modeling of movement and domination of space, while simultaneously pulling *away* through the abstraction of space into a grid, and the abstraction of time into discrete units. And so, as the complexity of the tabletop wargames increased, new abstractions and formal conventions were needed. One such abstraction in *Kriegsspiel* is the use of single tokens to stand for whole military units,[35] collectives figured as individuals in a kind of functional allegory. Others include the ascription of different rates of movement to different units (infantry, cavalry, artillery, etc.), but the increased complexity of rules that this differential movement demanded led to the institution of an independent referee or director to ensure their correct interpretation and application.[36] Hellwig's game included some historically and physically inaccurate relationships—for instance, the relationship between the distance that infantry could travel in a day and the firing range of artillery. In *Kriegsspiel*, this was 4:3, meaning the firing range was much further than on an actual battlefield. It was, however, considered by Hellwig to be essential to balance gameplay: "Here, at the dawn of wargames, Hellwig discovered the trade-off between realism and playability, which history bore out to be among the most fundamental choices in wargame design."[37]

This toyetic paradox of simulation can be tracked through the development of the wargame. After the defeat of Napoleon and Prussia's liberation, Reisswitz's son developed the game, introducing probability and statistics—innovative features that fully institute the wargame as a simulation in the modern sense.[38] The mathematics of probability were harnessed to simulate chance and emergent complexity in a significant break from both chess and from the Newtonian mathematical underpinnings of the Enlightenment. Peterson explains that during the Napoleonic occupation, Prussian statisticians compiled probability tables from the large amounts of data they had gathered about the range and effectiveness of firearms. The younger Reisswitz used dice to randomize results from within the ranges set out with these probability tables. As Peterson puts it, "this allowed combat in his wargame to encompass the uncertainty of real events without rendering outcomes arbitrary. It was not chance he admitted to the game, but simulation."[39] The role of the independent referee was developed too, from an arbiter of complicated rules to something closer to that of the software in a contemporary computer wargame: establishing starting conditions and moving each army's units so that neither side had full view or knowledge of the other. In some versions of the game, there were three game boards, one for each player with their own forces and limited knowledge of their opponents' positions, and one controlled by the referee, with a god- or CPU-like omnipotent view of all the information. This latter is a clear forebear of "fog of war" mechanics in contemporary computer strategy games.[40]

On the one hand, we see the instability of the teleology of military simulation as a mode of modeling that belies its abstract origins in the ever more accurate capture of real-world dynamics and possibilities. On the other, its origin in toys and games is no historical quirk but rather a persistent and significant factor in both the machinic form and heuristic operations of the simulation—and its consistent entanglement over the centuries with its playful and popular cultural instantiations. For wargames, it is worth saying, remained *games*. The tabletop innovations of the late eighteenth and early nineteenth centuries developed game conventions and mechanics that have proved remarkably persistent. From the start, *Kriegsspiel* and its descendants have mobilized the playful operations of everyday amusement, pleasure, distraction, and sociality as much as the serious training of the strategic mindset. Hellwig imagined an audience for his game beyond the military; it would teach the art of war, but also "provide, to those who need no instruction, a pleasant entertainment."[41] Thus, although in 1824 it was adopted for the military academy's training and research program,[42] it was also adopted by the Prussian royal family, who played it for entertainment as well as for formal military training.[43] Reisswitz himself had played Hellwig's game recreationally in his youth.[44] When one reads these game rules, mechanics, and conventions, now so familiar from board games, tabletop wargaming and role-playing games, and turn-based and real-time strategy digital games, it is easy to imagine a whole set of playful pleasures attending the ostensibly deadly serious motivations. Would these planners, most probably themselves raised with toy soldiers, not have had moments of less instrumental play, testing out improbable scenarios, even actual games in the full, nonserious sense? Even if professional propriety forbade full-on play, surely there must have been significant pleasure in the manipulation of tokens and rules, the imaginative conjuring up of a world of domination and victory, or the ludic and puzzle-like challenges of tactics and strategy in a formalized agonistic space, free from actual world consequences? And on another level, the simple fact of two people playing together brings in the need for the abstraction of rules, balance, and turn taking at the level of game design. Rules of engagement, movement, damage, and resources must at least be shared and understood as the game commences, and likely adapted and negotiated to fit time constraints and to facilitate satisfying play. "There has always been a tension between realism and playability in wargames," Meriläinen et al. argue, "between accurate simulation of combat situations and the recreational flow of the wargaming experience."[45]

Wargaming picked up an enthusiastic following in both military and everyday culture over the nineteenth century, with civilian and officer clubs in Germany and a *Kriegsspiel* club established at Oxford University in 1873, and overlapped with lively new markets for war-themed toys and board games.[46] Robert Louis Stevenson used the new cheaper mass-produced figures for wargames of his own design in the 1880s, marking out terrain in chalk on his attic floor and mobilizing around six hundred units, each unit representing one hundred actual soldiers.[47] The Britains company's innovations in hollow casting at the end of the century took the amassing of large toy forces to a wider and more youthful public, encouraged as well by their publication of suggested wargame rules to accompany the figures. By the time H. G. Wells wrote his two books on wargaming (*Floor Games* in 1911 and *Little Wars* in 1913), burgeoning toy industries in the UK and Germany meant that the toy army was now within the reach of the middle class and found its place within the new domestic dynamic of leisure and hobbies, bringing about "a second wave of invention . . . as hobbyists repurposed these wargames to emphasize entertainment over education."[48] To emphasize the divergence of the wargame from preparation for actual warfare (whether in the nursery or in the control room), we might note that Wells himself saw his games not as celebrations of or training for war but rather as attempts to model its shortcomings: "his simulation of command tried to teach players to hate and avoid war—while still enjoying it themselves" (figure 3.3).[49]

The operational efficacy of the serious war simulation, while predicated on the fundamental "as if" move of the toy and game, is driven forward by the "what if" of simulation. What if the infantry attempted to breach the enemy's lines on their left flank, followed by the cavalry? Or instead, what if the cavalry led the charge? The "what if" lies at the instrumental, operational end of the imaginative play spectrum, underpinning for example the engineering of construction toys (the "as if" / "what if" distinction is explored in more depth in chapter 4). Like the scientific simulation with which it shares its genealogy, the serious wargame offers a speculative, future-oriented temporal mode. It is an elaborately engineered thought experiment. As Will Wright, the designer of *SimCity* and *The Sims*, explains in relation to play with an early flight simulator, simulation games offer "behaviour space" and "possibility space" within which to conduct "What happens if I . . ." experiments that necessitate engaging with and exploring the game's internal model.[50] So, from starting conditions (number and arrangement of forces and resources, environmental and geographical conditions), the game/simulation facilitates the playing out of cause and effect into the future. The child's play with soldiers as if they were actual troops tends to operate in the moment, a dynamic emerging from the moment-by-moment imaginative manipulation of the tokens, the only teleological force perhaps a sense from the start of play of the goodies and baddies and hence the eventual victors.

These are different modes, but they are by no means mutually exclusive. One can imagine a child, perhaps a little older, with a fascination for military strategy whose floor games might draw on a degree of historical and tactical realism, a more or less fabulous playing out of effects in time. And between

THE WAR GAME IN THE OPEN AIR.

Fig. 3.—BATTLE OF HOOK'S FARM. Positions of both armies after their first move. The Red Army is in the foreground.
(See page 73.)

Figure 3.3

Illustrations from *Little Wars*. H. G. Wells, 1913. Top: The War Game in the open air.
Bottom: Battle of Hook's Farm. https://www.gutenberg.org/ebooks/3691.

the serious wargame and the child's toy play lies the realm of adult wargaming, itself a diverse mix of historical accuracy and phantasmagorical speculation. Some wargame practices mix these closely, pitting, say, Roman legions against Napoleonic forces: each army is animated with technical and strategic fidelity, but the battle itself is fantastical, impossible outside the imaginative technics of the toyetic. Many computer simulation games offer similar whimsical but rigorously regulated battles between impossible adversaries, including *Age of Mythology*, which allows wars between forces from different mytho-historical universes—Norse versus ancient Greek armies, for instance, each augmented by their own divine pantheon, and *LEGO Battles* (pirates versus medieval knights versus space explorers).[51]

Dungeons & Dragons is an important example of this systemically consistent but thematically fabulous tendency. Derived from both tabletop wargaming and other playful traditions, including role-play, its game mechanic is predicated on the mapping and navigation of imaginative and narrative space, with the probabilistic algorithms of dice rolls to open up chance and dynamism within the game's encounters and events. Significantly too, though, *D&D* culture involves the collection and painting of miniature figures, toy-like objects that are not necessary to play the game but which add a visual corollary to its maps, dice, and tables. In this, *D&D* continues a dual lineage of tactical wargaming that can be traced back to *Kriegsspiel*, two distinct notions and practices of simulation: as Foley puts it, "the "toy soldiers and cannons" world of play, with its focus on the arts-and-crafts modeling of the environment, troops, and matériel; and the "staff officer *Kriegsspiel*" world of play, with its focus on situational assessment, double-blind issuance of orders, and refereed outcomes."[52]

Unbox: Miniature War

The toylike tokens and figures pushed into battle across wargame maps are tiny for good material reasons: for a satisfying battle, as many as possible should fit into the floor or table space available, while still within the reach of the player-general's arm. But there are aesthetic aspects to the wargame token too, at least those termed "miniatures," those characterized by a level of elaborate detail in their form, clothing, insignia, and weapons. As Susan Stewart explains, the cultural and phenomenological workings of the miniature as a type of artifact are inseparable from relationships of scale with hands and eyes. That is, it is the tininess itself of miniature books, sculptures, paintings, and figurines that, before any particular text or image, catches the attention and the imagination. On the one hand, the holder and viewer of a miniature marvels at the apparently impossible skill and technique of their makers—the actual scripture in a thumbnail-sized bible is significant only in the fact that its hundreds of thousands of words can be written at a near-microscopic scale. On the other hand, where the miniature does function as a more conventional cultural artifact—a miniature painting or elaborate dollhouse furniture, for instance—it opens up a phenomenological relationship with the viewer that is at once material and imaginary. The spectacle of its ingenious manufacture adds to a sense of an otherworldly space and time hidden within the everyday: "That the world of things can open itself to reveal a secret life—indeed, to reveal a set of actions and hence a narrativity and history outside the given field of perception—is a constant daydream that the miniature presents. This is the daydream of the microscope: the daydream of life inside life, of significance multiplied infinitely *within* significance."[53] With its miniature dimensions, the mimetic toy in particular, once animated in play, instantiates this interior daydream world with a narrative temporality, no longer "an extension of the time of everyday life; it is the beginning of an entirely new temporal world."[54]

For all its didactic and serious pretensions and its rule-bound cosmology, the wargame is bound up in the space-time of the miniature. In fact, the genealogy of wargames and their fantasy role-playing descendants represents an intense and industrial generation of daydream worlds within the everyday: *Kriegsspiel* itself was dreamlike in its abstracted manifestation of violent conflict, and later wargames played with and reimagined history. Even the most serious war simulation is predicated on the divinatory procedures of the "what if." In the 1970s, the tabletop role-playing game *Dungeons & Dragons* effected a significant split in wargames, away from the historical realism and "god" view of the wargame and into a more intimate, fantastical, and social activity. In this sense, *D&D* brought two miniature toy forms together, adding to the wargame's rule-based and conflict-driven universe the role-playing dynamic, architectonic world, and family-scaled set of imaginative characters of the dollhouse. In *D&D*, role-playing and narrative background effected a shift in scale and game mechanics. A Dungeon Master or Game Master took on a central role in managing play through the balancing of rule sets with the pacing of satisfying action. From its rather niche cultural position at the turn of the twenty-first century, *D&D* has undergone a marked revival in popularity in recent years, proving highly adaptable to new hybrid on- and offline modes of social play. Its place within game culture and the games industry had, to a certain extent, been held open by the success of the related game system *Warhammer 40,000* (or *40K*),[55] which retained the fantasy theme of *D&D* (albeit

Figure 3.4
Unpainted *Warhammer 40,000* Ork miniature. 28 mm scale. Games Workshop, circa 2018.

with a futuristic science fiction rather than swords and sorcery cosmology) but eschewed the role-playing dynamic in a return to a wargaming system.[56]

Whereas the scale of *D&D* adventures requires only a small squad of figurines, one for each player, plus any monsters encountered—and can easily be played without figurines at all—as a tabletop wargame, *40K* demands whole armies.[57] The size of armies in *40K* is determined by a points system. Different units are awarded points according to size and strength, and the player has free rein over the makeup of their army, so long as it doesn't exceed the total number of points allowed to each player. Contemporary game miniatures, then, are polyvalent objects, like their cast silver and lead ancestors valued in quite different registers: as exquisitely detailed and relatively costly commodities to be collected and displayed, but also as quantifiable elements with a game system. In the game, the figurine functions as a placeholder in tactical formations on the battleground and carries a set of numerical values (strength, range, and so on), and as such its baroque styling is superfluous, as in *Kriegsspiel*, an abstract token would work just as well in ludic function. But with the late twentieth-century tabletop role-playing and wargames, this styling effects a significant twist in the wargaming line of descent. The painting of miniatures was embraced in adult wargaming's attention to historical detail in uniforms and insignia, but it spun off into new hobbyist and player-community dimensions with *D&D* and its competitors. *D&D* and *40K* figurines are deployed in a "miniaturing" craft culture that goes far beyond the exigencies of the play battle.[58] The metal, plastic, and resin figures often come in kit form, requiring construction by the player, and painting the resulting objects is an art itself. Players often adapt figurines, adding extra clothing or weapons from other figures or shaping their own with modeling putty.[59]

To crafting, we might add collecting, socializing, displaying, and storytelling. The British producer of *40K*, Games Workshop, relies on and nurtures this hobbyist culture, deftly negotiating commerce and community, with its stores and staff organized around game tournaments, introductory sessions for new recruits, and construction and painting workshops for figures and battlefield dioramas. There are echoes here of the centuries of dressing and decorating dolls as, first, an everyday craft-based creative practice and then a commercialized one, but there are also direct connections with other twentieth-century toy-hobbyist pastimes, notably the construction of model railways. In the model railway too, the simulation of logistics and territorialization is both rendered miniature and manifested through the technical (the machinery of railways, points, and signaling) and the historical-aesthetic (the modeling of stations, figures, and surrounding towns and countryside in tiny and precise detail).

At a more fundamental level, one that connects with this book's emphasis on the relationships between the imaginary and the technological, these types of game are made possible by the toys as tokens, and the ludic theater of war as a real space, whether tabletop, game board, or virtual gameworld. The complexity of the battle, arising from the simple rules of movement and efficacy of the military units (whether determined by agreed convention, dice rolls, or digital algorithm) requires visualization and interaction. The toys/tokens augment the imagination. First, they do so in visualizing the military units as distinct soldiers, artillery units, and so on, generally in precisely molded historical detail, offering them to an informal role-playing dimension (formalized in *D&D* and its descendants). Second, and more practically, they spatialize and fix formations, and allow the testing of tactical maneuvers and countermaneuvers. In this regard, the abstract tokens of Reisswitz are at least as effective as detailed lead, tin, and resin miniatures. Computer games merge the two, offering greater and greater visual detail (historical and fantastical) as graphic processing developed, and delegating to themselves

Figure 3.5
The strategy game from table to screen: *Advance Wars: Dark Conflict* on 3DS console.
Nintendo, 2008.

the complicated quantification and calculation of strength, power, effects, and environmental conditions. But the logic remains the same: the toylike tokens and rules of movement and damage are embedded in the materiality of the toys and their board, freeing the imagination to adopt the tactical and strategic vision of a general or god (figure 3.5).

The tangled genealogy of the wargame/simulation is further complicated by significant historical and technological change, not least the rise of the German toy industry in the eighteenth century, late twentieth-century consumer and media culture, and the recent systematization of toy production and consumption (from marketing to the digital and networked). With wargaming, the postwar moment brings to bear a quite different set of techno-political dynamics, a complex of the rapid development in electronic and digital computing in World War II and after, and the concomitant technological demands of the Cold War. Formalized military wargaming was central to a new scientific and rational approach to conflict, and was "a key progenitor of computerized modeling and simulation principles and procedures. . . . These practices drew on a rationalist enthusiasm for the schematic, mathematical simplification of complex real-world dynamics into abstract principles and procedures."[60]

The popular image of war planning is the darkened control room, dominated by a large table with the theater of operations modeled as a map or relief terrain and populated by tokens of infantry units, tanks, and warplanes, pushed around by shovel-like sticks, tracking actual positions and supply lines, or testing out the ramifications of possible tactics—and, as such, is reminiscent, of course, of the tabletop or floor wargame. However, wargaming itself is now a primary practice in the military, not for the management or tracking of live conflicts but rather for testing out future scenarios.

If World War II transformed the technology of wargames through the computerization of prediction and simulation, World War I had smashed the underlying principles of the Prussian model, if not its components and appearance. The material simulation stayed the same (grids, tokens, dice), but the system or world it modeled changed completely. The Napoleonic-era theater of more or less evenly matched and organized armies, open space, and predictable ballistics was trampled by the new realities of protracted trench warfare, tanks, and chemical weapons. From the 1940s, new paradigms of command and simulation were modeled to address the diplomatic and coalitional imperatives of nuclear-era brinkmanship. The new computer systems and procedures both modeled, and provided models for, these new, less tangible battlefields—for instance, in the game theory of Herman Kahn at the RAND Corporation. In the 1960s, Andrew Wilson noted the new urgency of operations research, systems analysis, code breaking, and cybernetics in the Cold War era, but connected it directly back to Prussian wargaming, via the post-Enlightenment "quest for true principles"' in the tactics, strategies and logistics of war.[61] Patrick Crogan points out that wargaming and these related technical processes are now widely used across all branches of the US military, including the Department of Defense and the chief of staff's office.[62] With the computerization of simulation, this quaint image is displaced not only by screens and computer-generated models but also by quite different and new modes of the virtualization of mapping and prediction.

In the 1950s and 1960s, serious military simulation and popular wargaming diverged somewhat, with popular family board games such as *Risk* (1959) and *Stratego* (1961), and adult-oriented ones such as *Diplomacy* (1959) and

Tactics (1954). Particularly in the US, new commercial and hobbyist companies such as Avalon Hill produced war-themed board games, dice, miniatures, and rules for a niche but commercially viable audience.[63] Even here, there seem to be significant points of connection and technical–ludic reciprocity between military simulation and popular game culture. The designer of *Tactics* and founder of Avalon Hill in the 1950s, Charles S. Roberts, was invited to visit by the RAND Corporation because of their work on game theory. They were impressed by his game *Gettysburg* and its combat results tables, and it has been suggested that his widely adopted hex map grid, introduced into his games in the early 1960s, was inspired by RAND's innovations in cartography for wargaming (figure 3.6).[64]

The serious and the popular technics and epistemological models of wargame simulation fully reconverged from the late 1970s with the availability and popularity of the home computer and videogame console. These three strands (war simulation, wargaming as entertainment, and board games) retangled with the advent of the digital game. Early Avalon Hill games such as *Tanktics* (1980) worked with the technical limitations of early home microcomputers by augmenting a graphic-free game with actual game board and

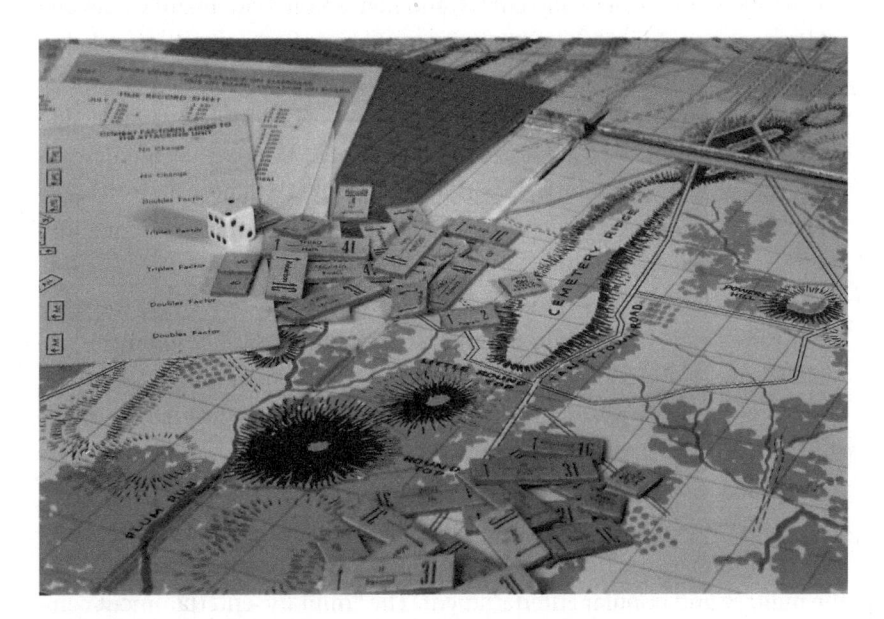

Figure 3.6
Gettysburg board game. Avalon Hill, 1958. Photo: Dave Gibbons.

counters, with the software calculating positions and combat results,[65] but within a few years, both turn-based and real-time strategy graphical games were available.

In toyetic terms, albeit still terms that resonate with the interplay with military ludic-technics, the most important change to the game simulation is the automation of its key aspects. Early digital versions of wargames and tactical role-playing games (TRPGs) were sold on their promise to provide an always-available and willing opponent—that is, the computer itself—and, as with *Tanktics*, to automate complicated or tedious processes of dice rolls and table checking. From here, a whole world of variables, complexity, and movement could be driven by the software. Although clearly continuous with the mechanics of dice and pencil-and-paper recording of variables, automation brings about a paradigm shift in gameplay. To pinpoint a single moment or technical development as effecting this shift would be to oversimplify, but we could take the arrival of the real-time strategy game (RTS) as emblematic at least, with early examples in the early to mid-1980s but with *Command and Conquer* in 1995 as a "major evolution."[66] The game marked a significant break from the turn-based play mechanic and sequential algorithmic calculation of movement and effects, and hence from both board games and tabletop wargaming. The toylike aspects of the tokens or units receded as they became animated and semiautonomous. The game engine determined their agency on the fly, the player's control of—now invisible—variables and parameters mediated by increasingly complicated interface elements such as cursors, menus, tables, maps, and shifts in scale. With ever more detailed animation, topography, and atmospheric effects, the wargame wove into itself a new genealogical line—that of popular screen media.

Crogan tracks the direct historical and technological descent of the computer game, war-themed and otherwise, through the simulational and virtualized innovations of Cold War and post–Cold War military planning. If tabletop war planning shared a technical basis with toy soldiers, the contemporary virtualized systems are much more closely and extensively intertwined. Data visualization, the remote-control systems (and embodied practices) of drones and UAVs, predictive and dynamic models, and so on—technologies, technical practices, and aesthetics even are shared across the military and popular entertainment. The "military–entertainment complex" is comprised of "an increased interchange of personnel and software between the US military organizations and defense firms and the commercial gaming and simulation industries."[67]

Given the radical and interconnected transformations in technology and geopolitics since the eighteenth century, it is remarkable many core features of *Kriegsspiel* and its descendants persist in contemporary digital and tabletop ludic theaters of war: rectilinear and hexagonal grids and maps, turn-based versus real-time strategic mechanics, mechanics of randomization (dice or number generation), ambiguities of unit size, the simulation of combat through actual or virtual dice rolls and probability tables, the use of hidden information from the simple mechanics of sightlines and guesswork in *Battleships* to the adoption of the referee (whether delegated to software or doggedly human as in TRPGS). *D&D*'s emphasis on individual role-play and its heritage in literature rather than history marks a clear departure from established wargames, but the game still relies on the established wargame infrastructure of combat systems, maps and dice, and miniature figures (see "Unbox: Miniature War"). *D&D* and the other fantasy- and science fiction–themed tabletop role-playing game systems it inspired reciprocated, in turn influencing traditional wargaming with innovative TRPG mechanics—for instance, experience-point and hit-point systems.[68] As Jon Peterson puts it, "the tools of simulation pioneered by wargames continually infiltrate new genres."[69] He gives the example of the collectible trading card game *Magic: The Gathering* (1993). So, we could include, by extension, many other contemporary games and game systems, such as *Yu-Gi-Oh!* and *Pokémon*, whose simulation of combat or movement can be tracked back too to the long-established quantification and randomization mechanics of classic playing cards.

Conclusion

From their origins in the toy soldier, an ambivalent tool for both the child's inconsequential distraction and his inculcation into or training for adult martial values and mindsets, wargames have evinced a tangled interplay of the serious and the frivolous. The drawing of a direct line of descent between *Kriegsspiel* and contemporary informational and virtual warfare is useful and convincing, but it should not overlook the continued existence of toy soldiers and wargaming for adults as well as children, objects and activities that have informed the design, mechanics, and overall metaphorical or allegorical shaping of serious modeling and simulation and that have spawned new, less instrumental and disciplinary models—from nonmilitary themed board games and computer simulation games, transmedial card games, and fantasy action figures to historical reenactment (e.g., in the US and England, the "live" reenactment of their respective civil wars), and live action role-playing. In the same post–World War II period, children have continued to spend their pocket money on sets of cheap monochrome injection-molded plastic figures of GIs, "Cowboys and Indians," and animals, worlds of war mixing with other everyday and fantastical rule-free dramas.

I have speculated that military planning at the turn of the nineteenth century must have had a playful and imaginative dimension that exceeded the demands of its instrumental uses, a feeding back from the nursery. and an inevitable condition arising from any complicated and satisfyingly interactive system. As Jon Peterson notes, "wargames are speculative, almost thought-experiments" embracing "real settings of the past, present or future, or they may be located in imaginary settings with purely fantastic combatants."[70] From their inception, wargames were regarded as toys as well as tools. My aim here is not to assert the primacy of imaginative play over post-Enlightenment or post–Cold War epistemes and technical regimes, nor any utopian possibilities for "transgressive" or resistant moments. Rather. it is to track and speculate on the instabilities and ambiguities that run through dominant technoculture at its most terrible (the simulational worldview and worldmaking/destruction of the military–industrial complex) because of these heterogeneous genealogies of games, toys, and play immanent to it. As I note in the introduction, and as the wargame demonstrates, toys, games, and play can be conservative and disciplinary, but along with the serious simulations and machines that I argue are a subset of toys and games, they afford a latitude of play and emergence that must be understood and described rather than necessarily celebrated.

4 Construction Toys

What if themes of architectural modernism at the beginning of the twentieth century had been absorbed, refracted, and reassembled within a theory of cultural modernity in which children and toys played a leading role, a theory that continues to illuminate the problematics of culture at the end of the century?[1]

Like toy soldiers and wargames, construction toys at times chime with their historical and technological moment, epitomizing in miniature prevailing architectural styles and engineering techniques, and at other times, they diverge, depicting past (or future) aesthetics and systems. Detlef Mertens here sees, in the early twentieth century, a paradigmatic instance of the former: the foundational role of toys and play in the design, construction, and modes of thought in modernist architecture and urban planning. From their origins in building blocks, construction sets promised distinct modes of imaginative engagement with the wider adult modern world—promises that persist today in both their marketing and popular and critical reception. Of all commercially produced toys, construction toys have promised the most in terms of flexibility in both physical use and in imaginative application. Indeed, this promise has often been predicated on the inherently imaginative process of production itself, a playing or toying with modern construction (figure 4.1). Architectural toys of the late nineteenth and early twentieth centuries are, for the architect Norman Brosterman, "boxes of possibilities" and "potential architecture." Differentiating between sets with recognizable architectural elements and the abstraction of simple building blocks, he asserts that the former are "abstractions of reality in a more comprehensible, miniature form," while the latter have "another level removed. In their unbuilt form they are ideas for ideas of things."[2] Construction toys, from the simplest stacking cubes to the sophistication of *LEGO Technic* and Meccano,

Figure 4.1
Children playing with a large construction set. Illustration from *The Wonders of a Toy Shop*, Dean and Co. Printers. London, circa 1845. © Victoria and Albert Museum, London.

promise abstracted architectonic or systems thinking and practice—of material relationships and their experimental instantiation rather than directly applicable architectural or engineering skills and planning.

Materiality and Imagination

What role does the materiality of toy systems play in the imaginative and speculative worlds they create in play? Although block- and brick-based systems have dominated construction toys since the eighteenth century, changes in materials, technologies, and engineering have inspired other systems, notably Meccano, the girders and bolts of which offered a material and technical alternative to bricks in the playful modeling of the built and industrial environment. This chapter asks, then, how construction toys—as objects and systems with distinct aesthetic and mechanical characteristics—relate to the design, planning, or imaginative grasp of the built environment and of industrial and postindustrial modernity more broadly. It also asks what conceptualizations of this relationship are possible—concepts that will also help explain toyetic operations in general: modeling, planning, systems thinking, simulation, and material-symbolic synecdoche. The ambiguous role of imagination in these relationships will be of particular interest as both an ideological and Romantic framing of construction play and commodification and as a lived, everyday dimension of play. All of this will be grounded in attention to the mechanical operations of construction play itself, particularly the relationship of children's bodies (eyes, minds, fingers) and the technical possibilities of the toy systems.

Although the focus of this chapter is on modular sets and systems for more or less open-ended and flexible construction, the category of "construction toys" is far from fixed. I will touch on other types of model buildings with which they overlap, including toy towns, farms, and dollhouses, many of which are predicated on a degree of construction of individual buildings and the arrangement and placing of buildings, figures, topographical features, vehicles, and so on. Toy and toylike miniature replicas of buildings such as houses and bakeries have been found in Egyptian tombs. So, they are as old as dolls and toy warriors.[3] Building blocks themselves are not always architectural in reference: wooden cubes for stacking and arranging have been a persistent feature in the education of infants and young children since at least the seventeenth century in England and the eighteenth century across Europe. Decorated with numbers and letters, their combinatory mechanic was designed to aid letter and number recognition rather than building,[4] and they were often more closely related to children's books—for instance, the alphabet books popular in the time of Queen Anne.[5] The nineteenth and early twentieth centuries saw a popular interest in printed card booklike products that could be cut out and assembled into townscapes.[6] Purposely manufactured blocks and bricks for the open-ended construction and reconstruction of models of buildings and cities are largely the product of the industrial era, with architecture-themed building block or brick sets not commonly available until the late eighteenth century.[7] Such sets varied in their degree of mimetic reference to actual buildings. Many of the architectural

Figure 4.2
Wooden town. Europe, mid-twentieth century. Photo: Dave Gibbons.

toy systems in the early twentieth century were characterized by a degree of geometrical abstraction that matched toyetic simplicity and truth to materials in toy production with the emerging forms of modernism, but others evoked past styles and in detail (figure 4.2). An example of the latter is the popular American line *Lincoln Logs*. Designed by John Lloyd Wright, these sets offered wooden elements shaped like logs from which to construct cabins, forts, ranches, and other structures that evoke the North American frontier myth. It is worth noting here that for all their nostalgic and Romantic connotations, these toy-cabin construction sets were also the product of very up-to-date developments in architectural engineering, as their system was inspired by Lloyd Wright's father Frank's new techniques of floating cantilever construction.[8]

The styles and materials of construction toy systems, and the toy vehicles and industrial machinery that relate closely to them, demonstrate complicated and shifting synchronic relationships with the industrial and urban environments of the time of their design and manufacture. At certain moments, these dimensions appear to align, with materials, form, and imaginary in lockstep. Dan Fleming argues that the mass production of construction sets and tin toy vehicles "had much of the industrial revolution about it and relied on that machine revolution's inherent appeals, the appeal of the new steam engines and the new machines of land and sea."[9] The construction sets of the early twentieth century included numerous systems that modeled the modernist aesthetics and ergonomics of the day, and did so in modules fashioned from the very materials and processes of contemporaneous industrial production. Meccano is an example of this: Frank Hornby's invention was inspired by the early industrial machinery of cranes, but also manufactured as standardized steel components isomorphic with larger-scale industrial production processes.[10] There is tantalizing evidence of the direct influence of construction set play and modernist and industrial architecture and planning, in terms of both aesthetics and process.[11] For example, the construction set *Tinker Toy*, introduced in 1914, exploited mass production, the president of Toy Tinkers, Inc., claiming in 1924 that, in their factory, "design, plans and preparations, automatic machinery, expert labor, simplification, standardization, synchronizing of production, all work together."[12] Although the images on construction-set packaging necessarily depicted simplified town and cityscapes, they nonetheless offered their young consumers in the early twentieth century the opportunity to model something of the urban and industrial world around them rather than the anachronisms of the forever-Edwardian dollhouse or bucolic farm sets. Indeed, in important ways, construction toys were in the vanguard of modernity—as Fleming puts it, they "were totems of the very revolution which included in its defining characteristics the processes of their own manufacture (this would not happen again until computer games)" (figure 4.3).[13] If we put aside for the moment their tiny scale and functional uselessness, back in the eighteenth century, they were the first mass-produced, standardized, and prefabricated buildings, and hence too the first modeling of future cities as arrangements of largely unadorned rectilinear and modular units. As wooden bricks were joined by stamped and die-cast steel, and molded plastic materials, systematized and modularized for flexible and economic construction, these sets are clear examples of toyetic synecdoche in materials and modes of production, design, and construction.

However, as the *Lincoln Logs* demonstrate, the historical and temporal relationships between toy construction systems' material constitution, technical design, historical architectural styles, and imaginary visions of a built and lived environment are by no means fixed, and slide against one

Figure 4.3
Clockwork train set. Lithographed tin. USSR, 1950s. Photo: Dave Gibbons.

another. Toys look back to idealized pasts, but they also capture moments in the now, and sometimes suggest futures. Fashion dolls and toy vehicles are persistent examples of this, and much dollhouse furniture has been made in contemporaneous styles. From the late twentieth century, toys that model future worlds or parallel fantasy universes have been very popular, from the tin spaceships and clockwork robots manufactured for a global market in postwar Japan, via the science fantasy storyworlds of commercial TV–toy tie-ins in the 1980s (see chapter 6), Airfix and Revell model kits of actual and science-fictional spacecraft, to the transmedia science fiction–fantasy mélange of contemporary LEGO and *LEGO Bionicle*. And toy culture has its own peculiar dynamic of continuity and shifting historical significance: a toy set purchased as the epitome of contemporaneous modernity—a train set in the 1930s featuring the latest engines, for instance—is transformed, within a generation or two when handed down to children or grandchildren (or held by an adult collector or hobbyist), to signify a vanishing industrial world through historical interest and nostalgia.

Materials and manufacturing processes are part of this historical slippage: a lost pastoral life is industrially blow-molded in the late twentieth-century

Figure 4.4
Meccano crane with electric motor, from Meccano *Motion System 6520* set, 2001.

plastic farm set; children stack skyscrapers from wooden blocks; and the modular steel strips and bolts of Meccano shape both futuristic spacecraft and industrial cranes (figure 4.4). Some toy construction systems bridge architectural and technological periods and prefigure fabrication methods and aesthetics to come. The architect Richard Rogers's childhood love of Meccano is held to be a key inspiration for the exoskeletal engineering of his 1970s landmarks such as the Lloyds Building in London and Paris's Pompidou Centre, and his studio used it as a medium of modeling and display.[14] Such buildings not only carry the look of a Meccano framework from the outside but also, inside, evoke its flexible organization and demarcation of space, echoing the endlessly manipulable character of construction toy play. If wooden blocks and simple building sets of the nineteenth and early twentieth centuries are the rather anachronistic product of the persistence of craft production and skill in the industrial era, then Meccano is more fully of its actual time, mode, and materials of production. Toys, for all their mimetic and symbolic aspects,

Figure 4.5
LEGO history: wooden ABC blocks (rear), early 1950s; acrylic System in Play sets, 1970s. Design Museum Denmark, Copenhagen.

are also synecdoches of their industrial and material environments. As noted above, the punched steel strips and bolts of Meccano not only approximate the visual appearance of a crane on an early twentieth-century building site, they are also made from the same materials and through similar processes, and hence are synecdochical of mass and standardized production of steel units. The salient difference here is, of course, scale, and hence mode of use. The construction set shrinks the manufacture of industrial systems to the scale of the hand, rendering the forces and technological infrastructure of modernity and urbanism tangible and manipulable.

LEGO is another example. Developed from the ubiquitous and diverse wooden brick construction systems of the late nineteenth and early twentieth centuries, its innovations in the engineering and molding of thermoplastics in the late 1950s and early 1960s anticipated the larger-scale application of synthetic materials in consumer goods in general and new systems of modularity in construction in particular (figure 4.5). In recent decades, LEGO has proved central to the development of virtual construction, architecture, and urban planning through its influence on games such as *SimCity*, *Minecraft*, and the LEGO Group's own extensive range of virtual construction platforms and digital games and to serious planning simulations. LEGO has become by far the biggest manufacturer of construction toys and, from the late twentieth century, has also become a dominant global player in children's media and digital culture. So, LEGO is paradigmatic of the new industrial milieu from which construction toys are produced and, in convoluted ways, into which they carve new kinds of symbolic space, virtual construction, and sociality—a development to which I will return later in this chapter.

Constructions of History

But there is something of this historical-material prefiguration in the very essence of the construction toy. The simplicity and modularity of sets of eighteenth-century wooden blocks were a necessary product of their material and modes of production, and at first glance, their visual similarities with the geometric and unadorned buildings of the modernism to come, of Le Corbusier or Lloyd Wright, could be taken to be the arbitrary function of the production of bricks and timbers for construction throughout history. A set of plain wooden blocks with square and circular sections are just as likely to be arranged into a castle or ruined temple as a modernist utopia. However, there are direct connections between construction toys and modernist principles, notably via the influence of Friedrich Froebel's radical educational theories and inventions in the 1830s. These inventions included a range of play objects, "Gifts," in different materials such as paper patterns, strings threaded with colored balls, and sets of wooden shapes, including cylinders, cubes, and spheres. The types of play that the Gifts were designed to instigate were not to be narrative driven or fantastical, not imaginative in the sense of role-play or storytelling, but rather a play with the materials and objects themselves, the relationships of form and scale and the natural laws of gravity that determined them: "A child was to reach out and take the world by the hand and palpate its natural materials and laws, gravity and grace, pliancy and rigidity, to discover its harmonies and limits."[15] We see here a formalized harnessing of the nonmimetic, sensorimotor toy into a pedagogical system, and hence to a toyetic philosophy in which the workings of the hands and fingers are central. The hands-on and the constructional have particular connections in play as making, or working, as Walter Benjamin put it: "Children are particularly fond of haunting sites where things are being visibly worked upon. They are irresistibly drawn by the detritus generated by building, gardening, housework, tailoring, or carpentry. . . . In using these things they do not so much imitate the works of adults as bring together, in the artefact produced in play, materials of widely differing kinds in a new, intuitive relationship. Children thus produce their own small world of things within the greater one."[16]

This said, Froebel's Gifts were intentionally nonrepresentational and non-mimetic. Children playing in his system were not to imagine castles or houses. So, despite his immersion in the Romantic culture of his time, Froebel held to values that were to resonate powerfully with modernist abstractionist ideas to come. The Gifts have been widely interpreted as playing a key role in the interplay between toys and the technics and aesthetics of modern architecture and city planning, and for the particular mode of, and ideas about, play with objects and its relationship to knowledge.[17] Through play and education at the turn of the twentieth century, they forged direct links between the materially determined abstraction of play objects and the new ethos of modernism with its celebration and exploitation of the geometric and rectilinear, the modular and the unadorned, and its valorization of abstract relationships of scale and play as systemic arrangement and juxtaposition over mimetic fidelity to period style or building type.[18] To give just one example of the role of the Gifts, Anna Lloyd Jones, mother of Frank Lloyd Wright, bought sets of the Gifts for her son at Philadelphia's Centennial Exhibition in 1876. Interestingly, these sets were manufactured by Milton Bradley, a printer and board game manufacturer, whose company would go on to become the largest board game company in the United States. Bradley had begun printing and marketing sets of brightly colored paper shapes, part of the wider range of objects and materials that Froebel had designed and systematized.[19]

Like those of dolls and soldiers, the genealogy of construction sets is interlaced with strands of thought about the education and training of children through objects. The Gifts are a particularly marked example of a systematic approach to design and the pre-scription of play, but faint resonances with Froebel's emphasis on formal relationships and tactile manipulation are evident throughout the claims made and rationales given for the value of construction blocks in children's development—from the early alphabet blocks to LEGO bricks. Construction systems in the nineteenth and twentieth centuries took the simple stacking mechanic of the wooden block and generated a wide and ingenious range of designs for the combination and connection of units into elaborate structures. Between the primitive geometry of infants' blocks and the Gifts, on the one hand, and the more or less prefabricated toy house sets, on the other, the engineering of these sets explored the interplay of abstract flexibility, technical detail, and stylistic specificity. This ratio varies according to either the designers' aims to offer more or less latitude in play or, often, to the age of the child: colorful cubes for infants; elaborate models—often with instructions—for older children (and adults).

Imagination and Technology

For my toyetic argument, there are two questions to ask of this construction play. First, what are the relationships between the mechanical design of particular construction systems and the imaginative structures generated in their playing? Even open construction can only be effected through the material possibilities of the toy system itself: the strength of the connection between units, and the types of arrangements and shapes these connections and units form. Standard LEGO tends toward the architectural, Meccano to the machinic. And, as we have seen with dolls and soldiers, imaginative play often meanders far from the serious framing and expectations of models of domesticity and warfare. So, in what ways do these microindustrial systems in play engage with or depart from serious instruction in architecture, planning, and engineering? Second, what are the synecdochical relationships between the physical, cognitive, and imaginative processes of construction in play and the processes of construction in the industrial world at large? That is, putting any specific historical or symbolic elements of particular sets to one side, in what ways might everyday construction and design with Meccano or LEGO resonate with or *model* macroscale industrial processes of construction and design? The tangibility and manipulability of toys in general and construction sets in particular are salient here. On the one hand, this is a straightforward matter of children learning technical processes and material affordances through hands-on models and construction—at the very least, Meccano play demands proficiency with a spanner and nuts and bolts. But, on the other hand, we see a more nebulous relationship of ideas and ideals about the processes and procedures of construction in a broader sense, of the relationship between imagination and creativity and the material

manipulation of toy systems. For instance, Friedman notes that manufacturers and parents encouraged children to play with these toys "not simply
to teach dexterity and design skills through play, but to mold the behavior,
aspirations, and desires of future citizens and consumers."[20] Construction
toy design effects a general orientation of the child's imagination toward
particular modes of design and assembly—but what of their *toying*? In what
ways can *play* with construction toys be regarded, or speculated upon, as
foundational to the shaping of process, of modes of imaginative and technical enquiry? What, as children build, are they modeling? Technical complexity brought with it a significant fault line in the discourses of the workings
and value of construction toys in children's moral and vocational development, a fault line between competing notions of imagination and creativity.
These concepts are predicated (again, like dolls and soldiers) not only on
the toys' symbolic and representation of the adult world—here of the built
environment—but also on the physical and cognitive behaviors toys suggest, scaffold, or inadvertently facilitate. Like the tactical deployment of a
miniature lead army, it is the mobilization and dynamic arrangement of
a system of units that characterizes construction toy play. This mobilization
can be closely directed, through the following of a set's instruction booklet
to complete a predesigned model, or "open," driven by the child's symbolic
preoccupations in the moment of play itself, or somewhere between.

The shape of any moment of imaginative play is inseparable from the
materials and forms of the play objects and materials from which it unfolds
and through which it is articulated. This articulation can be loose, trivial
even, as when a toy is deployed as a prop or to-hand token that, in its general scale and availability, suits a particular moment of fantasy, or it can be a
process tightly driven by a set of instructions, or it can be somewhere between
the two, more loosely suggested by the toy's packaging and branding. These
latter are "preferred play practices," as Maikke Lauwaert calls them, as "toys
and play practices are intimately connected, and the design of a toy facilitates certain play practices (and not others)." Whereas studies of toy play
culture have often focused on the textual and communicative dimensions of
toy form, packaging, and media, a full toy theory demands analyses of the
interplay of toy semiotics with their technical characteristics and operations;
in Lauwaert's terms, of the symbolic and the mechanical: "The structure of
a toy, its technological specificities, its materiality, the rules and manuals,
examples and guidelines, its 'reputation' and connotations create a network

of facilitated play practices. Both the material and immaterial aspects of a toy or computer game create a window of opportunities within whose boundaries the players can act."[21]

To follow instructions in the construction of a model is not to acquiesce in some unimaginative conformism, but rather to mobilize a distinct set of cognitive and motor abilities and pleasures. There is something like puzzle solving in the translation of graphic diagrams into the fiddly three-dimensional parameters of the physical parts, a hands-on engagement and appreciation of often ingenious designs, aesthetic pleasure in the emergence of a scene or vehicle from a pile of modular abstract elements, maybe sometimes too the realizing and appreciation of the engineering and plastic imagination of the designers. In this sense, recent LEGO making could be considered closer to the construction (and then display) of Airfix and Revell scale models of historical aircraft and vehicles. The technically adept and obedient manufacture required here, and its performative and exhibitory pleasures, resonate with much adult play with LEGO. To track the interplay of the mechanical and the symbolic in construction toys, and hence their effects in technoculture at macro- and microlevels, we need to address three key factors: the ethico-political assumptions embedded in the academic critique of everyday media and technologies, the contemporary mediatization and virtualization of construction toys, and the conceptualization and description of the workings of imagination in play.

Of all the concepts brought to bear on the study and commentary on toys, imagination is not only the most prevalent but also the least coherently defined and understood. Contemporary toys and children's media are often evaluated on the degree to which they foster or restrict children's imaginations and imaginative play. Imagination itself is often invoked as if it were separate from the everyday materiality of lived experience, bodies, environments, and artifacts: to imagine is to take a flight of fancy, with any technical or environmental engagement only of the most simple and nondeterminant. It is rare to have a discussion on children, toys, technologies, and play, for instance, without someone asserting that children would rather just play with a cardboard box—often, it is joked, with the box that an expensive and complicated (but neglected) plaything came in. The cardboard box and other simple materials (sand or sticks maybe, or early LEGO), it is asserted, facilitate the child's free imagination, unconstrained by either dramatic themes and images of commercial packaging or by the pre-scripted functions of technically complicated toys.[22] But a cardboard box in play is no less a technical artifact than a videogame: the issue is not one of removing "technology" to free the imagination. Rather, it is to describe the ways particular material and mechanical characteristics of objects facilitate and scaffold particular modes of imaginative play. To put it more simply, there are different kinds of imagination that more or less correspond to different kinds of play equipment. The genealogy of construction toys—of both their attendant rhetoric and their mechanical form—offers resources for the critical examination and disambiguation of imagination in play. Let's start with the contemporary moment and current assumptions about the nature and value of imagination in technical play as epitomized by the transmedia and toy behemoth LEGO. LEGO has come to dominate contemporary debates, assumptions, contradictions, and hermeneutics of children's culture and imaginative play in the twenty-first century.

LEGO and the Construction of Imagination

In their corporate pronouncements, marketing, research, and charity work, the LEGO Group and the LEGO Foundation work hard to position and maintain imagination, creativity, and play as universal categories that seamlessly operate across everyday consumption and global corporate activity.[23] Along with learning and fun, imagination and creativity constitute LEGO's brand and self-proclaimed values.[24] Free play leads the child from curiosity via imagination to systematic creativity, but the packaging, colors, and availability of LEGO bricks and the mechanisms and materials through which they click together are given the flexibility and creativity of their use in play "unbounded" by such material factors.[25] The technical underpinnings of the LEGO System in Play were established by the early 1960s: the stud-and-tube linking mechanism, the adoption of thermoplastic for most of the LEGO pieces, and the decision to make all subsequent sets and products compatible and hence interchangeable.[26]

Academic and popular criticism of LEGO is nearly always predicated on the neo-Froebelian perception that the toy has lost its original flexibility and abstraction, a prelapsarian design where the simply colored and unadorned bricks suggested nothing in themselves to their owners and were open entirely to the workings of the child's curiosity and imagination. LEGO's subsequent fall was incremental, beginning the 1960s with the provision of illustrations on the toy's packaging, suggestions for possible models and constructions, followed by the inclusion of more specialized pieces (notably windows and wheels), instruction booklets, sets designed to be constructed as one single model (e.g., a fire station). Next, the storyworld framing of construction with the introduction of the LEGO Space sets in the late 1970s and early 1980s, followed by, in the twenty-first century, the full mediatization and transmediatization of sets and lines with LEGO's own proprietorial lines such as *Bionicle*, *Ninjago*, and *LEGO Friends*, and with media franchising—first *Star Wars* in 1999, and now most popular franchises from Marvel and Disney to *Lord of the Rings*, *Indiana Jones*, and *Batman*, and movies, videogames, and online platforms. For Gary Cross, the LEGO System lost its initial value as "unbounded creativity" with the introduction of LEGO Space; the company "had adapted to the all-pervasive marketing techniques of the noveltymakers, sacrificing its initial educational value."[27] Maaike Lauwaert situates the watershed moment in the mid-1990s, with a shift in LEGO's industrial strategy from prescribing construction as the preferred or encouraged mode of play to story-based action and role-play.[28]

For all the anxiety about LEGO play's framing by the characters and storyworlds of commercial children's media, this notion of imagination and creativity as ideally developed through engagement with narrative and with role-play is uncontroversial. However, ideas of imagination are far from fixed and stable, and they shift significantly over time and, as Lauwaert noted, even in the different stages of LEGO play at any particular event of play: from construction itself (which in itself could mobilize different imaginative practices such as following instructions or "free" building) to the handling or display of a finished model. Imaginative play as story or role-play based is a recent configuration in construction toy play at least, one that was much less evident in the earlier history of LEGO as a product, and in the genealogies of construction sets from which it emerged and with which it competed. Many pre-LEGO construction toy systems were not "imaginative" in this contemporary sense, at least not in their design, packaging, and marketing. For instance, *Tyor* wooden construction blocks in the US at the start of the twentieth century were advertised as "constructive, scientific, amusing," and the contemporaneous *Structo* set was clearly directed toward the boy's ambition: "you don't have to wait until you grow up to get training in mechanical building." *Structo* bragged, "Fathers can't resist the fascination of *Structo*, because it does the real things that big men do in real life. It is not a toy. It is a miniature of the mechanical world for boys."[29]

In my ethnographic and memory work on LEGO construction play, I proposed two dominant categories of imagination in the rhetoric of the toy and its historical and contemporary devotees, neither of which transcend the material and mechanical form of the toy system itself but rather are fully predicated on it. I call these "engineering-imagination" and "symbolic-imagination."[30] The latter is dominant today, with LEGO's potential for the expression of symbolic, narrative, and performative imagination key. Children building worlds through which to tell their own stories and invent their own characters through open-ended building of new structures and dramas would epitomize this preferred style of play. "Engineering-imagination" is still evident today, but much less so than in the early years of LEGO and in construction toys more generally. Engineering-imagination assumes that the imaginative operations and developments in construction play are geared toward engineering and design not story or character. Here, play progresses through material and technical challenges—building a bridge, perhaps—and the imagination works on how the bricks can be connected to solve it. Engineering-imagination persists in LEGO's educational activities and in its robotics sets such as *Mindstorms*. Kate Maddalena notes that, in some of its pronouncements, LEGO positions its putative player as a "maker-learner" and hence an "engineer-scientist," and LEGO bricks themselves then are "media firmly and deeply enmeshed in the ethical and epistemological commitments of technoscience."[31] Engineering-imagination is still very much about the creative, the bringing of something new into being. But any value given to LEGO by engineers, educationalists, and scientists cannot be straightforwardly instrumental or didactic. LEGO is too idiosyncratic a technology to teach precise and varied engineering skills. Rather, it nurtures a physical problem-solving mindset, a machinic or systematic imagination—a forming in the mind of a solution to a problem with the resources to hand. The products of the playful engineering-imagination don't model structures that will be realized in the industrial macrosphere of course; they remain in the world of the virtual. But we might think of a child as a potential future engineer, playing with LEGO as the process of imagining a technical solution to a problem or imagining a problem as rationale and motive for constructing a solution in the first place. The design problem and challenge is an epiphenomenon of the process of creation, of the play. We may build a LEGO bridge because there is a gap to be spanned, but we are just as likely to look for a suitable gap because we want to build a bridge. Any productive or instrumental end is an artifact of the will to create, to play.

Engineering-imagination loosely corresponds with the "what if" mode of play that I outlined in the Introduction: "What if I were to use this set of parts in this particular structure to span this gap?" Symbolic-imagination, then, would correspond to the "as if" gambit: "Let's play with this brick construction as if it were a dragon and as if it were alive and could talk." Importantly, though, these modes are both fundamentally reliant on the mechanical and material nature of LEGO and the System in Play. The "what if" is a material and mechanical necessity, fully immanent to any construction: clicking bricks together demands a hands-on expertise in the technical dimensions of the system's studs and tubes, their physical possibilities and impossibilities. As Jonathan Rey Lee puts it, "to build anything with this system is to engage in an architectural logic manifested in a material process resembling bricklaying—even a brick-built mountain or giraffe structurally implies construction."[32] The "as if" move of even the most phantasmagorical or inchoate fabrication is also, by necessity, an imaginative process of mechanical experimentation and testing, facilitated and scaffolded by the material possibilities of the bricks themselves. Units are selected according to their scale, dimensions counted out in studs, and functionally operative elements such as wheels or hinges. A desire to create a fantastical structure or creature is realized through more practical and technical cognitive engagement. As one respondent's account of their five-year-old sibling's play demonstrates, the child "approaches it in a very matter-of-factly way most of the time, doesn't refer to pieces as 'Oh I need more scales to complete this dragon!' but rather just 'I need a green, 4×4 one' or whatever, and he likes to build as fast as possible. Of course, he likes playing around with the pieces once they are completed."[33] Engineering, design, and creativity are all familiar concepts and phenomena in adult, serious discourse—but the certainties of these categories are revealed to be unstable, paradoxical even, at the mechanical microlevel of play events, in the flow of any particular moment of play, where engineering and fantasy, instruction-following and flexibility, and construction and destruction intertwine.

Unbox: Toy Cities

Roaming the streets and outskirts of the city in *LEGO City: Undercover* is a markedly similar experience to playing a *Grand Theft Auto* game. Walking or driving, one can seize cars from their mildly outraged drivers and careen through the streets, across parks, embankments, even into gardens. Minifig nonplayer characters (NPCs) roam in solipsistic A* paths, muttering to themselves in snatches of looped monologue, barely troubled as one mows them down and their solid little bodies flip and bounce. There is some hand-to-hand combat in the form of police arrests rather than killing, but unlike *GTA*, these levels are primarily puzzle driven and, as such, are very much based on the mechanics of LEGO's current media franchise–themed games.

On one level, then, the LEGO in *LEGO City Undercover* is a remediation of the construction toy and of the well-established *LEGO City* line of playsets in particular.[34] Through it, the new medium of the videogame is encountered, as if through Marshall McLuhan's rear-view mirror, as images familiar to a child consumer in their bright plasticity, and reassuring to the parent in their cartoon skeuomorphism of comedy and affectless violence. Residual aspects of the LEGO System's modularity and of actual brick play are retained: although most buildings are solid and impenetrable, vehicles and much of the street furniture can be easily destroyed and rendered into bricks and studs that then either dissolve into nothingness or are gathered as the game's currency-like resource for unlocking abilities and devices. As the environment is explored, a sequence of discoveries drive progress through the game, generally involving finding special objects that can be broken down into a pile of bricks, then reconstructed as little devices to overcome obstacles (a machine, a ladder, etc.) or by swapping between a gradually increasing set of minifig characters, each of which has a particular ability or tool to solve particular puzzles—opening safes (a criminal), using dynamite (a miner), and so on. As such, little of the *construction* dimensions of actual LEGO remains. Even the moments of building that do present themselves to the player are resolved through a repeated pressing of the "A" button as the game automatically clicks the bricks together in a prerendered sequence. Fingers are shifted away from bricks to controller buttons, and construction itself is delegated to the software, with speed and spectacular animation offering some mediatized compensation for the loss of dexterous agency. The game plays down the imaginative processes of construction and design in favor of videogame-specific mechanics of exploration, accumulation, combat, puzzle solving, and the more general form and aesthetics of the LEGO Group's post-1980s mediatization trajectory and media universe. With its numerous cutscenes, parodic and jokey dialogue, and characters. the game often feels more like an interactive version of *The LEGO Movie* than a digital transduction of a construction toy.

Figure 4.6
LEGO City Undercover. Top: street scene. Bottom: Albatross prison interior. TT Games, 2013.

The buildings and development zones in urban development simulation games such as the *SimCity* and *Designer City* series change and grow, unlike the static buildings of *LEGO City Undercover.* They don't remediate the toys' dexterous assemblage of modules, as buildings appear and transform, driven by the software—with players merely adjusting certain conditions for this growth. Yet, the games are often discussed in terms that evoke both toys in general

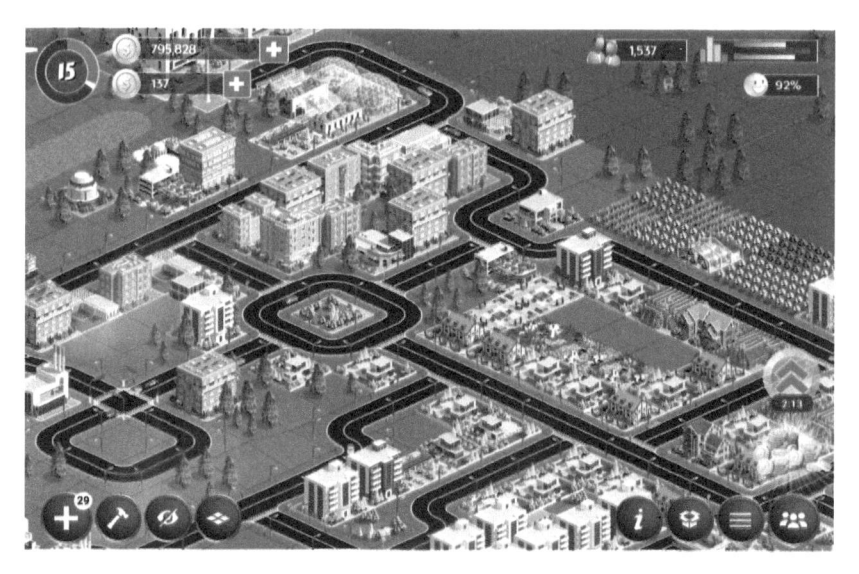

Figure 4.7
Designer City 2 (Sphere Games Studio 2018).

and LEGO's promulgation of imagination and creativity in particular. From the mid-1990s, Will Wright and Maxis, the producers of *SimCity* and other simulation games, referred to them explicitly as toys, in that they were characterized by an open-ended and imaginative exploration of self-created worlds, differentiating them from the goal-oriented or competitive nature of *games*.[35]

Although not so focused on the modern urban environment, *Minecraft* is often regarded as the digital inheritor of LEGO's open-ended mechanics and ethos. This is due in part to its visual similarity to the blocky units and abstraction of actual LEGO (leading to, inevitably, a line of *Minecraft*-themed LEGO playsets; see figure 4.9) and to its absolute plasticity, for unlike the Town Plan or LEGO videogames, buildings, trees, rocks, and the earth itself are fully malleable—available to be broken down, reconstructed, and transformed in the construction of objects and environments from dungeons to fully functioning virtual machines. Even the sky is constituted of functional blocks.[36] Like *SimCity*, though, to play *Minecraft* is to engage in a systems thinking that can model urban growth or architectonic forms but which is, at base, a simulational and gamelike mode of imagination. Players must, as Bart Simon and Darren Wershler explain, "learn this geometrical language" with a set of "tools and metrics for navigating the world as a more abstract mathematical

Figure 4.8
LEGO *Minecraft* set. 2022. Photo: Dave Gibbons.

construct."[37] These game-toy platforms demand of their players a grasp of their virtual spatiality, procedural mechanics, and resource management—with roots in both instrumental computer simulation and the archaic abstract and economic workings of the board game.[38]

Speculative Construction

Whether driven by a symbolic or an engineering mindset, building with LEGO is a technical practice. Connecting the pieces sets its own parameters and rhythms on the imaginative flow. It is design, but not in the conventional sense of satisfying a functional or aesthetic need through plans, iterations, and final realized objects. Rather, this is "aimless" design, a fully nonteleological process. Unless they are working from instructions, young LEGO makers tend not to look at pile of bricks, picture a final object or model in their head a car or house, and then work toward it, selecting the necessary bricks to complete a preformed mental model. Rather, they pick a few random bricks, a base plate, some wheels, and they just start clicking them together. That may then suggest a form or type to work toward. Like the division of stem cells, early decisions will set in train a process of individuation—toward something vehicular, robotic, architectonic, or more heterogeneously environmental. The emerging model might resonate with the player's own interests or obsessions, or it might be seeded by a momentary glance at a TV show or a topic studied at school that day. Wherever these evolving templates or plans come from, they evolve through the feedback from the little acrylic units. The box is rummaged in, a suitable piece found and clicked into place. Rummage, click, rummage, click. The model is not a model of anything but its own emergence, its own toying.

For all this apparent open-endedness and flexibility, though, the LEGO System in Play has its own particular engineering affordances. The workings of imagination are not transcendent but rather are distributed through the human mind and fingers and the construction toy system—the bricks and their system of connection, the workings of gravity, the characteristics of ABS thermoplastic, all paced out through a rhythmic temporality. In this distribution, the toy asserts its own desires: it prefers particular broad types of form that are more easily and satisfyingly constructed, and resists others that are not. As with any construction toy system, as Gilles Brougère argues, "function and representation strongly interact with each other. The final result will always bear the mark of the technical principles that enabled the toy construction to be built and the constituent parts are easily identified."[39] For all the specialized pieces that now help build themed and media-licensed models, the brick remains the base unit for most LEGO lines, and hence the architectonic persists as the primary broad type of form in the design of particular sets and product lines—*LEGO City* and *LEGO Friends* for instance—and in everyday play. Second to the architectural is the vehicular. The first specialized pieces were windows, doors, and sloping roof tiles, closely followed by wheels (1962) and, later, train and track components (from 1966). With these early sets, a child could construct stylized human- or animal-shaped figures, often imagined as robots due to the blocky forms the system necessitated. But with the introduction of minifigs in (1978), the LEGO universe, for all its heterogeneity, took on a fixed scale, with buildings, townscapes, and vehicles pinned to the dimensions of these thermoplastic Vitruvian men. The paradox of LEGO is that it facilitates the generation of an infinite variety of structures but only ever within a tightly bounded range of architectonic forms: nearly always buildings and townscapes or vehicles.

One only needs to place LEGO alongside a competitor system such as Meccano to get a sense of the contradictory takes on the relationship between system mechanics and notions of open and imaginative play. The stud-and-tube system overcame the gravitational challenges of earlier building-block systems: simply, it allowed the construction of larger models free from the risk of accidental destruction. However, as formed by *bricks*, these models were largely walls or blocky and solid vehicles. By comparison, structures that are extensions in open space are facilitated by the girders and bolts of Meccano and the more mechanical-anatomical cross axles and ball joints of *LEGO Bionicle* (2000–2016). Before *LEGO Technic* (1977–), cranes and bridges could be built in LEGO, but they tended to be unstable, as the stud-and-tube connections work best in gravity-friendly stacks, whereas in reaching out across space, structures become rickety and brittle. Conversely, to construct a house or street in Meccano would be time-consuming and largely unsatisfying. This is one—technological—reason why LEGO's industrial strategy of mediatization has proved so successful: its buildings-and-vehicles tendencies lend themselves to the design of play sets that model spaceships, boats, and cars, and to architectural distillations of familiar movie and TV sets (Hogwarts, the Death Star), as proprietary tableaux or spatial vignettes in a highly stylized economy of objects and signs (see "Unbox: Toy Cities").

So, however flexible and open-ended LEGO construction may be, it is predicated on the clicking together of bricks (at least until the advent of digital LEGO in videogames and virtual construction applications). LEGO's success as a commodity and media franchise in a global cultural economy is inseparable from its persistence as a material and technical platform: simply, the studs and tubes and material characteristics of the plastic pieces. Defiance of gravity, tactility of clicking and separating, the absolute application of the system so that all sets can be connected, going back decades and over highly diverse lines and franchises. For all the criticism over the waning of imagination in LEGO, the obdurate flexibility of the system always returns us to its facilitation of open-ended construction and all the narrative, symbolic, and engineering possibilities this allows. Through their various connective mechanisms (even if this is only stacking), all toy

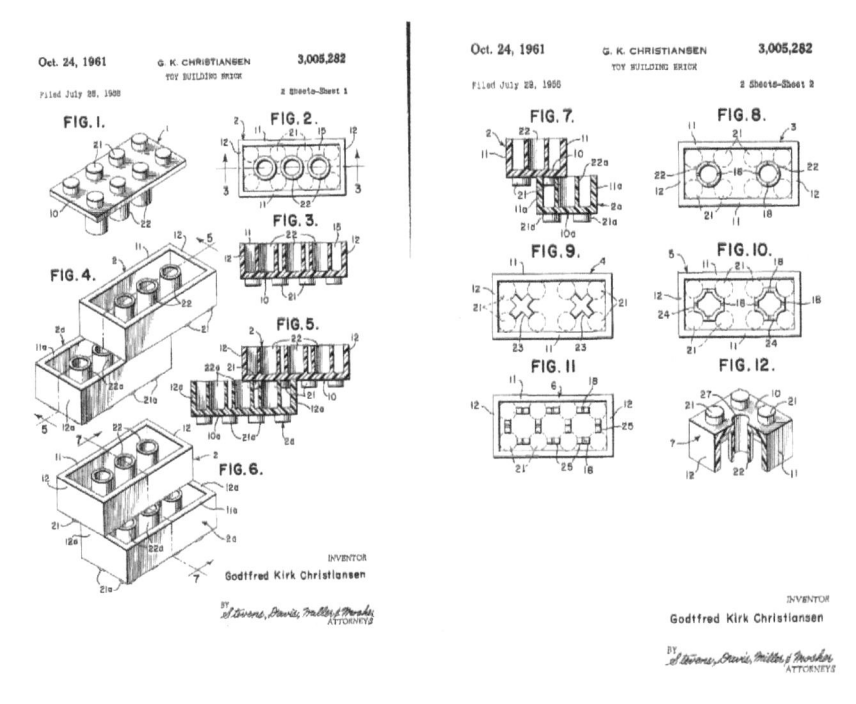

Figure 4.9
LEGO System in Play: US patent for a "toy building brick," 1961.

construction systems by necessity shape their possible modes of play and imaginative engagement.

My interest here is not to identify preferred play practices or to single out and celebrate particularly creative modes or moments of construction play. Rather, it is to address the question of how imaginative play emerges from and through the picking up and assembling of construction toy pieces, how the imagination is shaped and distributed in the complex of design, materials, the contingencies of moment-by-moment rummaging in the box, and the temporality of selection, placing, the extension in time and space of both material assemblage and immaterial drama, challenge and scenario. And further, to develop a theme that runs throughout this book: that imagination is not a settled concept, centered in the human brain, but rather a technical achievement emerging from the coming together (in play specifically, the *collusion*) of the mind, body, cultural, and physical environment and objects and systems—not least toys. Imagination—and hence imaginative play—is distributed across and emergent from the human and nonhuman, the intangible and the material.[40]

Although today LEGO appears to have effectively trademarked these claims for the essential interplay of imagination and construction in their marketing and educational activities,[41] competing assumptions about the didactic and character-building nature of children's building with toys goes back at least to Froebel. We might critique Romantic notions of creativity and imagination, particularly when articulated by global corporations, as ideological and illusory. However, the fact remains that construction toys are used to *construct*. They are not images or narratives (although they may generate images and narratives); they are material and technological systems, the design and technics of which facilitate certain kinds of symbolic and engineering activity and limit or foreclose on others. The ideological dimensions of LEGO marketing have been thoroughly critiqued. My argument here is that the role of the toyetic technology of the LEGO System in Play in the exercising of imaginative engagement with construction, fabulation, and wider socioeconomic milieus demands a more nuanced articulation of imagination and technics.

Models and Systems

What, then, of the relationships discussed at the start of this chapter between construction toys and their toying and the historical and economic times from which they emerge as products and with which they are articulated, however loosely, in play? To start with, play with construction toys collapses design and construction: the child is at once building an architectural *model* and a building or city in simulacral form. Neither "engineering" nor "symbolic" therefore are fully adequate modifiers for "imagination" in modeling play. A Meccano bridge could be a representation of an existing road or rail bridge, assuming the a priori presence of this source bridge known to the child builder. As a representation, it would be necessarily abstracted, stylized, and scaled down through the mechanical characteristics of the set. Or the bridge might be a fantasy structure, an architectonic environment for a paracosmic or media storyworld—Bifröst or the Bridge to Terabithia, perhaps. In the flow of play, it can both of these in turn or at the same time. But a toy bridge is also always a *real* bridge, albeit a small one. It can span the gap between pieces of furniture and offer safe transit for real, albeit small, vehicles. Educationalists and toy producers might see the value of the bridge not in its own particular and contingent existence but rather as a fleeting instantiation of the child's potential lifelong trajectory of creative and imaginative development. Their bridge is a plan, a model—not for an actual bridge to be realized but of potential bridges, of a future orientation of the playing child's imagination toward the physical and dexterous demands of instrumental construction and engineering. The bridge, then, is not a *potential* structure but rather fully *virtual* in the philosophical sense: one point in a line of flight for imaginative and material emergence.

The notion of toys as paradigmatically simulacral finds purchase in the ambiguity of the model and suggests new manifestations and extensions. Like the tabletop wargame, construction sets are models in two significant and temporally or causally distinct senses: in the sense of a representation or depiction *of* contemporaneous or historical phenomena (historic battles, actual cityscapes), and in the sense of a design or plan *for* a future instantiation (a strategy, a blueprint). The temporality shifts from a starting point of the copying of something that exists, that is actual, into the modeling of something that does not yet (and may never) exist. As with everything toyetic, these are not exhaustive or mutually exclusive categories. The architect's model or blueprint might be an instrumental plan for a soon to be realized structure, or it might be a speculative design, a plastic thought experiment never to be built but rather to open up discussion and imaginative engagement with possible utopian futures.[42] On the bedroom floor, we see the child's construction, modeling something that ostensibly exists (a house, a castle, a bus) but which is likely to be a *type* rather than a faithful copy of a specific structure or vehicle (a castle, say, but not a model of any particular castle) or a more fantastical extrapolation of features of fortified buildings drawn from direct experience and media images. In both cases—the castle-constructing and the speculative design—it is the modeling and the model themselves that are salient, not a source to be copied or a potential building to be realized. They are "copies without an original" or perhaps "models without a future." Just as I argue that to ask what any particular simulation is a simulation *of* is not the most interesting question, here the question is not what the construction toy *models* but rather what the nature *of* the model is in its own right, in the processes of its modeling and the imaginative uses to which it is put in moments of play: a microcosmic plan for fantastical structures and events that have never existed (until now) and will never exist again (in a few minutes).

The relationships between construction toys and the industrial and urban worlds they purport to image are therefore ambiguous and ambivalent. Some—early LEGO, for instance—bear no direct similarity to specific actual buildings and townscapes. Other sets are more referential in design, closely resembling particular architectural styles, built environments, engineered structures and vehicles, or even specific buildings. These may be contemporaneous and modern (Erecto, Meccano) or nostalgic and bucolic (*Lincoln Logs*, farm sets). As we have seen, historians of architecture and toys have suggested an opposite direction for influence: the stylized and simplified forms of building blocks or the open frameworks of Meccano type sets shaping the modernist aesthetics and engineering of a generation of children who grew up to be architects. Underpinning many claims and assumptions for the toyetic potential of the construction toy, however, is a broad sense not of any direct causal connection between a child's play structure and either their immediate urban environment or their future designs, should they grow up to be an architect or engineer. Rather, it follows a less distinct notion of the learning of both physical fundamentals (connecting structures, gravity, etc.) and abstracted processes of relationships between parts and wholes, units and systems. Here, it is not the toy itself that depicts the built or engineered environment, it is also the *toying*, the playful construction that echoes actual design and construction. Or, more accurately, play prefigures the child's future professional life and aptitudes, whether inculcating precise mechanical, spatial, and relational skills or instilling a more generalized and nebulous creative and technical aptitudes. So, this toying-learning can in turn be tightly instrumental (e.g., the instructional claims made for early construction sets) or more loosely nurturing of a general imaginative and creative set of cognitive, aesthetic, and dexterous aptitudes (e.g., more recent LEGO). At times, it is particularly polyvalent: Froebel's Gifts are a foundational instance of a system that deliberately eschews symbolism in favor of relational thinking; abstract but material relationships of shape, scale, and assemblage. The Gifts made no assumption about the type or scale of system their play might open up to the child. For instance, these early blocks were adopted by crystallographers in France and Sweden in the eighteenth century to "materialize the morphological features of crystals and their growth patterns" (and Froebel himself was a crystallographer).[43]

Players toy with the emerging metropolis in *SimCity*, and the game has an exploratory and speculative dynamic that resonates somewhat with the engineering-imagination of actual construction toy play.[44] But the notion of "toy" here takes on very new attributes that are far removed from predigital construction sets. Traditional LEGO and Meccano, for instance, are *systems* in their modular and extensive design, but they are not dynamic and organic systems in the sense that Wright is describing. Effectively, in *SimCity*, the toy is the simulation itself, the computer simulation as an automated and largely autonomous model unfolding over time, with construction the open-ended output from a nonlinear and nonhuman interplay of dynamic variables (figured as population, tax rates, crime levels, and so on). The player toys with the system from the outside, adjusts parameters, and can pause, "speed up," and "rewind" time, return to earlier save points, and hence try different tactics and aim at different trajectories. But in the main, the simulation-as-toy toys with the player, generating challenges for the player to respond to, offering rewards in the form of new buildings, facilities, and screen-animated growth, insisting the player is swept along with its own algorithmic momentum.

This "systems thinking" (to use a contemporary phrase) can be tracked throughout the genealogy of construction toys. It informs both the generalized principles of engineering-imagination and the creative claims for symbolic-imagination but is not limited to the physical artifactual world of the former and retains a scientific sense of structure, causality, and physical relationality lacking in the latter. Construction sets, from the Gifts on, have been produced or adopted by schools for teaching mathematical and engineering principles and for more open, imaginative development: wooden blocks from kindergarten up, to more specialized and complicated systems in the twentieth century, including Knex, Meccano, and LEGO. As such, its genealogy can be tracked back to Froebel via scientific applications of LEGO, scientific educational kits, and specialized building systems—for example, molecule modeling sets. Thus, to paraphrase Kate Maddalena, a construction toy system such as LEGO has always been digital. LEGO bricks are "palpable pixels," tied to "the history of computational logics and atomistic epistemologies that powerfully shape both the world itself and the possibilities for human existence in it."[45] Both plastic and software-based LEGO share the building block characteristics of being "non-semantic, manipulable, discrete."[46] LEGO demonstrates a remarkable plasticity in its metaphorical application to broader dynamics, epistemes even, of modernity and modern subjectivity. As Nick Taylor and Chris Ingraham put it, "As modular media, LEGO bricks suggest a world-making process that is aggregative and assembled, consisting of discrete parts that, together, add up to a completed whole. They also imply a recombinatory logic: the supposition that all world-making is provisional and capable of revision, deconstruction, multiple configurations."[47] Again, it is significant to this book's "what if" approach that we can simply think about a toy in these terms; it speaks to the nature of the toyetic in general, linking back to different ways in which construction toys have connected with and built on toyetic thought, from abstract reasoning to open-ended creativity. Also, "what if" here is unavoidably a postdigital question: in general terms, as nondigital play and its real–unreal worlds—after computer games—cannot now be unthought as "virtual."[48]

Conclusion

I would remind the reader here that my framing of the "what if" question in this book demands that we look beyond the metaphorical and the allusional for the efficacy of the toy in wider technoculture. To return to the historical frame with which this chapter opened, construction toys are also synecdochical: made from the industrial processes, materials, built, and economic environments they also depict and simulate. In the early to mid-twentieth century, this was steel, plastics, mass production, and modularization. With digital construction in the late twentieth and twenty-first centuries, simulated cities are both microcosmic images and fully part of the informational and networked infrastructure of industry and culture. And the processes and operations—physical and imaginative—through which they are assembled and animated are fully part of (albeit often ambivalent and nonlinear parts) of modes of thought and imagination claimed for and operationalized by postdigital modernity, from the apprentice engineer or architect of the 1920s to the creative media consumer and embryonic coder of the 2020s.

5 Robots

The most ingenious mechanical devices of antiquity were not useful machines but trivial toys. Only slowly do the machines of every-day life take up the scientific advances and principles used long before in despicable playthings and overly-ingenious, impracticable scientific models and instruments.[1]

The pen twitches spasmodically, writing furiously, apparently in midair, with a magical yet clumsy suggestion of an invisible hand. After a few seconds, it falls back to rest, and a small card pops out into a tray in the front of the cabinet. The coin-operated machine is called The Wizard's Pen, but this is a markedly industrial manifestation of wizardry: behind the glass is an assemblage of metal components and red electrical wire wrapped around spools. A sign reinforces this contradictory spirit: the card is "read from your own personal mystic rays," but at the same time the user is asked, "How is it done? Can you work it out?" I certainly couldn't "work it out" myself, although I guessed that the pen is animated by an intermittent electromagnetic field. I also guessed that the visible components and wires were decorative and not functional. Overall, the machine presented a mix of magic and magnetism, of credulity and belief versus detective work, of divination through technical ingenuity that, as we will see in this chapter, is nothing new. The Wizard's Pen dates from around 1930, and by then, electricity and electromagnetism were familiar and mundane phenomena: this machine was wringing out the last drops of their magical charge for few seconds and an old penny (figure 5.1). The card, printed in the style of a handwritten script, addressed me with the ambiguous yet portentous language of popular divination devices such as horoscopes and fortune cookies—and the numerous fairground, seaside pier, and amusement arcade machines of which this is one:

Figure 5.1
The Wizard's Pen. Arcade machine, UK, circa 1930. Sea City Museum, Southampton.

> In public you give the impression of being cautious and unimaginative, but we both know your yearnings to do something daring and frivolous.
> You're careful—your friends sometimes think <u>too</u> careful with your money. They also think you would never do anything to attract attention. Give them a surprise they won't forget—Spend a penny now and watch their faces!

The conceit that this card was written by the pen itself channeling some supernatural technicity is barely sustained, a rather sorry novelty. Yet, divinatory devices, however unconvincing, have a lasting appeal, and they tap into a wider technocultural genealogy in which the collusion of mechanical process and a lusory or performative imagination generates powerful operations of nonhuman animation—animation in terms of both movement and of intelligence or life itself.

Automata and Androids

The Wizard's Pen is an automaton, a self-moving machine. As such, it is a descendant of the remarkable mechanical androids of the eighteenth century, invented by the Jaquet-Droz family and Jacques de Vaucanson and fashioned as large dolls. Elegantly clothed with china heads and hands and with jointed limbs, they simulated music playing, drawing, and writing for well-to-do audiences and royal courts in France and across Europe. Despite its contemporary science fiction feel, the term "android" is actually of this era, used to describe Jacquet-Droz's creations in Diderot's *Encyclopédie*, denoting the human-like. Jacquet-Droz's Writer, for instance, is a simulacrum of a boy seated at a desk, able to write texts of up to forty characters long with a quill pen and ink, its head and eyes moving as if following the script. Its internal workings include a set of wheels to program the sequence of letters to be written (figure 5.2). A similarly child-shaped Draughtsman could sketch four different images, including a dog, Cupid, and a portrait of Marie Antoinette.[2] Such automata are thought experiments realized in mechanical form, at once spectacular novelties and prompts to philosophical and scientific reflections on the nature of life, reason, and consciousness. They are devices that, in their design and in the showiness of their presentation to audiences, prompted philosophical or religious reflection on the workings of the soul, consciousness, or the invisible realities of the microscopic. My aim in this chapter is to take the toylike characteristics of self-moving machines seriously, to keep attention on the toyetic dimensions of synthetic animation as a technocultural mode immanent to science and technology from the ancient to contemporary AI and robotics, but one that should not be separated from toys and toy play.

The terms "simulacra" and "automata" date back to ancient Rome and Greece respectively. Although they have come to overlap, and precise categorization is difficult, sketching a general sense of their meanings will help us to address questions of the material and semiotic workings of different kinds of animated devices. In myth, the machines and figures fashioned by the engineer-god Hephaestus illustrate a widely accepted distinction between the terms. Machines such as his tripods, wheeled devices that traveled around Olympus by themselves, and animated mechanical girls are all automata, in that they are "self-moving things," but the latter only are also simulacra because they are crafted to resemble living creatures.[3] Over time, simulacra have also come to refer to static artificial likenesses (e.g., paintings and sculpture)—that is, artifacts that are not necessarily self-moving. The mythic Galatea was a statue carved by the sculptor Pygmalion, coming to life under the force of his desire for her. Hence, she moves from static, albeit uncannily lifelike, simulacrum to simulacrum-automaton, a self-moving thing in part still characterized by its mimetic character. The tripods were functional machines, self-moving but, in appearance and wheeled movement, unlike any human or animal. Along with these mythical machines, ancient Greece

Figure 5.2
The Writer. Jacquet-Droz family, France, circa 1774. https://commons.wikimedia.org
/wiki/File:Automates-Jacquet-Droz-p1030495.jpg.

saw the design and construction of actual automata such as fountains, water clocks, and self-playing musical instruments. These, then, would be automata, although here the distinction is not a hard one, as they often incorporated simulacral animated figures.[4]

Cultural and literary histories of both automata and dolls trace key intertwined aspects back to Greek myths of Pygmalion, Pandora, and the giant mechanical warrior Talos (recounted around 700 BCE but from stories that were even then archaic), via the Golem of Jewish folklore, the early nineteenth-century fiction of Mary Shelley and E. T. A. Hoffmann, to children's literature and science fiction cinema.[5] As noted in chapter 2, the dream of animating inert matter or artifacts links simulacra from statues to dolls to robots. Alongside and intertwining with these fictive threads is a history of *actual* working self-moving devices that is rich and wide ranging. Animated figures and tableaux adorned temples in ancient Greece, singing blackbirds and early water clocks were evident in third-century BCE Alexandria, and the first clearly recorded inventions were fountains and mechanical theaters constructed in Egypt by Hero of Alexandria in the first century CE. Pneumatic theaters, fountains, water clocks, mechanical clocks, and animated figures populated the Christian and Islamic worlds of the medieval era, and mechanical calculators and clockwork were developed in the seventeenth century.[6] As both spectacle and philosophical reflection or model, and notwithstanding that the social and economic conditions they mediate have changed hugely, these automata explicitly or implicitly tested the boundaries of life and death, the human body and the machine, the animate and the inanimate.

There is extensive and fascinating scholarship on the history of automata from classical antiquity, through the Middle Ages in the Christian and Islamic worlds and China, to the eighteenth and early nineteenth centuries, much of which addresses their implications for the exploration of technological imaginaries of life and consciousness. Critical reflection on recent developments in ideas about robotics, new cyborgian intimacies between the human body and mind and computer technology, and artificial intelligence often draw on this long genealogy of automata.[7] Philosophical and historical studies of automata from the eighteenth century and before generally acknowledge their toylike appearance and being but downplay any relationships with children's play objects in favor of serious adult concerns: philosophical reflections on the nature of consciousness and life, evidencing the persistence of the irrational and magical in the rationalist discourses and methods of Enlightenment natural philosophy, or exploring the relationships between self-moving devices and epochal shifts in technological paradigms and imaginaries. I will argue, however, that these grand automata were characterized by key toyetic aspects: a performative mode of demonstration combining wonder, amusement, and technical materiality; an articulation of contemporaneous materials and mechanics with distinct technological imaginaries; and a strong and persistent relationship with play, games, and the toylike. On the one hand, then, this literature is an important inspiration, and support, for this book's toyetic thesis: toys and toylike machines shifted from the margins of technoculture to a central importance in philosophies of technology and the human body and mind. On the other hand, though, the continuity or contiguity with the child's toy and its playing in everyday life is generally treated at best as incidental. One aim of this chapter is to shift attention back to the toy itself, to see the automaton's purchase on protoscientific and natural-philosophical enquiry as inseparable from its affinity with the child's plaything with its cheap distractions, simulacral trickery, and hands-on play.

In some regards, the automata of antiquity, the Middle Ages, and the Enlightenment are among the least toylike of the objects I'm directly addressing in this book (figure 5.3). Expensive in design, manufacture, and upkeep, they were never play objects for children.[8] As objects whose attraction lay in their capacity for self-movement, they were not—at least ostensibly—designed to be manipulated and animated by the hands. In this, they appear to have cultural as well as visual resonances with the expensive and delicate porcelain dolls that also emerged in this period: to be displayed but not touched, the hint of simulacral life in the doll fully realized in the automaton. As a category of toylike technology, they are—more so even than construction toys—the most self-consciously designed and put into practice for broader nonplay, nonplayful reasons. So, what might an eye for ordinary toys, games, and play see in the design, use, and reflection on nonhuman mechanical behavior and its imaginary and material effects, from ancient parerga to contemporary robots and AI?

Toying with Automata

Before we identify and address these base toyetic characteristics and implications of the automata, let's address the two main reasons why they have been

Figure 5.3
The Elephant Clock by Badī az-Zaman Abu I- Ìzz ibn Ismā Ī l ibn ar-Razāz al-Jazarī.
Jazira, Mesopotamia, early thirteenth century. https://upload.wikimedia.org/wikipedia
/commons/0/0b/%22The_Elephant_Clock%22%2C_Folio_from_a_Book_of_the
_Knowledge_of_Ingenious_Mechanical_Devices_by_al-Jazari_MET_DP234075.jpg.

so persistently referred to in relation to toys. First, most of the eighteenth-century automata looked like large dolls and, with their ceramic faces and elaborate clothing, were made using materials and technologies similar to those in upmarket toy production at the time. No doubt, their imaginative impact as automata was heightened by the simulacral sense of the doll as symbol or model of the boundary between the inanimate and animate. Second, although such devices were often in the vanguard of technological development and their mechanical innovations were subsequently put to productive use, instrumentality was not the motivation for their production, and their audiences in the courts and salons of Europe in the eighteenth century did not watch them as such. Engineered for presentation and performance, for wonder and contemplation, and not as prototypes or models for future tools and systems, they were mechanical thought experiments, asking their audiences to take the short imaginative step from watching a machine that is ingenious but explicable to one that can—preternaturally—think and reason for itself. The Writer captured this unsettling proposition as he scratched on his pad, in a play on Descartes, a question that might speak for subsequent simulacra, "I am not thinking . . . Do I therefore not exist?"[9]

In particular historical moments, self-moving machines personified the technological paradigm of their day. Fashioned from dominant technical processes, principles, and materials, they also conjured up imaginaries of these very technics. And again, very often, these are imaginaries of *animation* in the sense of bringing-to-life as well as movement, of "living technology." Writing after World War II and the beginning of the modern information era, the cyberneticist Norbert Weiner argued that "at every stage of technique since Daedalus or Hero of Alexandria, the ability of the artificer to produce a working simulacrum of a living organism has always intrigued people. This desire to produce and to study automata has always been expressed in terms of the living technique of the age."[10]

Talos, for instance, the bronze giant created by Hephaestus built to patrol and defend Crete, was an expression of a Bronze Age technological imaginary. In form, material, workings, and processes of manufacture, Talos was rooted in the actual technics of his time, extrapolated through divine intervention into fully realizing his imaginary potential. Hephaestus himself did not simply will his creations into being through divine power, he physically forged, cast, and assembled them, and Talos's powers of animation and autonomous behavior were possible due to the tube of ichor that ran through his hollow body. Ichor is a divine substance—the blood of the gods—but is figured as the primary transformative material of the Bronze Age: molten metal.[11] Emphasizing the material reality from which ancient automata were fabulated, Adrienne Mayor calls them "cultural dreams, ancient thought experiments, 'What if?' scenarios set in an alternate world of possibilities, an imaginary space where technology was advanced to a prodigious degree."[12]

Automata, then, are more than allegories, as they, like Talos, are fashioned from the materials and through the processes that they, at the same time, symbolize. They are synecdoches of a machine universe, from pneumatic and hydraulic antiquity, through early-modern clockwork, industrial steam, and, more recently, postindustrial digital and genetic technologies. With the predominance of digital computing at the turn of the twenty-first century, with its networked communication, virtual environments, intimate cybernetic circuits between the human and these new machines, and the animated characteristics that these machines prompted, came a critical revisiting of earlier automata to help theorize new models of the human and the technological.[13] In their genealogies of digital media, Lister et al. explore the relationship of the devices of Jacquet-Droz and Vaucanson to the philosophical concerns and mechanical possibilities of their time. Clockwork, in this period, was at once a practical motive technology and a model of how the universe worked: from the Newtonian movement of the spheres to the human and animal body, "this was the period in which philosophers and scientists devised the ambition of explaining all nature in terms of clockwork."[14] René Descartes, for instance, regarded the functioning of bodily organs as fundamentally mechanical, like a watch, or as a system of pipes, engines, and pumps. This blurring of the distinction between biological and synthetic entities carried through into his reflections on the nature of thought and being. Famously, he speculated on the figures moving in the street below his window: How could one know if they were conscious humans like himself or mere animated machines? Although not simulacra in the classic sense and hence not as imagination grabbing as the writers, chess players, and musicians, the simulation of human intelligence in automatic machines had begun a century or so earlier in the mechanical calculators of Pascal and Leibniz,[15] picked up in the nineteenth century by Charles Babbage and Ada Lovelace. As well as intelligence, Enlightenment automata modeled theories of the invisible atomic or corpuscular constitution of material reality through pneumatic technology. As Daniel Tiffany puts it, "the toy divines the invisible substance of things."[16]

Unbox: Cheating at Chess

The Chess Player was a wooden cabinet with chessboard and a life-sized android with carved wooden head and hands. Designed and constructed by the Hungarian inventor Wolfgang von Kempelen in 1769, the figure was dressed in Turkish style, and both it and the cabinet had doors that could be opened to display the inner workings. Its left arm and hand picked up and moved the chess pieces, its head and eyes moving to follow play. Its first heyday was in the 1780s, as Kempelen traveled with the device around Europe. It played, and beat, Napoleon and lost to Catherine the Great (although she may have cheated).[17] On Kempelen's death, the automaton was dismantled, reassembled, and sold on a number of times before touring widely in the early nineteenth century, including the United States.[18]

If The Writer hinted at the possibility of machine consciousness, the Chess Player seemed to fully realize and demonstrate it. As the figure clicked and whirred, it consistently beat its opponents, including accomplished players as well as ordinary members of the audience. It appeared to take the rule-based mathematical achievements of Leibniz's calculating machines of a century earlier, anticipate the breakthroughs of Charles Babbage, and add the complex and instinctual modes of human thought and reason that chess playing was seen to demand. As such, it is now often regarded as continuous with the genealogy of artificial intelligence,[19] its evident trickery somewhat skated over, for while it certainly fed into an imaginary of synthetic minds that continues today, it added nothing to the actual technical development of AI, as the play itself was directed by a human player hidden inside.[20] It was an ingenious and cyborgian mechanism in its own right, however, the human "director" disguised by mirrors and playing by candlelight, moving the chessmen through an innovative pantographic armature and magnets.[21]

There is a key toyetic dimension to the Chess Player automaton that I want to pick up on. The Chess Player's construction and career are characterized by many layers of deceit, secrets, and trickery. It is important to bear in mind that the automaton was not a fake or a fraud in absolute terms. Kempelen himself never directly claimed the machine really played chess without human intervention; he referred to it in the toylike terms "trifle" or "bagatelle" and as an "illusion." So, it always had something of the stage magic trick about it (as its later life in Barnum shows would attest).[22] Demonstrations of

Figure 5.4
Kempelen's Chess Player. 1769. Copper engraving from Freiherr Joseph Friedrich zu Racknitz, *Ueber den Schachspieler des Herrn von Kempelen*, Leipzig und Dresden, 1789. https://commons.wikimedia.org/wiki/File:Racknitz_-_The_Turk_3.jpg.

the automaton were characterized by elaborate, ritual-like performativity: the exhibitor opening its doors and drawers, passing a candle through its interior to "prove" its purely mechanical workings, before winding it up with a key.[23] Even in the Age of Reason, it appears, a taste for magic persisted. However, we should not assume that the reactions and desires of the automaton's audience can be divided into a straightforward distinction between credulous belief in enchantment in some observers and scientific and technical interest in others. Numerous pamphlets were written with theories of how the illusion was realized, and some audience members returned again and again to performances, trying to work out how it was achieved. Kempelen toyed with his audience, standing close to the figure as it played and fiddling in his pocket, suggesting he was controlling the figure's movements with a concealed powerful magnet and thereby feeding into one of the prevalent theories of the machine's actual operation.[24] Edgar Allen Poe, himself fascinated and unsettled by the automaton, theorized in a pamphlet that the relatively crude carving of the figure's face and hands—in an era when waxworks, for instance, would easily and cheaply provide a much more convincing simulacrum—was in itself a decoy, suggesting that if the device looked more machinelike, the audience would be more likely to believe it was fully a machine.[25] As with stage magic, and the cinematic special effects it—and automata—would inspire, audiences were at once entranced by the illusion and its implications (What if a machine really could play chess and think?) and hungry for the revelation of how the trick was pulled.

The intriguing suggestion is raised, then, that perhaps audiences *did not want* to see the actual fully realized moving and thinking machines. The pamphleteers expressed an anxiety about the essence and boundaries of the human, and the general public appeared to have been, as Gaby Wood puts it, "titillated by the possibility of automation," toying with the idea that "machines could be like humans, without ever having to deal with the reality. It was like playing with machinery, or playing with what was human."[26] I would note a marked similarity with the children's anxious response to the suggestion of a fully autonomous robot toy in "Unbox: Robot Imaginaries."

But why is it important to assert, as Tiffany does, that automata *are* toys? Toy-like attributes are more consistent in automata than would first appear and go to the heart of their simulacral and performative character. Even those with natural-philosophical and scientific pretensions are characterized by a playfulness, a spectacular, wondrous, or quasi-magical mode of presentation and public reception, reveling in the marvelousness of artifice and technical ingenuity (see "Unbox: Chess-Player"). Here are four other ways that the automaton overlaps the toy. The first addresses the practical and the technical: the toy is the most suitable technocultural form for the embodiment, instantiation, and public demonstration of new technologies, material forces, and their relationships. A toy is a concentration or condensation of materials, ideas, aesthetics, forces, and mechanisms into a figure easily grasped by the hand, eye, and imagination: the dimensions of scale, operability, a level of visibility, and, when we look at the ways in which these were presented, the spectacle and performativity. They were manipulable, operated by the designer or showman, but because this toying was in close proximity to the audience, it felt tangible. Often, the inner workings of the automaton would be revealed to the audience as part of the performance. Second, these are highly sophisticated and expensive machines, but ones with no straightforward instrumental end: they are generative of knowledge, wonder, and reflection but not of power or goods—luxurious and useless, they resonate with toylike aspects of consumer culture to follow in the nineteenth century.[27] Third, they epitomize the uniquely toyetic epistemological mode that I track throughout this book: a hands-on, material, and mechanical instantiation of the thought experiment: a cognitive, imaginative, and speculative "what if." "Okay," we might ponder, "this here-and-now marvelous machine *doesn't* think, but our operation of it helps us imagine one that might, and to muse on what an actually thinking machine would entail." Finally, this toyetic mode of speculative knowledge manifests in two overlapping ways: the speculative (the "what if" as above) and the deceptive. Figural automata are deceitful in their human- or animal-shaped forms; they appear natural and living but are synthetic and mechanical. Others, such as the Chess Player ("Unbox: Cheating at Chess"), play more elaborate trickery, promising displays of self-moving wonder while teasing their—more or less knowing—audiences with hints at the illusion. As a mode of cognition, then, one's apprehension of the automaton, like that of the toy, cannot be easily separated into comprehension and wonder, inquiry and credulity, knowledge and belief.

Again, the relationships of seriously playful technologies with children's toy play are not incidental and marginal but rather integral and consistent. For every courtly display of an expensive and awe-inspiring figure, there were innumerable ad hoc, playful, and functional devices, objects for children, strange funerary and memorial devices, and quasi-religious installations. Tiffany notes that the "first complex, self-activating machines in antiquity were not tools but toys, and more precisely, *singing birds* and other *parerga* (ornamental devices), including moving or talking statues employed at the sites of oracles."[28] There is surely something of the *parerga* throughout the subsequent genealogy of automata. Medieval churches were furnished with statues of weeping Madonnas and Crucifixions where Christ's head would move and His wounds bleed.[29] Whether pious churchgoers saw these as actual miracles or as ingenious but profane simulacra of the miraculous is not recorded. They were often not full automata, sometimes worked by nuns pulling levers inside the statues, or filled with liquid that would leak from the statue's eye when disturbed by living fish within them.[30] Unlike the ancient pneumatic and hydraulic automata before or the clockwork and protoprogramming of the eighteenth-century robots to come, these installations appear to be less a philosophical reflection on prevailing technological paradigms and more a practical use of economical and to-hand materials and mechanics—rope, wood, lead pipes—that modern eyes might recognize as prefiguring the construction methods and mechanics of theater sets, stage magic, and theme parks, all of which suggests playful and improvisatory modes of production and display that jar with contemporary views of the medieval world as bound by religious fixity.[31]

By the time the Chess Player's career ended, automata had long ceased to be courtly wonders, and their genealogy diverged into three main lines: toys proper, industrial machinery and the factory system, and new forms of popular and spectacular entertainment. Self-moving toys became very popular, as the once highly expensive clockwork came to be mass produced and the floors of nurseries and bedrooms were crisscrossed by speeding tin vehicles and wheeled animals. The simulacral aspects of the automaton continued to cross-fertilize with dolls, with new industrial techniques in ceramics and textiles leading to the fine delicate clothing and lifelike faces and hands of the expensive Victorian doll, the figure whose uncanny connotations and affects we encountered in chapter 2, and, as such, were connected to the lifelike and life-sized waxwork figures of contemporaneous popular attractions.[32] Some were animated: the clockwork doll—*la jolie catin*—had been popular in Europe since the mid-eighteenth century (figure 5.5),[33] and jointed limbs have always lent a sort of life to dolls in play. The industrial era brought new techniques for the simulation of skin, eye movements, hair, and the manufacture of elaborate and extensive costumes, recharging the ancient trope of the deceptive and alluring "living doll."[34] Today's postindustrial and postdigital industry brings a new slant to this ancient imaginary, with investment in, and instrumental fantasies of, robot sex dolls.[35]

As industrial machinery, the automata rediscovered their water- and steam-powered origins with the mills and factories of the Industrial Revolution. And the tangled genealogical lines between the programmable Jacquard looms and Ada Lovelace's innovative programming of Babbage's

Figure 5.5
Clockwork animated doll with *Polichinelle* (Punch) puppet. Automaton by Léopold Lambert. France, circa 1890. Doll and Toy Museum, Josselin, France.

inventions are well documented (along with their prefiguring of electronic and digital automata in the twentieth century—not least the computer itself). Less so are Vaucanson's later innovations in automating silk weaving that were to lead to the Jacquard loom—and his role in designing the first specialized factories.[36] As Wood puts it, "Vaucanson played a significant role in the widespread replacement of men with their artificial counterparts."[37]

The showman-like and performative aspects of the simulacrum-automaton sank into the new cheaper and popular cultural sites that industrialization and urbanization brought: rented showrooms in city centres, vaudeville theaters, sideshows, fairgrounds, and later amusement arcades. Here, they joined and fused with the spectacular novelties of magic shows, magic lanterns, panoramas, and mechanical and projected moving images. Machines such as The Wizard's Pen emerged from this disreputable milieu of the popular attraction and were as unremarkable as the human fortune tellers they simulated. But while they epitomize the fall from grace of the ancient and courtly self-moving devices, they also look forward to later twentieth- and twenty-first-century toyetic automata, media, and toys. Joining other coin-operated automatic and semiautomatic attractions on the pier and in the arcade, from animated tableaux to pinball, this is the technical and cultural cocoon within which automated moving images metamorphosed at the end of the nineteenth century. The scientific and optical philosophical toys of the eighteenth and nineteenth centuries along with their spectacular cousins—such as peep shows, magic lanterns, panoramas, and devices that brought still images into life—joined the automata in the fairground, interbreeding and mutating with them as animated tableaux and coin-operated mutoscopes. It is no coincidence that cinema itself has demonstrated its fascination with *animation* in many forms, not least a self-reflexivity on its own motive form evident in its early self-presentation as a technology of spectacular and illusory movement. A thematic and visual obsession with the animation of dead matter runs through cinema for both adults and children. And, as we'll see in the next chapter, automata emerged from the fairground, butterfly-like, as cinema.

Unbox: Robot Imaginaries

Eight children sat around a large table in a primary school classroom.[38] They were year 5, nine or ten years old. We asked them to draw robots, and as they did so, they talked excitedly:

—It could be a household robot . . . a microwave here, and a washing machine there!

—Mine looks like a snail!

—I'm thinking of Droidius from *Star Wars* . . .

—Brian! The confused.com robot! [Two of the children recite in unison the words of a recent TV advertisement for this price comparison website featuring a comic robot]

—None of the robots in adverts are proper robots.

The workshop leader picks up on this last statement. "So, what's a proper robot?"

—Uses proper technology, not just wires.

—You can program it!

—Brian's probably just remote controlled.

—R2D2!

—Mine's like a snail . . .

After this drawing activity, the project designer revealed and demonstrated the prototype robot toy. It twitched, then jerked into life, its front legs rearing up threateningly, something like a tarantula responding to a threat. Its servos whirred and the whole device clattered noisily against the melamine-topped table. With involuntary gasps and a collective "whooaaa," the children started back from the object in front of them that had instantly transformed from a boxy and technical-looking assemblage of gray plastic elements, joints, and wires into an uncannily alive-like creature.

The gray tarantula's movement was remote controlled by the project's lead designer. As yet, it had no autonomous or sensing capabilities, aspects generally taken as key defining elements of a robot.[39] There were, however, a set of material objects, intangible ideas, and excited imaginations that added up to a range of ideas—expressed through talk, drawing, and play—about robots in general, robots past and present, fictional and actual robots, and a robot toy to come. It was clear that the first associations that sprang to the children's minds were from popular media culture and not actual robots or, interestingly, toy robots. One girl pointed out, however, that none of these were real robots, and that Brian was probably remote-controlled. Others concurred, suggesting an understanding of some specific features of actual robotic technology, notably the distinction between remote control by a human operator and preprogrammed behaviors. Two of the children had recent experience of actual robots from a visit to a popular science center. They had taken part in a workshop in which they had programmed a robot to use sensors to distinguish between colored balls. No further detail was offered at this point, but the notion of sensors—and these children's hands-on experience of them—was to inflect the children's imaginary future scenarios for the robot from then on. The drawn

Figure 5.6
Two robots and none: robot toy design workshop. Bristol, UK.

imagined robots were boxy, with screens for faces, some with caterpillar tracks rather than legs, perhaps a mix of Wall-E and Brian. One drawing was even labeled "sort of Brian." Another, however, was more rocket-like in shape and inspired by R2D2, and one had a dome-like body above caterpillar tracks. Its creator announced repeatedly, apparently no less surprised than everyone else, that it had turned out to be a snail robot. It was clear that whatever these children's understanding was of an everyday life of robotic interaction, it was imagined primarily in terms of characters from popular media entertainment. However, this shifted significantly once they had seen and played with the actual prototype:

—Those look like lasers! [shooting noises] It could twist its head and kill you!

—I would build a LEGO city and make it destroy it! It would be like Godzilla! It doesn't look nice and kind!

—If it was mine, I would make it walk first. Then I would make its front legs come. [Gestures it rearing up with her arms]

—[Responding to a question about playing with friends with two robots] They could work together to destroy a city.

—Or battle together with their front legs! Ninja!

—If I had one on my own, I would make a park for it to go through, to follow and path and turn corners. [One of the children who had been to the robot workshop]. Sensors.

On the one hand, unsurprisingly, the children immediately began to imagine how the robot might be played with, what features might be added, and what playful possibilities they might afford. Their imaginative engagement with the physical and moving robots was kinesthetic and bodily expressive, as well as simply cognitive and symbolic. As they excitedly invented possible scenarios and events for the future robots in their everyday play, they gestured—the dramatic motion of the robot's front legs was performed, forearms held up with hands bent down at the wrist, moving rapidly up and down as a large spider or praying mantis might attack its prey.

On the other hand, though much of the conversation was shot through with a distinct unease about aspects of the proposed toy. The insect- or alien-like and combative-looking character of the design did not alarm them, but something about its potential autonomous capabilities caught the collective imagination in ways both exciting and unsettling. This became particularly evident when the project designer (PD) explained a key feature of the planned toy:

—(PD) Something else about these robots that I forgot to tell you. If you leave them by themselves, they can just walk around and have fun by themselves. Is that a good thing or not?

—(All) No!

—If you go on holiday, it could move around and break things, and then when you get back, it could have gone, or gone outside and you can't find it.

—Or it could just be walking on a table and just fall off and break.

—It's creepy—if you're reading in a room and it comes up to you [laughs].

—If they were like at the bottom of your stairs and they somehow climbed up the stairs to your closed door and started banging on your door because they wanted to come in. They know it's the door to your bedroom because they want that person to start playing with them.

This collective anxiety about nonhuman intelligence and autonomous movement was generated not by a general dystopian technological imaginary of robot supremacy and AI singularity but rather by the specific technical characteristics of the proposed toy and their imagined place and activity within the safety of the children's homes and bedrooms. The robot's material, mechanical, and behavioral aspects are inseparable from imaginative response and speculation.[40] The physical and behavioral capacities of the projected robotic toy were salient in a set of more or less anxious microimaginaries. These scenarios and designs were partly technical, practical speculations about the ways in which the robot might behave and behaviors it might be capable of, depending on actual components, and partly a much more detailed and collectively generated vision of how it might exist within and interact with their domestic space, family relationships, play, and dreams.

Digital Automata

While, by the 1920s, the early cinema had shed some of its reliance on technological novelty and spectacle and had achieved institutional and cultural prestige with relatively stable aesthetic and narrative conventions and technologies of production and viewing,[41] the amusement arcades continued as sites of hands-on and sensational mechanical trickery, spawning, some fifty years later, the first popular computer-based automata: videogames. In the rest of this chapter, I will focus on robotic, smart, and artificially intelligent toys and games, building on the discussion of earlier automata technological imaginaries and industrial synecdoche addressed above. My interest here, then, is the ways that these playful machines, both mechanical and virtual, articulate imaginaries of digital technologies with *actual* smart and artificially intelligent—self-moving—behavior.

The distinction between automaton and robot or AI is not always clearly drawn and tends to be determined by the presence or absence of certain capabilities and functions. Modern functional devices called robots generally have some degree of autonomous behavior through their programming and perhaps capacity for sensing and responding to environmental conditions such as obstacles, as for example in domestic robot vacuum cleaners.[42] Thus, folded and printed tin robot figures, animated by clockwork—early products of the post–World War II global mediascape—are *automata* but not actual *robots*. Similarly, recent toys styled as robots—often figured as animals or dinosaurs—but fully remote-controlled by a wired control pad or a smart device via Bluetooth feature sophisticated movement but have no autonomous, programmable, or sensate capacity. As the children cited in the "Unbox: Robot Imaginaries" attest, such nonrobotic robots are, however, fully part of a technological imaginary of computational agency. Indeed, Japanese-style tin robots are often used as a skeuomorphic emblem for actual AI and robotics in press reports, academic publications, and illustrations (figure 5.7). Between the full robot and the fully controlled

Figure 5.7
Twenty-first-century replica of mid-twentieth-century clockwork tin robot toy. Flaming Nora's toy shop, Bournemouth, UK.

movement of remote-controlled toys lie "smart" toys—various devices and systems that offer behavior that is both responsive to and semiautonomous from their players. Although there are no hard and fast distinctions between smart devices, robots, and AI, the latter tend to refer to more complex or advanced automata that operate at least partially independently of direct human control.

So, where does the automata imaginary lead us in recent and contemporary playful technoculture? In the late twentieth century, smart toy play generated renewed interrogation of the borders of the living and the thinking across the human and the technological. Sherry Turkle's observations of children's play with smart toys in the late 1970s and early 1980s illustrate this everyday philosophy vividly. Unlike earlier playful machines for children such as bicycles or clockwork toys, smart toys and games such as *Merlin* (Parker Brothers 1978) and *Simon* (Milton Bradley 1978) were black boxes—their workings hidden in solid-state electronics and silicon chips rather than visible and manipulable like gears and springs. As such, children's cognitive relationships to the toys changed, Turkle suggests: smart toys' opacity of agency, and capacity for autonomous behavior, necessitated modes of imaginative play that were psychological—that is, explored through theories of mind rather than bodily movement. "Children ask themselves if the games are conscious, if the games know, if they have feelings, and even if they "cheat," the computer encourages children to see computational objects as psychological machines."[43] Turkle's work consistently demonstrates that children are not deceived by smart toys and games. Rather, they work to interpret their being as synthetic but animate entities. For instance, one eleven-year-old girl, Holly, tracked these distinctions through fictional imaginaries and the material actuality of the device in front of her: "'First Pinocchio was just a puppet. He was not alive at all. Then he was an alive puppet. Then he was an alive boy. A real boy. But he was alive even before he was a real boy. So, I think the robots are like that. They are alive like Pinocchio [the puppet], but not 'real boys.'"[44] This enquiry into a third mode of being—between the inanimate object and the unambiguously living being—is remarkably consistent across the long history of automata engineering and fiction. As several of Turkle's informants put it, they are *"sort of* alive." In its degree of autonomous behavior (asking questions, responding to answers, competing with the child in games), the 1970s smart toy and its robotic and software-based progeny are quite different to other toys, ones that are, by and large, imbued with life and intelligence only by the imaginative and manual action of the actual child. In addition to the long-established "as if" realities of play with toys, these toys and devices bring a new degree of "sort of" life, and to play with them is by necessity to respond to them as if they were alive, again in new ways.

Programmable and sensing robots have been a feature of the toy market alongside smart toys in recent decades, and I will address some of them in this chapter, but their expense and mechanical complexity means that, with a few exceptions, they have not become as embedded in children's play culture as might have been expected. The more successful lines, such as *LEGO Mindstorms*, often cross over with educational applications, capitalizing on educational policies that espouse a basic literacy in coding for young children—and robot systems have been manufactured and marketed as a lively mode for the learning and testing of programming. Or they tap into the domestic and intergenerational hobbyist mode of serious play, well established since at least the early twentieth century with construction sets, scientific instrument sets, and the more elaborate train sets. Others play up game or toy connotations over the seriously robotic: *Simon* and *Merlin*, for example, or Hasbro's perennial *Furby* (from 1998). I suspect there are material-imaginary factors at the level of hands-on play too. Even a system as familiar and accessible as *Mindstorms* requires a level of achievement in programming to persuade the constructed robot to move, and the expertise needed ramps up quickly if the child wishes the robot to perform anything but the most rudimentary behaviors. Also, to program toys is a profoundly different behavioral, aesthetic, and imaginative process than their manual animation in play. To program a robot is to delegate and defer playful movement—whether exploration, sensing, gesture, or combat. In *Mindstorms*, the child clicks together blocks of code on a computer or mobile device, streams it to the robot, and watches hopefully to see if the expected behavior plays out, the toy now disconnected from their immediate control. Playful animation, then, is distributed in space and time, across the child's imagination, their grasp of the physical and engineered capacity of the robot, their ability to code, the Bluetooth connection between device and robot, and the ability of the code to instantiate that imagined movement and behavior more or less faithfully. The robot is manipulated by the child's hands, eyes, and imagination but at a significant temporal and mechanical remove.

If these proper robots have so far tended to occupy only a niche position in toy culture, I would argue that the contemporary heirs of automata and simulacra have found their fullest expression in computer games. Computer games mark a genealogical confluence of self-moving, animate technology with the ancient ludo-technics of the board game. I would suggest that the answer to the question of why children found smart toys such as *Simon* so compelling can be found not only in their autonomous and coded abilities but also in the structured temporality, spatiality, and mechanics descended from game rules and boards. Manipulation of them is structured and driven by a game mechanic—with *Simon*, for instance, the players memorized and repeated the sequence of colored lights that the device displayed. Player and device operated in the same real-time frame, and interaction was fast, reciprocal, and satisfying (or frustrating). I will return to the relationship between automata and games later in this chapter. For now, I would note that with computer games and toys, the notion that we are "toyed with" as much as "toying" reaches a new level of cybernetic intensity: *Simon* and *Merlin* coded their players' behavior.

In the late 1990s, the smart toy took a new turn, with the global success of the *Tamagotchi* line of virtual pets (Bandai, from 1996). These handheld egg-shaped plastic objects had small monochrome LCD screens that, in blocky pixelated graphics, displayed an animal face. With a simple game mechanic of feeding, playing, and general care and attention, the child carried the toy with them, pressing buttons when prompted to keep the virtual pet happy and alive. Such devices contain several key aspects of robots. Even if they don't move in actual space, they demonstrate autonomous behavior and modify that behavior through feedback from their environment. In this case, the environment is a narrow channel—the buttons that constitute an interface with the human player's actions—but an environment, nonetheless. From this little device and its simple rules and interactions, a distinctly dystopian technological imaginary was conjured up in both the popular press and academic cultural critique. The *Tamagotchi* craze represented the "technological erosion of emotion,"[45] the replacement of "real reciprocal relationships and surrogate, one-way imaginary ones," with technology "now a substitute for human relationships."[46] At the end of the millennium, *Tamagotchi* play seemed to some a dangerous blurring of children and technology, subjects and objects, and a waning of loving and caring relationships in an era of disposability and artifice (figure 5.8). Others were

Figure 5.8
Jurassic World: Dominion–themed *Tamagotchi*. Bandai, 2022. Photo: Dave Gibbons.

less pessimistic. Anne Allison saw in the *Tamagotchi* an emblem of a "global imaginary," a transnational cultural economy of Japanese hardware and media products embraced by children around the world. For her, the new intimacies between the human and (newly animate) nonhuman epitomized by the *Tamagotchi* are less catastrophic but no less revolutionary: they are driven by increasing virtuality and a concomitant "cyborgian fantasy."[47] For Allison, these toys are not the harbingers of an unsettling virtualized world. Rather, they are an imaginative palliative to it, as they "both reflect and shape an imagination that not only fits these postindustrial times but also helps kids adjust to a world where the border between the imaginary and the real is shifting so quickly."[48]

What neither of these *Tamagotchi* worldviews do, however, is consider the ways in which these overarching sets of ideas about an imminent posthuman popular technoculture actually drive or shape children's imaginative play with technologically sophisticated toys—or, indeed, whether they do so at all. Importantly, they don't fully account for the very particular contexts of play, neither the often ironic, phantasmagorical inversions of imaginative play, nor the particular mechanisms of the game form itself as a long-lived technocultural phenomenon. So, the *Tamagotchi* is presented and marketed as offering a loving and caring relationship. However, close attention to play with smart toys, robots, or virtual pets reveals a more nuanced and complex interplay of affect, mechanics, and instrumentalism, imagination augmented with patterns that are schematic, algorithmic, and procedural.[49] The child must learn which buttons to press in response to particular prompts and virtual events more for ludic than affective purposes (to level up the character, gain rewards, expend points or virtual commodities, and so on). As with other computer games, this is implicitly understood by the playing child: that it is a software system as well as an imagined companion. A child may appear to love the virtual animal and to get upset when it dies, but this is always within their knowledge of the game *as* a game, that "death" is failure in the game, within a structure that is coded as and geared toward a certain kind of play and a certain duration of play. This interplay of emotional and instrumental engagement with virtual creatures is evident in *Tamagotchi*, experienced as sort of alive and sometimes played with as if they are actual pets. To take the intense relationality of player and automaton (or any toy craze of the moment) and project it into the near future as an all-consuming dystopia is at once to recognize the *significance* of the toyetic but to profoundly misunderstand its tangled and tangential operations and effects.

So, without attention to the technical characteristics, possibilities, and limitations in moments of actual everyday play, and the nuanced and nonlinear set of relationships between ideas, imagination, technologies, and media characters they generate, critical work on smart and robotic toys runs the risk of perpetuating idealist assumptions. Multiple layers of the imaginary are central to the design, dissemination, and adoption of playful technologies, and are anchored in the material and technical characteristics of the play objects and systems themselves and—importantly—in the embodied and imaginative playful relationships and events they engender. As Minna Ruckenstein notes, "toys are designed both materially and semiotically . . . the materiality of toys intertwines with prominent ideologies and narratives."[50] It is only by describing the intimate and contingent relationships between specific toys and technologies and their playful use that we can both resist overly optimistic or dystopian predictions of the near future of children's playful technoculture and explore the nature of play in and as technoculture. Ruckenstein's ethnographic study of young children and *Tamagotchi* in Finland, for instance, emphasizes the complex interrelationships between the material characteristics and capacities of technological toys and their cultural framing as articulated in children's play. She notes a small but significant battle between young girls and their teachers over a technological and affectual imaginary of official approval. The teachers were invested in ideas that cuddly, animal-shaped toys were socially and pedagogically superior to digital games and battery-operated toys, and actively intervened in discussions with children about toys to encourage "bonding" with their preferred toys. As one girl showed both her *Tamagotchi* and cuddly dog to the class, she was asked which was best. "'This one,' she said, holding up the *Tamagotchi*, 'because it can be fed.' The teacher resisted, 'It is a bit cold, like a machine. Beautiful soft doggy: such a cute face.'"[51]

Jackie Marsh's observations of a three-year-old girl's play with her app-augmented *Furby* is an excellent example of the articulation of a meta-level technological imaginary with an ethnographic eye for the details and textures of the lived moment. Marsh teases out what we might call microimaginaries—contingent on and spun into existence by the intersection of the material affordances of the toy and the fleeting images, dramas, gestures, and concerns that characterize young children's imaginative play: "She always plays a number of times with the toilet feature of the app, in which Furby is encouraged to use the toilet, and then she flushes it by pressing the button in the app and creating clouds of air freshener around the toilet. At one point, Amy pretends that she has Furby's feces on her hands."[52] Marsh notes here that the app's AR function "has promoted imaginative play that moves beyond the inorganic organized objects contained within the play."[53] My interpretation of this is that while the app and toy play is no doubt predicated by an imaginative acceptance of AI and autonomous behavior, this dimension is not reflected on philosophically by Amy (as it was by Turkle's informants). Rather, it is taken for granted as the interactive and gamelike aspects of the app pull her into a much more hands-on engagement with virtual life—here, hands-on in both actual and virtual terms. In this moment, the global strategies of Hasbro, the design and programming of a particular toy system and the playful, scatological, and embodied imagination of a child collude in the simulation of a pungent dimension of (artificial) life. Thus, while Allison's cyborgian fantasy projected a posthuman future from emergent popular technocultural products, here it is lived in the here and now, fully contemporaneous, everyday, and generally unremarkable.

Artificial Playful Intelligence

With computer games, smart toys, and domestic/educational robot systems from the late 1970s on, the toyetic technological imaginary slipped fully back into synchronic step with the prevailing technological paradigm for the first time since the start of the Industrial Revolution. Videogames in particular are synecdochical of the era of information processing, digital networks, virtuality, and simulation, offering their players hands-on engagement with animate and responsive synthetic entities, environments, and processes. Digital game play is a persistent, everyday, and intense living with automata and artificial intelligence. NPCs are androids but constructed as finite state machines not clockwork dolls, programmed with default behaviors, patrolling a particular area of the game's world, for instance, but ready to trigger a new set of behaviors—fight or flight, say—in response to an input—generally, the player's actions (figure 5.9).

If NPCs are effectively soft robots, videogame avatars at first glance appear doll- or action figure–like in their manipulability via controller or keyboard, responsive in real time to the player's hands. But avatars themselves often

Figure 5.9
Soft robots: *The Sims 2*. Maxis/EA, 2004.

have semiautonomous abilities, including sensing their environment, the performance of pre-scripted sequences of movement, and the automated targeting of enemies in combat. Game figures such as the citizens of *The Sims* games fall between the autonomy of the NPC and the direct control of the avatar. At first glance, they look and feel like dollhouse dolls but are robots: the player sets values for their characterization and motivation and general instructions for their behavior, but the figures themselves behave unpredictably within these parameters and their virtual environment, according to fuzzy logic routines determined by the game software.[54]

I see two important and overlapping questions here. What do the concepts of automata and simulacra bring to the consideration of the nature of the digital object as a toy? And what does it mean to play with a toy if it isn't physical, if it can't be held in and manipulated by the hands? After all, this latter characteristic is one that I argue throughout is central to the toy as an artifact. Clearly, this attribute at least is transformed in digital games and, in turn, affects and transforms others. Emma Reay has tracked techniques in the design of some avatars to evoke or compensate for the tactility of actual toys. *Little Big Planet* in particular offers "overt toyness" in its depiction of characters as soft toys, action figures, and dolls—characters that can also be dressed, posed, and displayed. She suggests too that these avatars do not speak, so as to resonate with actual toy play, "creating space for the player to narrate their inner worlds as one might when animating physical figurines."[55]

Scale becomes much more ambiguous in the digital game, as the immediate relationship between its virtual characters and objects and the player's body and hands is loosened. As we play a videogame, are we looking at a small screen image of a full-sized world as if watching live-action television, a miniature world like a dollhouse or toy zoo, or even a normal-sized world but with miniature action and actors in games such as *Micro Machines*, *Toy Soldiers*, or the Ribbon Road track in *Mario Kart 8* set in a child's toy room? Early computer games were sometimes referred to as "microworlds," partly in reference to the novelty of their technological platform (microelectronics, microcomputers), but also due to players' apprehension of the gameworld as mediated by small, flickering, low-resolution screens, which, coupled with the simple graphics, gave a sense of interiority to the virtual activity.[56] Here, phenomenological echoes of dollhouses and the peep media (discussed in chapter 6) are coupled with an early digital-cultural imaginary of virtual worlds *within* machines and networks, notably William Gibson's cyberspace[57] and the mainframe world in the movie *Tron*.[58] By contrast, the experience of playing a game such as *Call of Duty: Modern Warfare II* today on a large and high-resolution screen carries little sense of the miniature. Rather, it feels much more like interacting with a live-action movie: a depiction of actual sized bodies and environments.[59] Thus, the ergonomic absolutes of the toy's material scale now pertain only to the mechanical interface: hands grasp and manipulate the controller, the mouse, the keyboard buttons. Manipulability is reengineered and mediated, recast as *interactivity*. With digital games, the child takes an agential step toward the screen image of television, grasping and interacting with it—but they are taking a step away from the physical toy, loosening their grip on its movement and placement, delegating some of its mechanical and imaginative operations to the software.

Thinking Machines

In the Introduction, I argued that, historically, the toy has occupied a material-cultural position between the ritual object and the instrumental tool, neither fully sacred nor simply functional. Public and scholarly engagement with automata and simulacra over the centuries suggests a broad imaginative or conceptual grasp of the toyetic that is analogous to its liminoid state: just as the toy and the toylike exist between the persistent categories of the tool and ritual object, there is a toyetic psychology, a mode of thinking and playing with technology that does not fit into the modern binaries of rationalism/religion, scientific thinking/magical thinking, knowledge/belief, truth/deceit. The mix of credulity and curiosity in the Chess Player's audiences, for instance, resonates with those for magic shows, modern divination technics such as horoscopes and Tarot, as well as for the scientific wonders of optical toys and protocinematic devices and their descendants such as CGI special effects and the novelties of virtual and augmented reality systems. This toyetic attitude should not be reduced to simple notions either of the "suspension of disbelief" in spectacular popular culture or to some persistence of the "magical thinking" of young children and preindustrial societies.[60] We see instead a more generative grasp of automata—a delight at being tricked, along with wonder at the illusion and a simultaneous desire to know how it was achieved. In simulacra and automata, the "magic" lies in the sophisticated and novel mechanism itself, preternatural not supernatural. There is a play across the surface effects (the porcelain face and velvet costume, the uncannily animated chess pieces, the CGI wonders) and the revelation of the inner workings (the programmable brass spine, the mirrors and trickery, the "making of . . ." documentary films that accompanied early CGI blockbusters).[61] And we're close here to the kind of thinking that grasps the behavior of toy automata as sort of life: the child is not fooled that the device is alive, but neither is its movement simply a "dead" mechanical effect. But this is not "animism" in either the anthropological sense or the "magical thinking" of very young children's play with toys; the distinction between the animate and the animate, the subject and the object persists, but it is a liminoid zone rather than a hard border. We can see this in the robot workshop account above: the children were fascinated by the idea of an animated toy but deeply wary of full autonomy. Whatever animism is at work in children's play, it is completely bound up in the exercise of control and manipulability, an achievement of the child's imagination, motor behavior, and the mechanical/material characteristics of the toy. Remove the latter from the reach of the former and playful animation ends. In actual toys, this desire is channeled through the hands as well as the imagination. As we'll see in the next chapter, optical toys epitomize a hands-on examination of the preternatural in technology and nature. That is to say, we know these devices are not supernatural or magical, but they concentrate and render graspable the wonderful and the spectacular in physical reality, from the properties of light to the human sensorium.

Conclusion

The toyetic runs through the genealogy of automata set out in this chapter. Self-moving machines materialize philosophies of the body, mind, and being in a form graspable and manipulable by the hands and the imagination. Embodied and emblematic, they render complex and distributed systems, physical and mechanical properties, ideas and philosophies, human bodies and minds into devices amenable to play or play-like activities and contemplation. As with the construction toys in the last chapter, we see the gamelike dimensions of many forms of technical modeling, experimentation, prediction, and speculation. And with digital games, the overlapping of automata, simulacra, and simulation in ludic form is vivid and compelling. As the eighteenth-century automata embodied a technological imaginary of agency, life, and being, contemporary digital and postdigital toys and games are concentrations of a worldview of an informational and networked world of entertainment, communication, science, and industry, formed from the same components, plugged into the same networks, mediated by the same virtual spaces and interfaces, and animated by the same distributed cognitive modes of simulation, modeling, and prediction. Like the Writer and the Chess Player, they condense an emergent technological and philosophical paradigm into a synecdoche, a figure graspable and manipulable by the hands, eyes, and imagination.

Toys in play, though, rarely adhere to the images and frames of reference we might expect. Ethnographic studies demonstrate that in children's play with smart and interactive toys, videogames, and virtual pets, imaginative engagement varies wildly according to the toy or system in play, the contingencies of location, immediate social relationships, and even recent TV viewing of the children playing. They warn against simply assuming playful behavior from the instrumental fantasies of the toys' marketing and instruction, and challenge ideal (utopian or dystopian) imaginaries of virtuality, simulation, cyborgian, or globalized subjectivity. But the broader technological imaginaries are no mere abstractions or illusions. They shape the design and reception of toys as technologies, facilitating and scaffolding certain kinds of play while never fully determining it. The vividness of concepts and dramas of artificial life and nonhuman autonomy may ebb and flow in children's play, but it seems that the material realities and potentials of self-moving machines will always engender imaginaries of animation in nonhuman bodies and minds.

6 Cinema Toys

The cinema industry might be embarrassed at being dubbed simply "the most successful of the toys that move."[1]

The aim of this chapter is to rethink the relationship between the toy and popular media in the twentieth and early twenty-first centuries. Much of the discussion will relate to cinema and television, commonly bracketed together as *screen* media, but as we will see, the assumption that the screen itself—as both technical apparatus and as mode of image presentation—is an integral and defining component of popular media predicated on an aesthetics of moving images looks much less stable from a toyetic point of view. As Iona Opie playfully suggests above, we might regard cinema as just one, albeit "successful," type of toy within a much wider category of "toys that move," a category that for her includes optical toys, animated figures such as jumping jacks or *pantins*, and nineteenth-century interactive books. To these, I will add the huge panoply of cinema and television-related toy tie-ins and merchandising (figure 6.1). What if, then, these screen media-related playful objects and devices, from contemporary licensed figurines back through all manner of merchandising, including toys, games, and puzzles, to the optical instruments and novelties that predate the theatrical cinema industry[2] of the twentieth century, were considered not as very much secondary to the dominant forms of the feature film and the television program, at best "paratexts," at worst commodified detritus? What if media-themed toys, as manipulable, portable, tactile, mechanical objects, suggested an everyday aesthetics of movement—a kind of domestic media kinesthesia—that predates, postdates, and even envelops the industrial forms of cinema and television? I mean "kinesthesia" in two senses of the term here: a media aesthetics of moving or animated images and devices, and its phenomenological sense of embodied

Figure 6.1
Mickey Mouse roller skates (BDCM cat. 31570). Mid-twentieth century. Courtesy of
the Bill Douglas Cinema Museum, University of Exeter, UK.

movement and pleasure. In this sense, the "spectator" becomes a "manipula-
tor," with their hands and fingers as important as their eyes, and with touch
and mechanical operation as important as visual pleasure—indeed, a sense
in which the eye itself is a physical mechanism with its relationship to the
medium an essential material one of position, angle, light, and perception.
Could toys be seen, then, not only as the evolutionary precursors of cinema
or as harbingers of future digital media but also as fully integral to cinematic
culture and experience? Or, more ambitiously (and playfully), what if we
regarded cinema itself as a subset of toy culture rather than the other way
around? If cinema were merely "the most successful of the toys that move,"
what other material, technical, imaginative, and experiential dimensions of
a paracinematic genealogy of "toys that move" might we find?

Toys shaped like, or printed with images from, characters and stories
from popular film and television were hugely popular in the twentieth
century and, as such, represent a significant extension of popular screen culture out of the auditorium and into domestic space and activities. But no
doubt, largely because they were primarily consumed by children, they are
very rarely mentioned in media and film studies. If noticed at all, it is as

ephemeral merchandising—the epitome of a culture of mass production and commodification, particularly in the postwar period. Toys as merchandising are considered interesting in themselves only occasionally as a sign of audience and fan interpellation or engagement—or as ideological and industrial vectors for the induction of children into commodified media culture.[3] This said, critical attention to recent developments in transmedia has begun to take the toy more seriously—notably, the interplay of movies, merchandising, and toy lines in the LEGO and *Star Wars* systems.[4]

Toyetic Paracinema

There is one relevant type of toy that has been studied seriously and in depth, however: the "precinematic" optical toy. In the array of ingenious devices from the nineteenth century and before, from hand-spun thaumatropes to the protoanimation of phenakistoscopes and zoetropes, media and film historians and theorists have identified both the mechanical origins and perceptual underpinnings of twentieth-century cinema and a source of alternative mechanical and perceptual apparatuses—ones left out or marginalized—but which resonate now with more recent digital-based media technologies, aesthetics, and modes of reception and spectatorship.[5] Optical toys, and toy versions of cinematic technologies such as projectors, persist in the everyday and domestic alongside theatrical cinema and overlap with it in fascinating ways. So, I want to investigate popular cinema- and television-related toys as cultural objects and media technologies in their own right. That is, my focus will be on not only optical toys before cinema but also the toys and games that grew with and alongside mainstream popular screen media in the twentieth and early twenty-first centuries—and their other media-genealogical strands in pre-twentieth-century "merchandising."

Most of the objects discussed in this chapter are in the collection of the Bill Douglas Cinema Museum at the University of Exeter, UK. The museum's collection has a wealth of dolls, board games, card games, jigsaws, memorabilia, nineteenth- and twentieth-century optical toys, interactive books, and toy theaters. Its filing cabinet drawers open not to suspended files and documents but rather to cluttered and colorful cabinets of curiosity. Stuffed into these drawers are not only a familiar array of merchandising for relatively recent films and franchises, including *Star Wars* and Disney animated features, but also tie-in toys from the first half of the twentieth century, such as articulated Charlie Chaplin dolls, numerous Mickey Mouses, and Felix the Cat souvenirs. In handling and manipulating the objects, seeing them work or trying to get them to work, I was struck by the material and technical variety of the collection: figures of stitched fabric or blow-molded plastic; lithographed or stochastic printed cardboard theaters, models and board games; film stock from 8 mm to 35 mm spooled and threaded, set in motion by clockwork, electric motors, or hand-cranks; play driven by the twisting and pressing of dials, levers, and buttons; or the shuffling of cards or rolls of dice. The collection's objects offer rich clues as to how screen action, storyworlds, and characters have been animated in everyday life through children's imaginative play with cinema-related toys.

Cultural Economy of Media Toys

Many of the objects and games in the Bill Douglas collection were licensed from entertainment companies and film studios. The prevalence of Disney-themed objects was no surprise, given that company's early development and exploitation of merchandising and licensing in the 1920s and its innovative industrial synergies from the 1930s. Disney modeled a lucrative circuit of character design and storyworlds established in the animated feature films, rendered physical and spatial experiences in the theme parks, and filled domestic space and everyday imaginative play through toys and merchandising.[6] Although Disney systematized the toy tie-in, the company didn't invent it. Children's literary culture, well-established in the nineteenth century, saw its own tie-ins and spin-offs—for example, the Berlin-based toy soldier maker Söhlke diversified to produce figurines of characters from *Gulliver's Travels*, *Robinson Crusoe*, and *Uncle Tom's Cabin*[7] in the early part of the century, and by the turn of the twentieth century, the German stuffed-animal toy company Steiff was manufacturing cuddly figures of Peter Rabbit from the *Tales of Beatrix Potter*. In 1811, sheets of illustrations were printed and sold in London's theater district, depicting characters from a popular pantomime, *Mother Goose*. Printed paper and card toy theater kits, sometimes themed as particular plays or genres, were commercially successful, spreading across Europe and exported to the United States (see "Unbox: Cardboard Cinema"). Dan Fleming links these toy theaters with their "strong elements of spectacle and narrative" directly to late twentieth-century media-licensed and storyworld-based toy lines.[8] Thus, over the span of the twentieth century, the cultural

Figure 6.2
Tie-in toys: *Hulk* (Marvel/Hasbro); *Transformers* (Bandai). Photos: Dave Gibbons.

economy of children's media and toys would tie together licensed characters and themes through a process that shifted from merchandising to mediatization[9] to transmedia systems. The advent of television in the 1950s opened up new opportunities for licensed and themed products and brought the moving image and its toy extensions even closer together in the living room. Writing in the 1960s, Antonia Fraser could refer lightly to TV and cinema-related play objects as "mascot toys," a small subset of a much broader and historically deeper field of dolls, animals, houses, puppets, and so on, unconnected to commercial narrative and screen media.[10] Yet, within a couple of decades, the "mascot" was to grow to thoroughly dominate a children's culture now saturated in TV and cinematic licensed toys, games, costumes, and merchandising (figure 6.2).

In the 1980s, commercial television engineered a significant step change in the process of media-driven commercialization as new business models were devised in the US to exploit a relaxation in the regulation of advertising. A new synergistic format that integrated television programs, television advertising, and toy manufacture was devised. New TV series such as *Thundercats* and *Masters of the Universe* were produced using relatively economical "limited animation" techniques pioneered by Hanna-Barbera and were effectively thirty-minute advertisements for toy lines. *Masters of the Universe*, for instance, was established as a line of action figures in 1981 by Mattel, with the TV series launching a few years later.[11] At the same time, in Japan, storyworlds and toy worlds such as *Transformers* had a similar global impact on children's culture, as did—from the late 1990s—hugely successful transmedial systems such as *Pokémon*. With LEGO and Disney's voracious ingestion of media companies and franchises, there is now in commercial children's culture today little sense of a hierarchy of media forms—that is, we are not looking at films and TV programs as primary texts with toys as peripheral paratexts.

Studying the Domestic-Cinematic

What kind of imaginative and playful world does this commodified and mediatized—but material and mechanical—environment offer the playing child? I argue throughout this book against the tendency in critical studies of children's media culture to address toys, TV programs, videogames, comics, and so on as primarily textual, as a world of adult semiosis driven by economic and ideological imperatives. The briefest glance at young children in play and in their play spaces—a bedroom or living room floor, kitchen table, backyard—demonstrates the futility of this endeavor. How can one read off meanings and messages from the design, images, and playscripts of a commercially produced and mediatized toy or toy line when it is just one among many, a jumble of storyworlds and characters mixed up with whatever important or fleeting concerns occur to the children at that particular moment?[12] This is not to argue that the symbolic imagery and form of media-linked toys are inconsequential. Many children do buy toys (or have toys bought for them) to extend their imaginative engagement with a favorite film (or transmedial story universe) such as *Batman* or *Star Wars*. Rather, it is to suggest that the semiotic components of a toy are just one aspect within, and articulated by, its material, mechanical characteristics and the contingencies of the environments and specific moments of play. Did the Mickey Mouse plush doll in the Bill Douglas collection sustain an imaginative persistence in the character's crazy cartoon world, or was it something more talismanic—a memento or statement of identity, a precursor perhaps of the intensive fan cultures today? Of course, it could have been all of these, perhaps even within a single playing event. And just as the *number* of toys can be crucial, as in collections of toy soldiers, for instance, so too can the sheer *variety*. Hence, gameworlds emerge from juxtaposition and combinations rather than faithful adherence to movie plots or transmedia canon and lore.

Without direct observation of play or memory work, toys give up the secrets of their histories of imaginative animation reluctantly. This said, working in an archive, whether a formal museum collection or a set of toys found in a charity shop or attic, offers insights that examining photographs or catalogue descriptions do not. Handling a toy itself opens up ideas and intuitions about how it might be played with, at least in broad sweep of the embodied if not in semiotic and narrative detail. As Meredith Bak explains, reflecting on her own research in archives of optical toys,

> Playing with pre-cinematic apparatus in the archive enables the researcher to participate in a particular kind of interaction between object and user characterized by openness and potential rather than predetermination. Object in hand, it is possible to regard its design attributes, its material and sensorial qualities, and to consider it on its own terms . . . Within the archival setting, play holds out the possibility for the articulation of alternative experiences.[13]

The opportunity to touch and *work* the objects during my visit, then, proved invaluable. Material characteristics of scale, tactility, and manipulability can only be appreciated in the picking up, putting together, and working of the toys to piece together their intended uses and suggested alternative possibilities of play. Throughout, I was fascinated by hints of how imaginative play with favorite film characters and storyworlds might be brought to life and mechanized by play with these toys. In what ways might the material and technical aspects of a toy or game frame or shape imaginative play? I picked up an early Mickey Mouse toy. As a cuddly or plush toy, it is soft to touch and pliable in the hands, with the well-established tactile technics of the teddy bear. It is less poseable than many teddy bears and, like the cinema character it represents, is more anthropomorphic than zoomorphic. Like a rag doll, I could imagine it hugged for company, comfort, and physical intimacy rather than positioned on display as a talisman of investment in and identification with the Disney world. On the other hand, its light, soft, and durable construction does not rule out its animation in a boisterous reenactment of *Silly Symphonies* action. I placed Mickey next to a roughly contemporaneous and similarly sized model of the silent movie star Harold Lloyd. Both toys are material instantiations of cinematic characters—solid and tangible, unlike the illusory figures formed from the trickery of the cinematic apparatus. Each

Figure 6.3
Hollywood "mascot" toys, 1920: clockwork tin Harold Lloyd (EXEBD 68019); cuddly Mickey Mouse (EXEBD 68229). Courtesy of the Bill Douglas Cinema Museum, University of Exeter, UK.

offers an extension of the characters into everyday imaginative life, and each speaks to the pleasures of owning and grasping a small manifestation of their flickering screen world. But handling them strongly suggests they had very different histories of imaginative and affective animation in play. The Harold Lloyd figure has a cold, hard, tin body, with a lithographed surface and face uncannily animated by internal clockwork. An ingenious artifact, one might imagine an animated performance of its mechanism to a small audience of family or friends, but it seems unlikely that he was ever cuddled or confided in (figure 6.3).

Some of the museum's artifacts spoke clearly of their intended or preferred modes of play. Board games included rules for play in booklets or printed on the base of the box. Jigsaw puzzles offer little latitude for alternative or inventive play. Some of the more elaborate mechanisms held on to their secrets, however. There were a number of projection systems with no instructions and apparently missing components. Some came with packaging illustrated with suggested uses, or detailed instructions for assembly, use, and rules. Several sets promised "hours of enjoyment," and a sense of temporal and attentional frames is possible with card and board games, but in the main, we can only guess now at the effectiveness of these products of an early "attention economy." Some objects, I suspect, had primarily a novelty value—for example, little functional 8 mm movie projectors that offered performative presentation but not much sustained imaginative engagement. They could only run moving image sequences or loops measured in seconds, and the many "viewer" devices in the museum collection offered very limited sets of still images, some only holding one slide or celluloid frame at a time. Any extended use of or play with such devices must have been predicated on the pleasures of manipulating the machine itself—and its manipulation of the viewer's vision—rather than "consuming" the images and stories themselves.

A Darth Vader mask strongly suggested the role-playing of *Star Wars* dramas, not least because its main feature is a device that alters the wearer's voice with the mechanized wheeze of the film character himself. Here again, though, the technological capacity of the toy is as important as its fidelity to the movie costume: it is scaled to fit a child's head and constructed to place a voice-manipulation component in front the wearer's mouth and amplify the resulting sounds. The fictional Darth Vader's technologically augmented body and communication is realized in an everyday and playful cyborgian assemblage (figure 6.4).

The earliest devices in the Bill Douglas collection predate modern cinema by at least a hundred years. Optical and scientific toys—or, as they were first called, "philosophical toys"—are a broad category of toy-related technologies that has been subject to sustained critical study, with attendant serious historical and cultural claims made for them. The "philosophical" dimension of these objects refers to natural philosophy—post-Enlightenment research, experimentation, and theorization in natural history, biology, physiology, human perception, and physical phenomena, notably light. Given the focus of the museum, examples tend toward those that project or animate graphic imagery, including magic lantern projectors and slides, zoetropes, thaumatropes, stereoscopic viewers, mutoscopes, and numerous "peep" devices, including kaleidoscopes (see "Unbox: Peep Eggs and VR"). However, the collection also includes children's science sets, such as a British *Construments* kit from the early 1930s, containing lenses, prisms, glass plates, bulldog clips, and lightbulbs from which magnifiers, kaleidoscope, photoprinters, and projectors could be assembled. For eighteen shillings and sixpence, it promised to make "every boy and girl a scientist" (figure 6.5). The genealogy of these devices is tangled with the automata, with significant moments of confluence, as we'll see. And like the automata, they fascinate cultural theorists as

Figure 6.4
Darth Vader voice-changer helmet. Hasbro, 2007 (EXEBD 66445). Courtesy of the Bill
Douglas Cinema Museum, University of Exeter, UK.

Figure 6.5
Construments: The Hobby of Ten Thousand Thrills (EXEBD 69125). UK, mid-1930s. Courtesy of the Bill Douglas Cinema Museum, University of Exeter, UK.

evidence of the spectacle, wonder, and illusion of natural magic at the heart of early science, education, and Enlightenment rationalism and which, by implication, remains embedded in technoscience today. Whereas, according to film theory, the theatrically screened narrative movie sustains and negotiates a fundamental opposition between spectacle and knowledge,[14] optical toys and *Construments* keeps them in intimate interplay. Even the "precinematic" toys with no immediate didactic pretensions, such as zoetropes and phenakistoscopes, offer to their players at once the magic of animation and the mechanism to manipulate—and understand—its achievement.[15]

Toy Archaeology

Recent media archaeological approaches to film and visual media history have explored optical toys in great detail, unearthing both intriguing devices and records of their publicity, marketing, and reception. As with the genealogies of automata discussed in the last chapter, the toylike playful and experimental dimensions of these technologies and modes of use are taken seriously but are ultimately considered secondary to other objects of research. Speaking very generally, the concern is often with a sense of an alternate history of media evolution in the industrial era, of failed inventions that speak of different modes of making and consuming media, and of early ostensible dead ends that reappear later in new forms. From this perspective, cinema itself, as industrialized and institutionalized in the twentieth century, was never inevitable. Its individuation from the confluence of experiments in sequential photography with the toy-based trickery of persistence of vision was not a linear evolution but rather just one of a myriad possible combinations of mechanical image capture, processing, and display that *could* have emerged from the sideshows and phantasmagoria at the end of the nineteenth century. For instance, other toy tricks with vision were popular in the late nineteenth century, notably the 3D imagery of stereoscopic photographs and viewers. A simulation of binocular vision and hence the illusion that a flat photograph might have the same depth as the unmediated world, stereoscopy seemed to disappear with the advent of theatrical cinema but returned in a series of attempts to reinvigorate its spectacular realist effects—from 3D cinema in the 1950s, Imax systems at the end of the twentieth century, and 3D videogame consoles, VR, televisions, and feature films from the 2000s. As the film theorist Jean-Louis Comolli put it, in his essay "Machines of the Visible," "the historical variation of cinematic techniques, their appearance-disappearance, their phases of convergence, their periods of dominance and decline . . . depend not on a rational-linear order of technological perfectibility nor an autonomous instance of scientific 'progress,' but much rather on the offsettings, adjustments, arrangements carried out by a social configuration in order to represent itself."[16]

From the critical perspective of media archaeology and through its genealogical enquiries, optical toys do not simply disappear with the rise to popular cultural dominance of theatrical cinema. Some of their aspects and components are key to the nontoyetic cinematic apparatus: the exploitation of persistence of vision (over single or discrete sequences of images, or other continuous visual effects such as the movement of beads in a kaleidoscope), the reality effects of the camera and the photographic image (over the sequential drawn image or the abstract effects of kaleidoscopes), the projected image of the magic lantern (over the "peep" technics of peepshows, zoetropes, and kaleidoscopes). The apparatus of theatrical cinema and the aesthetic conventions of the feature film sublimate their origins in the showy trickery of the sideshow devices, simulacra, and automata: the spectator's acceptance of the reality of the projected image, and forgetting of its mechanical apparatus (projector, camera, all the artifice of the sound stage, edit suite, film processing labs, etc.), is achieved through a persistent play with knowledge that echoes that of these earlier audiences. Comolli argues that this new technology of delusion in the fictional film continues to operate on the play between knowledge and belief, coupled with the much longer established deceits of fiction itself, which are interesting because:

> they can function only from the clear designation of their deceptive character. There is no uncertainty, no mistake, no misunderstanding or manipulation. There is ambivalence, play. The spectacle is always a game, requiring the spectators' participation not as "passive," "alienated" consumers, but as players, accomplices . . . spectatorial representations declare their existence as simulacrum, and, on that contractual basis, invite the spectator to *use* the simulacrum to fool him or herself.[17]

Other aspects of the nineteenth century "frenzy of the visible,"[18] it has been argued, were marginalized or repressed in the twentieth century. The spectacular trickery of early cinematic shows—the "cinema of attractions" in which the novelty of the projector and projected image were the focus of audience fascination rather than the subject matter of the short films they projected—was channeled into avant-garde cinema, theme parks, and special effects. Animation as a cinematic form, for instance, predates photography-based systems but did not simply disappear as the latter evolved from it (figure 6.6). Rather, it was pushed to the margins—into live-action feature film special effects, dream sequences, credits sequences, and, of course, cartoons and children's films with which, as we have seen, it persisted in its material, toy-based form as well. So, optical toys and the early cinematic technologies they issued are for the digital media theorist and media archaeologist, as Jussi Parikka puts it, "toolboxes for digital culture research whereby the current debates concerning convergence and the digital can actually be complexified . . . Through the lenses of the digital, we start to see old media anew again."[19]

This language of returns and renewals, the reclamation of "lost" historical-technical alternatives to dominant media cultural forms and institutions, has informed the nonlinear and genealogical approaches I have adopted in the study of toys and the toyetic. However, in relation to cinema, it runs the risk of a credulous acceptance of theatrical cinema's own claims for cultural dominance in the twentieth century. Tracking popular media through toys suggests a domestic and hands-on mechanical kinesthetic culture that does

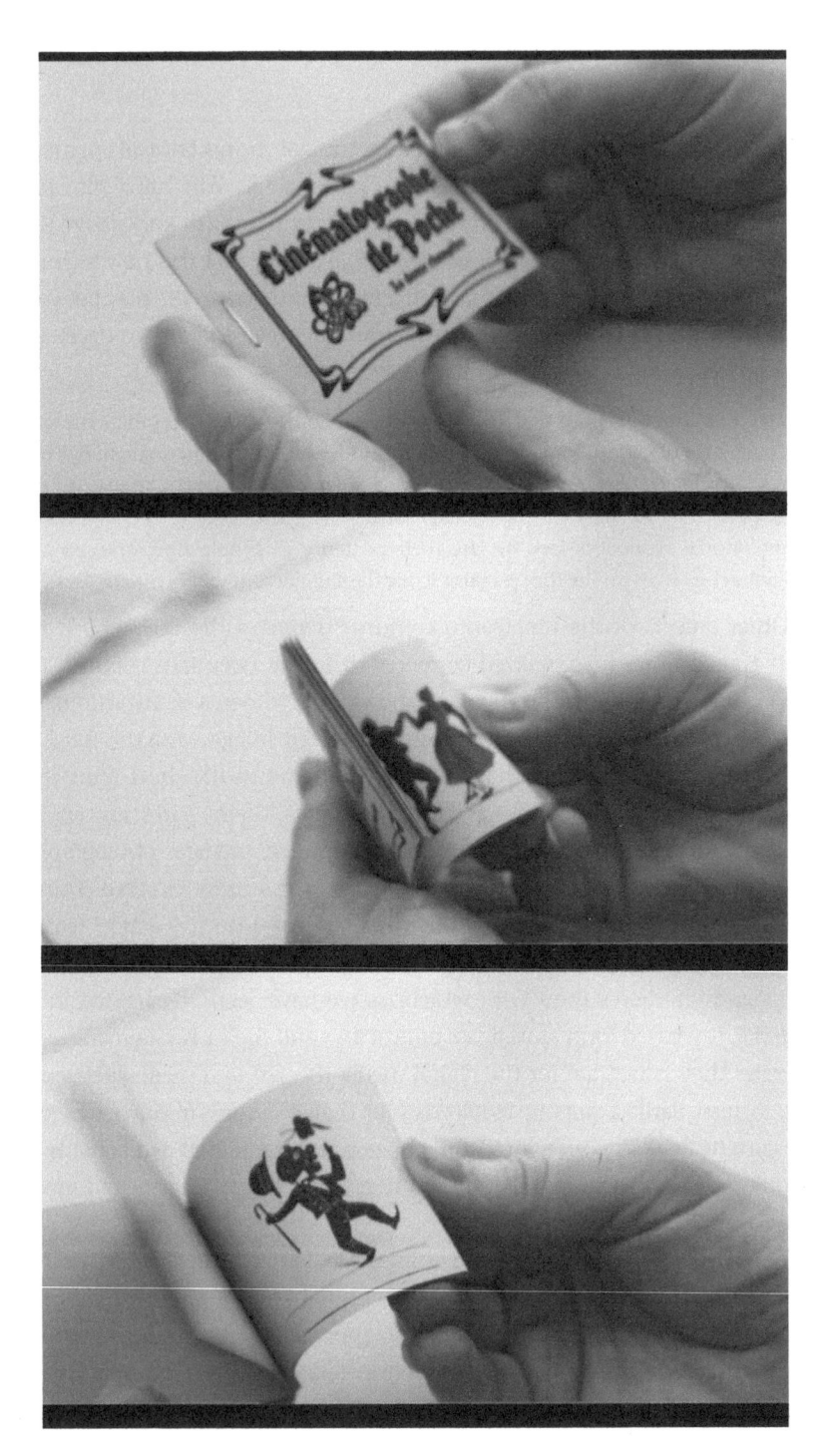

Figure 6.6
Handheld animation: *Cinématographe de Poche: La dance champêtre*. Flick book by Wiebke K. Folsch depicting a dancing couple (EXEBD 66218). Courtesy of the Bill Douglas Cinema Museum, University of Exeter, UK.

not fit neatly into the archaeology of cinema as even a tangled set of developments. Its lineage can be traced back as much to the industrialization of toy production in eighteenth-century Germany as it can to the *camera obscura*. It is the inventive and heterogeneous array of colorful and mechanically animated objects to which Iona Opie is referring in this chapter's epigraph, but also a much wider field of media technical forms, modes of spectatorship, manipulation, and play, and it involves the digging up or reclamation of nonscreen-based forms, from peep shows and paper cutouts to interactive and tactile objects. It is important to note too that these objects, along with many of the optical toys, were bought for, and engaged with, in the home. In the century before theatrical cinema *and* the half-century or so between the institution of the cinema theater as a distinct cultural site and the widespread adoption of television in the home, visual devices were a common feature of domestic media consumption and play. If research on optical toys and other precinematic devices tends to concentrate on their perceptual effects on vision, and hence on the emergence of a cinema of spectatorship, *and* their evolution into the collective, public apparatus of the auditorium, how might the interactive and mechanical capacities of these toys inflect a hands-on, *operational, domestic,* and *not-only-visual* model of popular moving media?

So, what if toys were neither mere evolutionary stages in the emergence of cinema, nor repressed and insignificant objects during a period of the dominance of cinema and television, returning only at their demise? What if the toylike and toyetic dimensions of moving image culture and technics persisted in the apparent hiatus of significance between 1890s and the 1990s, less coherent an industrial and technocultural form than cinema and television perhaps but at least as significant in the imaginative and behavioral undercurrents of everyday life? I would argue that this should be more than a thought experiment or counterfactual game. Rather, with a shift of perspective, it is a serious historical claim. If we took a step back and adopted a broadly anthropological rather than cultural-historical approach to twentieth-century screen media culture, then what would we see? How much time and imaginative energy would a postwar urban middle-class child in Europe or North America, say, expend in a week in the cinema auditorium compared to playing with "mascots," dressing up as, acting out, or drawing movie-inspired dramas and characters, peeping into viewer toys, projecting cartoon loops through toy projectors, playing movie-themed board and card games, or simply daydreaming cinematic worlds? Or picture the domestic environment of many children today: a space cluttered with commercial narrative and transmedia images and objects, the moving screen image itself floating free of the cinema screen and the television set, manifesting in the toylike devices of consoles, tablets, and smartphones.

Unbox: Cardboard Cinema

The *Beauty and the Beast* board game is an ingenious engineering of cinematic, narrative, and architectonic space into a slot-together cardboard construction. A tie-in with the Disney animated film of 1991, players first build the Beast's castle, condensed here into the building's ballroom (the main section of the board), staircase, and tower. Its central mechanic is a revolving disc within the ballroom board that at once drives the game, revealing characters and triggering events, and functioning as a kinesthetic and paracinematic toy device— evoking the swirling motion of the central characters, and the virtual camera, in the movie's baroque ballroom dance sequence (itself foregrounded in the film and its marketing as a technical and aesthetic achievement in the integration of 3D CGI with drawn cel animation).

The articulation of imaginative, mimetic play with popular film and hands-on manipulation of devices was evident in many of the collection's

Figure 6.7
Beauty and the Beast board game (EXEBD 67132). Disney / Milton Bradley, 1991. Courtesy of the Bill Douglas Cinema Museum, University of Exeter, UK.

board games and card games. These not only capitalize on the popularity of the films and extend their action and themes into domestic play, but also transduct the action and themes into mechanical devices. The games are machines both in the sense of being structured around a game mechanic (rules, dice-throw randomization, win states, and so on), but also more literally as moving mechanisms. Like *Beauty and the Beast*, the collection's *King Kong* game is particularly inventive in its translation of the filmic world into a cardboard and plastic mechanism with sliding, moving, manipulable characters and objects. The game strips the film's action down to the culminating scene of the monster's ascent of New York's twin towers.[20] A *Ben Hur*–themed game is more traditional in its structure and metonymic in theme: the board depicts the track and the tokens the chariots from the movie's central chariot race scene.[21] Other board games in the Bill Douglas collection have movie industry themes, effectively simulating—albeit in a manner stylized for simple game play—Hollywood Studios film production.[22]

Before plastic, cardboard and paper were ubiquitous toyetic materials: cheap and easy to produce, to cut and shape and print on. Cardboard playthings were often initially produced as an offshoot of more functional products or packaging and were often as disposable. As sheet materials, cardboard and pasteboard replaced wood in board game bases, toy buildings such as houses and castles, and simple mechanical devices from punchinello or jumping jack puppets to optical toys, and cardboard toys were generally packed and distributed in kit form, to be slotted or glued together at home. Cardboard and paper offered a cheap alternative material for multiple toys such as toy soldiers and tied in with other forms of print media, such as paper fashion dolls published in girls' comics. Papier-mâché has been used as a cheaper, lighter, and less fragile alternative to ceramics and composition for puppets and dolls' heads and even whole dolls such as *Gelenktäufling*, flesh-colored and jointed papier-mâché dipped in wax to simulate human skin, exported from Germany to Britain around 1850,[23] and instead of carved wood in toy animals and soldiers in the early German toy industry in the seventeenth century.[24] Cardboard continued through the twentieth and into the twenty-first centuries as a key toy material—from the ubiquitous plain cardboard box[25] to the playful design innovations of Charles and Ray Eames. Google has deployed it as architecture for smartphone-based VR viewers and consumer AI kits. To the material and practical aspects of cardboard (cheapness, lightness, foldability) is added "makerly" connotations for certain kinds of educational and hobbyist projects.

Unsurprisingly, given their industrial and formal relationships with book production, cardboard and paper toys and devices have often been constructed and folded into storytelling contexts. Since the eighteenth and nineteenth centuries, toylike and didactic paper objects for young children have played across picture books, pop-up books, picture cards, and blocks. Froebel designed colorful shaped cards to complement his wooden Gifts (see chapter 4), and Hans Christian Andersen, as well as his conventionally published stories, created numerous drawings and cut paper versions of his characters and others from contemporaneous popular theater. As Jacqueline Reid Walsh notes, the act of cutting out and manipulating these paper shapes reflects the coming-to-life or animation of toy objects in his stories, such as toy soldiers and toy theaters, constituting a precinematic animation.[26]

Ingeniously engineered books in the nineteenth century blurred the distinction between book, puppet theater, and mechanical toy with articulated figures and animals animated through pop-up and tab-pulling mechanisms.[27] Card and paper toy theaters are historically and technically closely related to the various forms of, and overlaps between, the dollhouse and the peepshow.[28]

Figure 6.8
Théâtre d'ombres (shadow theater), box with silhouette roll (EXEBD 69332). Paper and cardboard. France, nineteenth century. Courtesy of the Bill Douglas Cinema Museum, University of Exeter, UK.

Shadow theaters are among the simplest forms of paper and card protocinema (figure 6.8). A twentieth-century set might consist of little more than a tracing paper screen and some sheets of card and fastenings for the owner to construct their own characters and action. Shadow theater and puppetry as a sophisticated narrative and ritual medium appears around the world, particularly in India, China, and Southeast Asia, with the figures themselves fashioned from materials including leather and paper.[29] It seems likely that the casting of shadows of objects or the hands from the light of a fire is as old as the human management of fire itself (and is alluded to in Plato's "Allegory of the Cave"). As a literal *screen* moving image medium, shadow play is playful cinema in the overarching sense I am suggesting here.

The Bill Douglas collection bundles together optical toys and merchandising. As noted above, optical toys do not disappear with the advent of theatrical cinema, and the museum's collection has numerous examples from the late nineteenth century well into the late twentieth century.[30] As such, it provides convincing evidence for the everyday toyetic paracinema I am arguing for. Rummaging in the filing cabinets compels one to imagine new categories or characteristics. Take the *Kinora Picture Reel* of 1878 and the Disney-licensed *Beauty and the Beast* board game, for instance. At first glance, any connection seems superficial or tenuous at best. For media studies, these two types of toy are completely different and studied by scholars in distinct fields: by media archaeologists and film historians and by scholars and theorists of consumer/fan culture, respectively. From a toyetic perspective, similarities come into view: artifacts in a coherent cultural field of objects and technologies that animate images and sounds in everyday play. Across them, we see a hands-on manipulation of and toying with apparatus through very different mechanizations of mediated movement. The *Kinora*, a handheld or tabletop machine, uses a rotating stack of cards printed with sequential photographic frames, with a flick mechanism acting as a protoshutter to assist in the generation of the illusion of continuous movement. The mechanism is similar to that of the arcade and pier mutoscopes. In Britain, these coin-operated attractions are popularly known as "What the Butler Saw" machines because of their sometimes-risqué subject matter (e.g., a woman undressing) and hence doubly voyeuristic mode of spectatorship: the servant's peeping through a keyhole overlaid with the viewer's peeping into the machine. The *Beauty and the Beast* game is produced as a licensed spin-off from the Disney film—in transmedia terms, a "paratext." Yet, like the *Kinora*, it is a machine and a kinesthetic artifact in its own right. The playing of this game is no simple identification with favorite characters and stories (although this may, of course, be a component of any particular instance of play with the game), nor is it necessarily "secondary" in everyday significance or imaginative engagement to watching the film. Rather, it is a partial transduction of kinesthetic and semiotic elements of the film into a very different medium and mode of engagement—one that articulates and fuses with the much longer-established kinesthesia, semiosis, and (behavioral and social) dimensions of the board game (see "Unbox: Cardboard Cinema"). Both the *Kinora* and the board game are operated and animated by hand, and in each, the players are in control of the movement, including the speed of movement. The *Kinora* sequences started from a still frame and could be slowed down and sped up—the perceptual limits of the persistence of vision toyed with as the succession of discrete pictures flows into something like the real time and the live action. The play with the zone at which sequential still images flow into illusion at the threshold of visual perception is a consistent game. The thaumatrope is one origin here—a virtual image conjured by the simplest of movements of the fingers and the limitations of the retina. The Bill Douglas collection includes many flip-books, which use the same mechanical and perceptual principles as the *Kinora* and which, after the thaumatrope, are perhaps the most mechanically simple and ubiquitous cinematic invention. What is lost in the scale, sheen, and narrative immersion of theatrical cinema is compensated for in the close control and manipulation of the illusion.

The toying is effected here by the "spectators" themselves in the home, not the showmen at a public presentation. We can't know the extent to which this toying generated moments of astonishment or wonder, but surely the novel effects did grab the attention, and the persistent popularity of such toys over at least a century indicates a sustained domestic "machine interest"[31] of the cinematic apparatus, experienced not in the darkened auditorium with its remote screen but rather in the home and in playful and exploratory hands (figure 6.9). This cinema of minor attractions overlapped with hobbyist and science-educational modes of technical play mentioned above—of constructing, reverse engineering, and demystification, still coupled with playful performance and demonstration, no doubt. Projectors and viewers often needed to be constructed, kit-like, at the very least the

Figure 6.9
Peak Cine 16 mm projector (EXEBD 69230). Mid-twentieth century. Courtesy of the
Bill Douglas Cinema Museum, University of Exeter, UK.

connecting of a power supply for the bulb and the feeding of the film strip or
loading the cartridge. Some sets included blank strips of celluloid for users to
draw their own animated sequences. The apparatus was toyed with, and the
apparatus itself was a toy.

The tracing of connections and resonances within this motley collection
of home movie projectors, Mickey Mouse roller skates, jigsaws, Hollywood-
themed board games, and James Bond playing cards suggests quite different
mechanical, cultural, and aesthetic principles for cinematic and televisual
culture than the usual insistence on the projection or screening of images
with the illusion of movement in an extended narrative format. Instead, they

point to the importance of the hands-on and tactile techniques of manipulation and experimentation that link toy genealogy with contemporary digital media "interactivity." So, as well as noting the compelling resonances between the pre- and postcinematic apparatuses, I suggest that "precinematic" technologies and aesthetics did not disappear after 1905, were not "repressed" as such, to return, tentatively, in the 1970s and '80s, and more forcefully in the 1990s. Rather, theatrical cinema, and subsequently broadcast television, was one path through a much broader toyetic field. "Mascot" toys, cinematic and photographic toys, media tie-ins, and merchandising in the form of games, construction sets, and puzzles through to videogames and virtual worlds all constitute, if viewed through the kaleidoscope of the toyetic, an overgrown toyetic field in which *movement* is key, but with the *illusory moving image* just one (albeit persistent) type. What are these other paths, and what do they present to us as salient characteristics for an expanded notion of the cinematic as a technical and imaginary assemblage of playful movement? In addition to the factors already discussed (a lived "transmedia" environment of imaginative play with and display of popular cultural–themed artifacts and media, the domestic cinema of (minor) attractions of optical toys, viewers, and projectors), I would add two more, each of which is constituted by varying articulations of technological mechanisms and human perceptual and sensorimotor capacities: the mobilization of visual perception, and the persistent significance of touch in the toyetic dimensions of kinesthetic media. I'll address each of these in turn.

Static Cinema and the Mobilization of Vision

The achievement of the illusion of movement through the exploitation of the persistence of vision is the feature of optical toys most thoroughly explored in histories, archaeologies, and theories of media and screen technology. Rather than recount this well-documented history, I will draw attention instead to the techniques and devices that *do not* rely on the persistence of vision for their effects. First, then, let's address an apparently paradoxical suggestion that the *still* image presented in and by toys might count as a "cinematic" element. I would note that industrial movies are rarely wholly "moving"; they are bracketed and punctuated with still images, from title images and intertitles to freeze frames, and slow- or fast-motion sequences play with the illusion of the movie unfolding in real time. Avant-garde film often plays between the still and the moving image, notably Chris Marker's *La Jetée* (1962), and animated movies have performed similar experiments—or exploited the still image for mainly economic reasons.[32] A sequence of still images is often enough to keep the eye and imagination engaged, and toys exploit this willingness of spectators to follow sequences as well as flows of images. Over centuries, peep shows and magic lantern shows deployed a wide range of ingenious techniques to suggest movement, from overlaying and moving glass slides over one another or playing with light through pinholes and apertures. Some late twentieth-century toy projectors displayed only still frames, but their projectionists were encouraged to pick up and move the device to send the image flying over walls and ceilings, a practice identical to many magic lantern shows centuries earlier. Persistence of vision is by no means essential to cinema.

Several early twentieth-century devices worked through the winding of a short spool of film through a viewer. This was a relatively slow and uneven process, and the box contained no shutter mechanism to generate the illusion of movement. Rather, the viewer looked at each frame in turn, winding the spool to see the next. The Pathéorama is an example of this (figure 6.10). Produced from the beginning of the 1920s, it was a rather plain cardboard black box with a small lens on one side to peep into and a larger opaque aperture in the opposite side that let in light to backlight the celluloid strip that was wound through using a wheel underneath the box.

Another was the Stip Vuwer (figure 6.11). These were among the simplest "viewer" devices: small metal, plastic, or rubber containers again with a lens at the front and an opaque panel at the back. Rather than projecting their images, which required delicate mechanisms, powerful bulbs, and a power source, these are devices that are held to the eye and peeped into, a film frame slotted between the lens and aperture, backlit as the device is held up to catch ambient light (see "Unbox: Peep Eggs and VR"). In some models, one single 35 mm frame was inserted at a time; others allowed a strip of frames to be pushed and pulled through the device. One Stip Vuwer box made a feature of it being "unbreakable"—a characteristic one might assume was incidental rather than a core selling point but spoke to its surprisingly heavy construction from vulcanized rubber. Whereas the appearance and mechanism of handheld viewer devices such as the Pathéorama suggested something of the cine camera and projector, many Stip Vuwers made little or no reference to cinema itself, often sold as novelty souvenirs to commemorate national

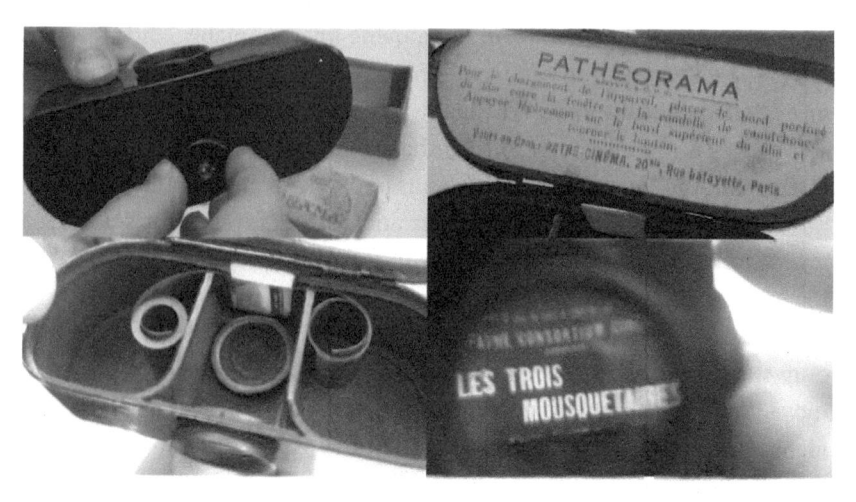

Figure 6.10
Pathéorama (EXEBD 48070). France, circa 1923. Courtesy of The Bill Douglas Cinema Museum, University of Exeter, UK.

events such as the Coronation of Queen Elizabeth II in 1953 or as tiny travelogue devices displaying photographs of exotic or holiday locations. As such, they fall somewhere between a commemorative postcard and a souvenir ornament like a snow globe with a miniature scene. Two examples in the Bill Douglas Cinema Museum's collection do, however, offer a miniature domestic evocation of the theatrical cinema experience. One is a set packaged in a large box with a selection of film strips depicting fairy stories, its packaging illustrated with drawings of boys and girls excitedly holding the viewer up to the light. No doubt the producers of this set were exploiting the popularity of Disney animated feature films, which at that time were dominated by fairy stories, but without infringing on copyright. The other is more playful, sardonic even, in its invocation of the theatrical experience. Its box proclaims it as an "unbreakable pocket cinema" and is printed with a line of expectant cinemagoers winding its way around the sides under the words "stips now showing." Here, the metonymic implication is that the device itself stands in for the auditorium space. Some of the 35 mm film strips and frames used in Stip Vuwers and the Pathéorama appeared to be leftover fragments of commercial movies rather than material produced specifically for the viewers. As such, the devices were synecdoches of cinema, both industrially (the latter was manufactured by the Pathé company) and materially (each used actual

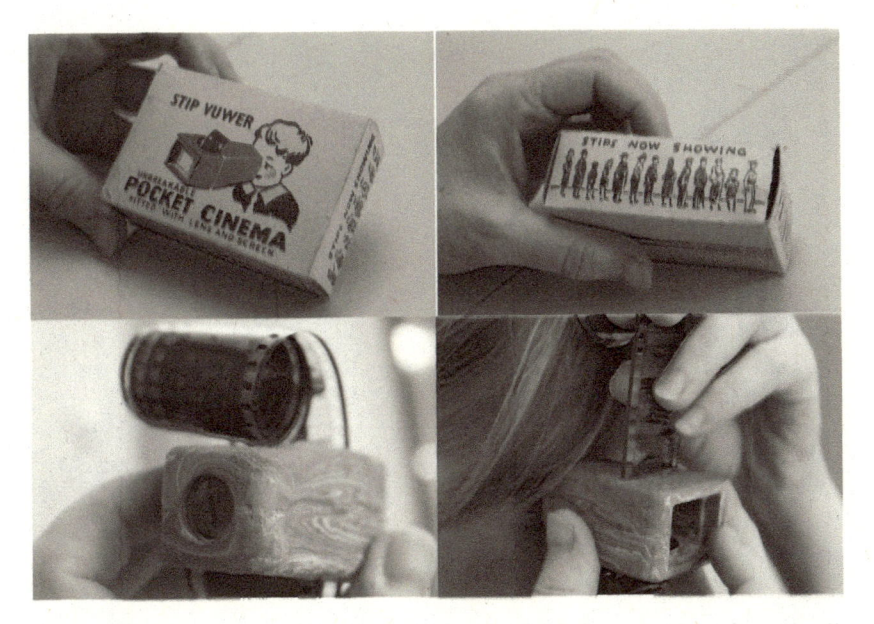

Figure 6.11
Stip Vuwer pocket cinema (EXEBD 69135). UK, 1940s. Courtesy of The Bill Douglas
Cinema Museum, University of Exeter, UK.

celluloid film stock), while relying on early perceptual techniques of peep
media and light for their operation, and with the toyetic attributes of scale
and manipulability.

Unbox: Peep Eggs and VR

The Bill Douglas Cinema Museum has an intriguing collection of "peep eggs,"
including elegant and expensive nineteenth-century alabaster eggs containing painted glass images, engravings, or applique objects such as minerals.
As a translucent material, alabaster allowed light into the tiny chamber to
illuminate the hidden object, and the viewer peered in through an aperture or
lens. Twentieth-century eggs were produced on a larger scale, first fashioned
from turned wood and then molded from rubber and plastic, and the collection includes a couple of very delicate examples fashioned from sugar. They
were often manufactured and sold as souvenirs, with a painted scene of a
seaside resort hidden within. Some were fitted with photographic transpar-
encies, often, like the Stip Vuwers, 35 mm frames that appear to be recycled

Figure 6.12
Peep egg–like film-strip viewer with 35 mm film still (EXEBD 48069). 1920s. Courtesy
of the Bill Douglas Cinema Museum, University of Exeter, UK.

"offcuts" from industrial movies rather than produced specifically for this
now-throwaway novelty medium. Although materially connected to theatrical cinema through the celluloid frame, the eggs stretch any conventional
notion of the cinematic—as characterized by the moving image. They use no
shutters, no persistence of vision, but they do sustain something of both the
perceptual mechanics that precede and persist through cinema: a luminous
image experienced in a dark chamber or *camera obscura*.

In their simple optics and their promise of secrets and revelation, peep eggs
follow a lineage of optical toys and devices that did not project their images
(like a magic lantern) but into which users "peeped," such as kaleidoscopes.
Erkki Huhtamo has traced the genealogy of "peep media" back to sixteenth-
century traveling peep shows and related devices such as catoptric theaters
and other mechanical spectacles that manipulated light through apertures
and mirrors. Peep shows were domesticated in the eighteenth century, and
their formal and perceptual links with *camera obscuras*, cabinets of curiosity,
and other philosophical toys are clear.[33] In the late nineteenth century, coin-
operated moving-image peep devices such as kinetoscopes and mutoscopes

were to be found in department stores, drug stores, hotel lobbies, and bars. Antonia Fraser saw direct connections between the Renaissance peep show, cabinets of curiosity, clockwork-automated images and tableaux, *camera obscura*–related optical devices, and dollhouses.[34] All "must be regarded as types of optical toys, which gratify the visual senses only, and are not intended to be used in play . . . They are 'toys of contemplation.'"[35]

For all their divergences and reconvergences over the centuries, these technologies have been characterized by a culture of interior attractions, the central "mechanism" of which is, as Huhtamo puts it, "the interplay of hiding and revealing."[36] Even the more prosaic images of cityscapes or historical events take on an illusory air or one of the revelation of hidden secrets. All are arcane in the dual sense of the mysterious (the floating, glowing image) and something hidden away—the word derived from the Latin *arca*, meaning "chest" or "box." Again, the effects of the peep image are generated through tricks of vision—not the persistence of vision but the play of light, lenses, and mirrors and the miniaturization of the image and its isolation from any actual context or reference of scale in the glimpsed and distorted interior of the chamber.

Stereographs, devices for viewing photographs with a simulation of three-dimensionality, added new perceptual manipulation to popular and domestic visual technoculture. Domestic and arcade versions of virtual reality systems (e.g., Oculus Rift and HTC Vive, or various cardboard holders for smartphone VR apps) bear both superficial similarities to and technical continuities with the peep egg and the stereograph. The two "viewers" (the human viewer and the device) must be pressed to one another, the eye completely subsumed; preternaturally lit and virtual images float in the visual field, cut off from any actual world reference of location or scale. The centuries-old illusions of linear perspective and stereoscopy are updated with the revelation of a hidden and enclosed virtual image that is no longer miniature but rather a full-scale simulation of the phenomenal world, open to exploration and interaction. VR reminds us that cinema has always been a peep medium.

Perhaps the most audacious condensation of the movie-going experience into a handheld toy in the collection is a contraption labeled "Teenie Movies" (figure 6.13). This is a shallow cardboard box roughly 10 cm × 15 cm, with a large square aperture cut in its lid. The box holds a paper scroll on two spindles, which protrude from its right-hand side to allow the user to wind the scroll past the aperture. The lid is printed with an image of a cinema auditorium with an audience looking toward the aperture, which

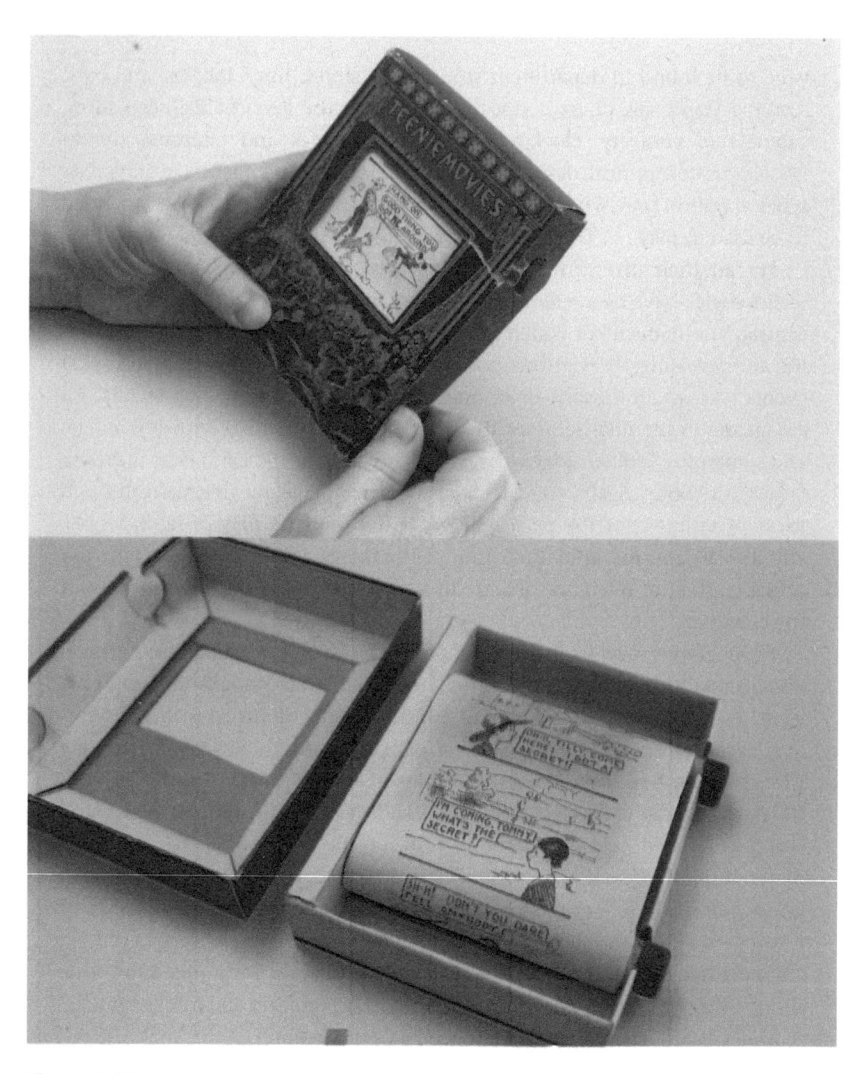

Figure 6.13
Teenie Movies (EXEBD 69249). US, 1920s. Courtesy of the Bill Douglas Cinema
Museum, University of Exeter, UK.

is framed by proscenium curtains to suggest the screen. The "movie" itself is a series of framed images printed on the paper scroll and is not even a continuous sequence in the cinematographic sense. Rather, it is a simple comic strip with speech bubbles and no continuity of movement or space between frames.[37] Teenie Movies feels playful and teasing: playing with this toy is nothing like the immersive and collective experience of cinema-going and the images little like the popular movies of the day, but it is here, in one's hands, here-and-now and not restricted to the Saturday morning matinee, manipulable and entertaining in its own ingenuity (see also "Unbox: Cardboard Cinema").

Tactile Cinema

Throughout this book, tactile manipulation by hands and fingers is placed at the core of toy play and technics.[38] This is a simplification, of course; hands and fingers are not separate from the mechanical or sensate capacities and operations of the whole body, or groups of bodies, in play. Optical and para-cinematic toys demand the factoring in of the eyes and vision at the very least. This resonates with media archaeology's insistence on the materiality of both media and the bodies that use them. For Jussi Parikka, "the body is already from the start deeply mediatic in the forms of perception, sensation and other capacities that it has been afforded with."[39] Thus, some media archaeological work on precinematic media, while not discounting visuality, resists any fundamental division between subject and image, conceptualizing "the primacy of sensation embedded not primarily in the gaze, but in the wider synaesthetic and physiological layer of *affect*."[40]

Although many media forms could be understood thus, the optical toys epitomize the phenomenology and engineering of visual perception—the mobilization and articulation of machine, hand, and eye. Against the classic cinematic apparatus[41] of the dark theater, the illusory moving images projected from behind and overhead, immersed in sound, people together but apart in their rapt attention to the dreamlike images, we can place the kinesthetic operation of the toy as *handheld*: picking it up, handling it, arranging, flipping, constructing. Those with sequences of images must be clicked or the strip handled and positioned with care, batteries fitted, mechanism wound and spun. Even the simplest viewers must be held and angled in relation to a light source, their hidden interior squinted into, their glimpsed image hard to manifest but vivid when achieved. From the peep egg to the late twentieth-century View-Master, they are designed precisely to fit in the hand and be manipulated by the fingers: these are haptic and visual assemblages.

Along with their symbolic and intertextual pleasures, then, a phenomenology of scale, tactility, and operability is key to the attraction of toys and toy play—the relationships of objects and devices to hands and fingers, their technical capabilities, and haptic surfaces. As Wanda Strauven notes in relation to nineteenth-century optical toys, the manual operation of cinematic toys is part of a larger history of *hands-on* media practices, media that are at least as tactile as visual, feeding into an archaeology of the contemporary touch screen, "through focussing on the manual operation of toys."[42] Strauven then traces an alternative technical and perceptual lineage for contemporary digital media, one that emphasizes the tactile over the visual, the hand over the eye, domestic space over public and commercial sites of media consumption, and the playful and physically engaged over the contemplative and immersed.[43] Drawing on Dulac and Gaureault, she notes that optical toys had a "player mode" as well as a "viewer mode" and were at least as much "pre-computer games" as they were "pre-cinematic"[44]: "the viewer became one with the apparatus: he or she was in the apparatus, became the apparatus."[45]

What I add to this convincing formulation is a historical and genealogical modification: the toy- and game-based media and sensory apparatuses of the optical toys are not repressed with the advent of theatrical cinema and TV to return with digital media; rather, touch, manipulation, and the domestic "player mode" persist throughout the twentieth century in toy culture.[46] From this perspective, the place of the videogame within my broad conception of the toy becomes not one of linear progression and "victory" over physical toys, but rather one of a shifting of material, economic, aesthetic, and ergonomic factors.

Conclusion

The "machine interest" of early cinema persists not only in the spectacular innovations of contemporary cinema and digital media but also, as the toys demonstrate, in everyday life—a kinesthetic and haptic culture of moving and manipulable devices, some visual some not, that runs alongside and through mainstream cinema culture. This is a domestic media technoculture that is less concerned with narrative and perceptual immersion and more about a mechanical and interactive putting-into-operation: the telling of stories and disorientation of the senses brought under control, manipulated, tested, extended, and reversed. A toying in, and with, a domestic space populated and animated by favorite characters and storyworlds, and played out with board and card games, figures, dolls, and vehicles, and out to construction sets, science kits—and hence a world of hands-on manipulation, interaction, construction, tweaking, collecting, puzzle solving, presentation, role-play, and performance. Following these "less successful" toys-that-move through the Bill Douglas collection, I felt a compelling sense of decades of this toying: of domestic tinkering, fiddling, constructing, presenting, performing. In this toying, the dexterous interaction with backlit and projected images, movie "mascots" and action figures, Hollywood-themed board games, card games and jigsaw puzzles, *Construments*, and cuddly characters are not peripheral to cinema, nor mere harbingers of digital play. Rather, they are constitutive of an alternative notion of a kinesthetic culture that is historically deeper and technoculturally wider than "cinema"—one that is generated through intimate collusions between hands, eyes, materials, mechanisms, and imaginaries.

7 Conclusion

In this concluding chapter, first, I will first sketch some of the key changes in toy manufacture, culture, and economies current at the time of writing, and second, I will draw together the book's main conceptual threads.

The Future of Toys?

A glance at earlier historical accounts of toy culture warns against extrapolating with too much confidence from the contemporary moment into the future. Writing in the mid-1960s, Antonia Fraser notes, almost as an aside, the popularity of the "mascot toy" at a historical moment just before the new mediatization of children's culture in general and toys in particular swept all other types other than the mascot to the margins and many of the long-established toys companies and manufacturing processes into oblivion. Dan Fleming's analysis of the television tie-ins and transmedia systems of the 1980s and 1990s is invaluable to grasping the distributed, networked, participatory systems of the Internet era but could hardly have guessed at their form nor the scale of the transformation of everyday communication wrought by social media, Wi-Fi, smartphones, and other mobile devices. Concomitantly, his account of videogames in the late twentieth century could not have anticipated the transformations in that young medium brought about by cheap broadband connectivity in the twenty-first century—from stand-alone console with, at most, four players to what is now a primary space for online and global play and sociality for children and young people. Marsha Kinder, at the end of the 1980s, presciently noted the coming transformations of the "GlobalNet," then still an unconnected set of discrete computer networks run by universities and the military. If I had written this book at the time I started thinking about it, around the mid-2010s, I would probably have taken the hybrid, toys-to-life games as my focus, given their popularity and industrial investment, their resonance with prevailing technological and economic trajectories and hence toyetic heuristic potential, and their centering of the material/virtual dynamics of physical play objects and software-driven gameworlds. But the early promise of these systems in the 2010s has yet to be borne out. The shutting down of the *Disney Infinity* line (2013–2016) demonstrated there was nothing inevitable about this particular commercial, formal, and technical trajectory. *Skylanders* and *LEGO Dimensions* remain popular but not dominant in the contemporary play product market, and Nintendo's *Amiibo* figurines persist, but these have always been a secondary add-on to the console games, not central to them.

Toy Systems

If the toy itself is rendered unstable in its ontological and phenomenological status in this postdigital media-technological environment, this instability is as industrial and economic as it is philosophical. The contemporary moment in the toy industry is one of flux, of significant investment by multinational media and entertainment corporations to capture both emerging technologies and the attention of a shifting, fickle audience. Although the toy today seems to be a much less stable object than it ever has been, material, physical objects, and devices do persist, albeit often in game/media formats that attempt to navigate the overlaps between software and hardware, digital networks, and physical objects. Such developments are better understood as *systems* rather than either sets of toys or games in their predigital form. By "system," I mean technocultural dispositifs, with a large degree of deliberate design, construction, and maintenance, heterogeneous in constitution but engineered with intention.[1] Like the entertainment supersystems and transmedia storyworlds from which they emerge at the turn of the twenty-first century, these systems configure play objects, characters, stories, and themes within commercial IP and via new technical and economic configurations of media devices, media imagery, digital networks, toys and toylike objects, social media, data collection, and participatory culture. And, in this, they build on the hugely successful evolution of the digital game from stand-alone arcade or console experience into its contemporary expansive and networked play environments. Game-based platforms with toylike characters, such as *Neopets*, *Minecraft*, and *Roblox*, have their physical components and merchandising, not least *Minecraft*'s collaboration with LEGO, but the core activities they offer are primarily engaged with on the screen. However, they are marked by significant new shapings of play, taking the millennia-old abstractions and economic forms of the board and card game—via the digital game—into new systems of attention and accumulation. As Sara Grimes has demonstrated, the contemporary commercial play landscape cannot be described without a grasp of (1) games; (2) the economic, technical, and formal structures of commercial online playgrounds[2]; and (3) their relationships with the prevailing digital media environment of social media, apps, data economics, and the new business models of microtransactions, including "free to play" strategies, downloadable content (DLC), microtransactions, and loot boxes.[3]

The design of, and play with, toys as systems predates computer media and networks. As we have seen, a toy soldier and a construction-set brick make sense only within the army or set: a system of rules and capacities in the case of soldiers, of modular combination in the case of construction sets. Part of the appeal of Playmobil, for instance, is the play of variation within a tightly designed aesthetic and mechanical system (figure 7.1).[4] The "multiple" toys I have discussed throughout this book, such as dollhouse dolls, could be regarded as kinds of protosystems, connected through form (scale, mechanics, and aesthetics) and behavior (the imperative to collect and combine, to expand the system). The LEGO System in Play is now one of the most prolific transmedia systems, but its history as a range of physical toys reminds us that systems, particularly but not exclusively construction sets, often had a sophisticated technical infrastructure before mediatization and the digital. Such systems in the mid to late twentieth century tended to be intensive rather than extensive. They were designed to work mainly or solely with their own mechanical and proprietorial system universes.

Unbox: Unboxing and the Mechanics of Surprise

"It gives you more information than just seeing an advert. It's more interesting because these videos give you more details about how something works and then they show you how it works." Nine year old Verity here is researching what birthday or Christmas presents she might ask for via the YouTube phenomenon of unboxing[5] in which children record and share video sequences of their opening, display, and operation of packaged toys. On the one hand, this is clear-headed consumer research on her part, as the video presenters offer in-depth assessments and demonstrations of the products; on the other,

Figure 7.1
Playmobil. Photo: Dave Gibbons.

it is a media-cultural practice with its own playful and performative dimensions. For instance, Verity also makes her own videos, but only for friends and
family, as she is nervous of being made fun of online. So, unboxing is part of a
new playful and productive media culture, or "space of affinity"' as Benjamin
Nicoll and Bjorn Nansen put it, of children's consumption practices and media
presentation that spans from private play with performative and media genres
and media technologies through the participatory and creative practices facilitated by YouTube and other platforms, to the handful of child stars working
as "brand influencers" with global commercial media operations. In recent
years, toy marketers have shifted a substantial proportion of their advertising
expenditure from television to social media and "kidfluencers."[6] Unboxing,
then, brings together children's consumption and production, in that the phenomenon encourages children's own user-generated content across a range of
networked media platforms and practices.

The origin of unboxing lies in adult online consumer reviews but has
proved particularly popular with children, in part, no doubt, for its resonances
with well-established patterns of gift receiving and the writing of birthday
lists and letters to Santa Claus in anticipation of desired toys. The surprise-
reveal format in children's gifts can be tracked back through the wrapping

Figure 7.2
Mechanical and hybrid novelty: Kinder Surprise fish-catching whale toy, with AR
connectivity. Ferrero, 2023. Photo: Dave Gibbons.

and unwrapping of presents themselves, party games such as pass the parcel and other playful activities such as bran tubs, tombolas, raffles, and lucky dips at fêtes and fairs. Surprise mechanics are integral to many contemporary toy systems, prefigured in part by products such as Kinder Surprise, popular across Europe since the 1970s (although banned in the US for its small parts). Manufactured by Italian confectionery company Ferrero, these small chocolate eggs contain a plastic capsule, which in turn conceals a tiny plastic toy (figure 7.2). The toys themselves often require some construction, made up of smaller parts so that they can fit in the capsule, and many are ingenious little machines with working parts. In this, they appear as a combination of Baudelaire's cheap mechanical street toys (chapter 2) and a secular and year-round version of Easter eggs, with an echo maybe of the peep egg and its hidden contents (chapter 6), particularly in recent developments in which AR markers and QR codes open further hidden images and animations via websites and smart device screens.

Supermarket toy aisle shelves today are stacked with boxes of capsules and packets with hidden LEGO minifigs, *Minecraft* characters, or the recent *Mashems* line, in which capsules hiding soft thermoplastic figurines are organized according to popular children's media franchises, from *Toy Story* to *Paw Patrol* and *Barbie Fashionistas*. Whole toy lines, then, are predicated on the sale of opaque capsules, bags, and packages, with surprise objects hidden inside. *L.O.L. Surprise!* dolls, for instance, a transmedia system of doll-related figures and accessories, and the *Gashapon* phenomenon of vending machines selling capsule toys, the unwrapping or unveiling of which is often a social event, the "reveal" a performative metaplay on the pleasures of acquisition, ownership, novelty, and reward.

These surprise systems rely on the well-established toy-cultural play modes of revelation and chance, but like collectible cards, they mix the benign techniques of "surprise" with more manipulative mechanics of false scarcity and "rare" items, impelling the collector to keep feeding in money to attain the desired items. All aleatory play systems of acquisition and collection have this dimension, from lucky dip onward: one is impelled to keep playing—and paying—until a reward that feels more valuable than the investment of the stake (and the time) is achieved. But recently, mechanics derived from commercialized gambling have been applied to digital games as monetization models based in pseudorandom "gifts" and loot boxes in free-to-play games and other videogames. Loot boxes are engineered to eke out microtransactions through the promise of a desirable virtual object or character. It is significant that the loot box is figured as a box, often an elaborate, solid-looking chest or strongbox. In such games, it seems that the toy itself is the prop around which a more complicated and nebulous game of revelation, performance, and satisfaction is played. Whatever value the toy or toylike virtual items may subsequently hold for the child, whatever games and imaginative play, or display, it may foster thereafter, at the moment of unboxing, its capacity as a distinct play object is less significant than its fleeting moment of novelty.

Toy Supremacy

This book began with two clear propositions and a set of speculative and playful suggestions. The first proposition is that toys and toy play are due renewed theoretical, historical, ethnographic, and philosophical attention at a time of rapid technical change in children's everyday lives. The toy is a cultural and material object worthy of sustained analytical and descriptive study. Toys are the infant's first engagement with the material-cultural world into which they are growing. Aptitudes with fingers and hand-eye coordination, relationships between objects and with gravity, texture, color, and mechanics are all developed with play objects. As D. W. Winnicott has shown, the body/play-object relationship is one that drives subjective development as well as sensorimotor skills. We differentiated our bodies and selves from the world through toys—a process that, Winnicott suggests, stays with us into adult life, sublimated into art production and consumption. In a late capitalist culture characterized by intense media environments and (aspirations at least) to commodity acquisition and possession, the toy both inducts the child and provides a model for adult cultures of consumption. And, of course, toys, games, and related media are in themselves a globally significant industry. Tracking the history of toys, before and after capitalism, suggests rich lived cultures of children's solitary and social play, of complex relationships between adult ritual and profane imagery and the objects given to children, of intergenerational care and distraction, and of nebulous but compelling imaginaries of technology, cosmology, and sociality rendered into hand-sized and stylized objects. Dolls, for instance, have been central to the child's passage into the adult symbolic order of social roles, religion, and marriage, but they also speak of intimate relationships and practices of care and love, with miniature bodies and clothing crafted by adults for their children.

Second, the toy should be grasped as technological: a technical object, its material constitution and form essential to its imaginative and embodied animation in play. Many toys are machines in their own right, with moving parts, operational elements, or motors. For all its tremendous variety in materials, form, mechanical ingenuity, and symbolic characteristics over centuries and around the world, the toy can nearly always be characterized by a few key interconnected technical aspects: scale, manipulability, and operability. Toys are necessarily scaled to work with the child's body, from the sweep of the arms in the driving of wheeled vehicles or animals to the mobilization of the whole body, as with kinesthetic objects and devices such as Hula-Hoops and pogo sticks (discussed in "Unbox: Unimaginative Toys" in chapter 1).

Scale and Tactility

Overwhelmingly, though, toys have been made to relate to the scale of children's hands and fingers. They fit in the hand or can be positioned and arranged by the hands and fingers. The touch of their surfaces suggests modes of play, and the haptic inflects the imaginative: hard plastics and metals, soft fur fabric and pliable vinyl. Many, perhaps most, toys are smaller than the objects or bodies they make reference to, but this is due in the main to material and technical demands rather than necessarily aesthetic reasons. They are smaller so that they can be held, hugged, and manipulated. A teddy bear is much smaller than an actual bear, but it is the same size as the cuddly Mickey Mouse discussed in chapter 6, which is, in turn, much bigger than an actual mouse. Each is scaled, up or down, to be animated, posed, and hugged, dimensions pegged to the child's hands and arms. For some toys, however, scale is integral to the aesthetic and imaginative affects of the object, in particular those for which the *miniature* is salient. These include dollhouse figures, furniture and household objects, and the figurines of tabletop wargames and fantasy role-playing games. Their pleasures lie in their exotic tininess and details. There is craft to this, from the making of tiny furniture and costumes to the assembly and painting of *Warhammer 40K* miniatures (see "Unbox: Miniature War" in chapter 3). Simply *looking* at the miniature is a historically persistent mode of play, as with early expensive dollhouse with their locks and prohibitions on children's access to their interiors. In this regard, there are strong historical and media archaeological connections between dollhouses and paracinematic devices and toys such as zoetropes, View-Masters, and VR. Each can trace a genealogy from the *camera obscura* and the cabinet of curiosities. "Peep media" play on the revelation of tiny and detailed images (see "Unbox: Peep Eggs and VR" in chapter 6). Here, Susan Stewart's notion of the miniature as a secret world within mundane everyday time and space pertains, at once an aesthetic and a phenomenology generated by the play of perception, narrative, and materiality.[7]

Operability and Manipulability

If the toy seems unsteady in contemporary children's play, the notion of "toying" remains salient. Mobile devices, chiefly phones and tablets but also handheld games consoles, lend themselves to text communication and hypermediated game interfaces and are, as Wanda Strauven has demonstrated (see chapter 6), hand-held and touch-driven play objects closely related to optical and other toys. Software applications, mobile apps, digital platforms, cultural and aesthetic conventions of memes, short videos, and new forms of slang all offer themselves up to be toyed with but, at the same time, more

Figure 7.3
Postdigital reinvention of one of the earliest toys: *#Selfie Fun Phone* rattle. Fisher-Price 2022.

or less tightly channel or scaffold imaginative and social play—they toy with their users. Or, more accurately, they constitute, and collude with these user-players in highly heterogeneous systems, networks, and moments, in which the toylike is never far away.

The attributes of the toy set out in this book's Introduction persist today, transformed in digital media but little changed in the resilient physical toy. The technical, embodied, and sensate interplay of hand, eye, imagination, and material and mechanical form shows no sign of decay (figure 7.3). Alongside, or beneath, contemporary toy culture's multinational systems lies the continuing mass production of cheap plastic objects and figurines, and craft and designer toys have their smaller but lively market. Toy store and supermarket shelves are still full of "traditional" toys, wooden, plastic, metal, tied into media licenses or offering nonproprietorial play worlds. Chinese production in recent decades has reduced the costs of production and distribution significantly at widely varying scales. Books, cuddly toys, and scientific toys are still bought for children, and—along with their iPads and game controllers—children still pick up any obliging object to hand to animate it in moments of imaginary world building. And connected platforms engage with the technological and social imaginaries and paradigms, as did the automata, the dollhouse, and the construction set.

From the perspective of the hands-on and the manipulable, the radically new forms of online participatory and creative culture for children and young people online resonate with the much longer genealogical dimension of craft toys, interactive books, the assembly of and tinkering with optical and cinema toys, the dressing of dolls, collection, swapping, and display. *Roblox* and *Minecraft* are nothing if not creative platforms, as were *Neopets* and *EverythingGirl.com* and LEGO's early online activities.[8] Thus, digital playgrounds such as *Minecraft* could be regarded as the mutated offspring of the nineteenth-century paper toy theater: media characters animated in a kit-like environment, making and manipulating the apparatus and performing to friends, both in the game and through video platforms. They also offer ways of thinking about the interplay of novelty and continuity in the prevalence of digital play objects from the late twentieth century. Videogame avatars, nonplayer characters, virtual vehicles, weapons, furniture, and animals are removed from the direct touch of the player's fingers but are animated by manipulability at one remove via the computer keyboard, mobile device touch screen, or console controller. They are operable in the mechanical sense I use here—that is, they have their own machinic drives: an NPC car in a racing game is a little machine with some residual similarity to the windup clockwork tin cars of the early twentieth century, but now with AI-determined speed, steering, and other ludic capabilities. Thus, the expression of imaginative agency through manipulation is also distributed across the human player and the play technology: the dramas and actions of videogame figures and objects are determined by the interplay of the player and the game software, a collusional fuzzy logic of play.

Toys Not Tools

The book's more speculative gambit, then, was to suggest that the toy, rather than being the most ephemeral and inconsequential type of object in technological and material culture, might instead be rethought as central to the development and adoption of new technologies and materials, both instrumentally and imaginatively. What if the toy were positioned as central to material and technically underpinned culture—today and over the course of human existence—rather than as a marginal, trivial object? What if toylike objects preceded functional tools in the origins of human technics? And play preceded design and instrumental use in the fashioning, application, and imaginaries of tools and machines? If, broadly, the instrumental were augmented or decentered by the toyetic? What, then, would be the implications for our theorizing of technoculture? What different emphases and concepts would be needed? Considerable evidence has been gathered to support this suggestion. Wheeled toys (see "Unbox: Wheeled Toys," in chapter 1) demonstrate that one now universal and fundamental machine, the vehicle moving on axled wheels, originated not in practical solutions to a pressing need for transporting people and freight but rather across the hazy activities of religious ritual and the distraction of children. The logistics and tactics of warfare in the Napoleonic era were first mapped and played out in tabletop games (chapter 3), and their development through to today's military–industrial–entertainment complex suggests an unstable core to post-Enlightenment rationalism, one characterized by practices, objects, and models that flicker between deadly serious planning and frivolous or experimental play. Current developments in, and imaginaries of, artificial intelligence and robots can be traced back through genealogies of children's toys, playful popular entertainment and the myths, cosmologies, and actual machines of medieval Islamic and Christian cultures and classical antiquity (chapter 5). Through their stylized simplicity, construction toys have influenced architectural styles, modeled urban futures (and pasts), and simulated abstracted modes of modularity and assemblage (chapter 4). The tangled genealogy of contemporary screen media in the optical devices and spectacles of the eighteenth and nineteenth centuries and the persistence of hands-on merchandising "ephemera" alongside cinema and television strongly suggest a popular kinesthetic and tactile media culture in which the projected animated image (whether cartoon or live-action feature film) is just one element (chapter 6). Twentieth- and twenty-first-century computing and artificial intelligence emerge from ludic hacker cultures and thought experiments and are modeled in, and disseminated through, game and toylike systems. Children's online game platforms such as *Neopets*, *EverythingGirl.com*, and *Minecraft* have generated new modes of (monetizable) sociality, surveillance, and creativity that have driven (adult) Internet cultures and economies in the twenty-first century.

Toying with History

Over the sweep of human civilization, the toy appears to have been predominantly at times a description of contemporaneous figures, activities, and environments, replicating for the child manipulable models of their wider worlds of domesticity, warfare, agriculture, animal husbandry, and so on. The toy can be historically and culturally specific—for instance, a tin clockwork Zeppelin airship from 1910s Europe or a Barbie Chelsea Vet Career Playset (on sale at the time of writing). Alternatively, it can be abstract and stylized, such as the rudimentary baked clay figures of the archaic era or the contemporary bright geometric play objects for babies and infants. But with modernity, social and technical change becomes a pressing feature of adult and childhood life, and the symbolic relationships between toys and their social milieus stretch and slip. From the late medieval era, for instance, dolls took on new a role as a conduit for fashion, either dressed in contemporaneous costumes in the child's toy, or sharing the latest adult styles as tangible models circulating among the well-to-do across Europe. With industrialization and urbanization from the eighteenth century into the twentieth century, toy farms, block-built villages, and grand dollhouses captured lost or fading industries, environments, and lifestyles in the projection of nostalgia onto (and construction of) childhood "innocence." But the same broad period also saw the toy take on the capture and epitomization of contemporaneous inventions and infrastructure. The archaic form of the toy warrior multiplied and organized along rationalist lines of strategy and logistics, the wheeled toy shaped itself after every new vehicular innovation, from steam locomotives to racing cars and—shedding its wheels—from the biplane to the robot and spaceship. While some wooden block sets were carved or printed with the ornamentation of early-modern European architecture, others offered a more stylistically and conceptually abstract form and process of building and assembly: alternative presents and futures of

Figure 7.4
Postindustrial phantasmagoria: *Hot Wheels* cars. Mattel, 1968–. Photo: Dave Gibbons.

the built environment, technical systems, and hence of modernity itself (figure 7.4).

It would be a mistake, then, to assume the toy always trails *after* the wider social and technical world, refracting and simplifying it for children's tastes and capabilities. The toyetic is, at times, reflective or descriptive of contemporaneous technologies and technics, but at others—particularly times of marked technocultural change—it is integral to and fully generative of imaginaries of prevailing technological paradigms. The material-imaginary genealogy of automata, the handheld and peep-into devices that spawned and transcended cinema and television, and the modular systems and plans of construction sets are all models that are graspable by the eye and imagination (if not always directly by the hands) to epitomize and disseminate new machines, processes, and systems. The toy form itself is ideal for the role of condensing, encapsulating, and personifying mechanisms, systems, and ideas, rendering them vivid and graspable, accessible and immediate. And even where toys proper are not directly involved in the process of invention, there is always a toyetic logic to the prototype, the experiment, the thought experiment, the proof of concept, the model, and the plan.

Synecdoche

To start and end analysis of the significance and effects of toys with their representational or symbolic attributes and effects, then, is to misunderstand the material-semiotic operations of play and toying profoundly. Throughout this book, I have suggested another approach to thinking about these operations: that of the synecdochical. Toys are not only representations of prevailing (or past, or future) cultural, social, and technical phenomena; they are, in various ways, *part of them*. On a basic level, this manifests as the scaled-down and supplemental deployment of materials to hand and fabrication processes of adult industry and craft, and hence immanent to and expressive of prevalent technological paradigms: the toy mammoth carved from the mammoth's tusk, cast metal from the Iron Age onward, carved wood, knitted and stitched garments, clockwork, die-cut and folded tin, lithography, thermoplastic, and software. From the early-modern period, toys have encapsulated historical moments both symbolically and materially—for example, the clockwork automata that figured the Newtonian universe as and through technologies of temporal measurement and mechanical self-regulation, or the computer games that at once realize and innovate the emerging relationships of intimacy and control in the information revolution from the 1970s. These are more than allegories. These playful devices did not merely provide images of prevailing technocultural paradigms but rather embodied them and set them in motion.

Toyetic synecdochical relationships are not always those of direct synchronicity, particularly in the modern era. The historical and imaginary slippage noted above intersects with material and economic contingency, on the one hand—clockwork was a cheaper and more practical technology for motive toys in the nineteenth century than the dominant steam power—and cultural factors, on the other—notably, adult notions of what aesthetically and morally appropriate materials might be.[9] Conversely, from the perspective of the toyetic, some technical and cultural phenomena generally regarded to be historically specific to the modern and late-modern period start to suggest their own deeper genealogical roots and continuities. For instance, the aesthetic attributes ascribed to the commodity fetish in recent cultural and media theory—spectacular novelty, superficial differentiation, the illusory, and the deceitful—epitomize the toyetic throughout its history. At the start of this book, I wondered what the implications might be of extrapolating from the essentially *artificial* nature of the toy to toylike technologies and then more generally to the histories and cultures of technologies at large. The toy is fundamentally not, as Brian Sutton-Smith asserted, what it appears to be. Whether the miniature facsimile of the dollhouse, the stylized and vividly colored abstractions of animal-shaped toys for infants, or the algorithmic videogame avatar, toys may seem at first glance to depict the existing world for developing hands and minds, but unlike the staid and fixed forms and images of sculpture and painting, the toy's relation to its referent, especially in play, is generally either much looser or much closer.

If we apply this synecdochical perspective to contemporary toy systems, it is evident that (along with the AI developments discussed in chapter 5) in this postdigital era, the toyetic is at its most closely enmeshed with dominant, instrumental, material, and economic paradigms; more tightly connected than ever through material infrastructure, processes, and protocols of data sharing and aggregation, and feedback via targeted marketing. The centrality of media culture to the global political economy, new modes of media production and delivery based in streaming services, more bottom-up developments in both funding and disseminating playful media production (from crowdfunding to *Twitch*), to the exploitation of networked sociality and play for data and targeted advertising by the social media and tech giants, notably Facebook/Meta and Weibo. And the material platforms on which this economy is based: personal computers, networked games consoles, mobile devices, broadband, and cellular data networks. The twenty-first century is, as a number of game scholars and cultural critics have argued, the "ludic century"[10] with the agonistic, aleatory, and simulative dynamics of games restructuring cultural forms and industrial strategies from television and cinema to the corporate exploitation of play mechanics in gamification and notions of imagination and creativity for productivity and market edge.[11]

The designers of platform architectures and the behavioral manipulation embedded in apps and social media—and, by extension, networked communication in all its social and industrial operations—have learnt from the economics and sociality of children's connected play spaces and videogames. Sara Grimes links awareness of the business side of platforms and privacy concerns, "biased algorithms and the always-on surveillance enabled by devices associated with the internet of things" across children's digital playgrounds with issues such as Cambridge Analytica's use of Facebook user data for intervening in the US presidential election in 2016.[12] The game and its toyetic dimensions are integral to these new modes of behavior, economies of value and extraction, models of gamification, and its app and social media instantiations. Games are both a major player in the postdigital cultural economy and, in significant ways, the template for it.

If, as this book has (more or less playfully) maintained, toy culture is at least as important as adult popular and high culture, toy play behavior is at least as important as other social, technical, and productive behavior, then what models of an emergent regime of networked, artificially intelligent, and data/surveillance-driven world do they offer? What kinds of toying with what kinds of toys? Is it possible to glimpse a technological imaginary of this systematized and distributed play—a picture, however indistinct, of this new networked environment of culture and sociality for children and young people, one that dramatizes dominant paradigms (like the toy theater in the nineteenth century) or models and allegorizes them (like the eighteenth-century automata or twentieth-century toy robots)? Maybe this is impossible for now, as it is too recent; we are too immersed in the fog of these banal virtualities to see their underlying contours. We need, at the very least, much more ethnographic attention to everyday connected play.

Or, as I suspect, is it that the very technologies, mechanisms, and platforms in play *are* those of the dominant technological paradigm and its economic workings? I have emphasized the importance of synecdochical relationships between toys and the broader material, economic, and technical environment relationships that, over centuries, can be tightly forged or more loosely articulated. The digital playgrounds, virtual spaces, ludic and surveillant economies, platforms, smart devices, and the corporations that produce them *are* the paradigm. The articulation of toy technology and prevailing technological and economic paradigms today is perhaps as tightly in step as any time since the wood carving and artisanal economy of sixteenth-century German forest towns. The toyetic now both nestles completely within this networked world and is a key innovator in the generation of new modes of engagement, attention and monetization, aesthetics and interfaces. If, in earlier modes of capitalism, the toyetic and the ludic have lagged behind industrial change, figuring the factory system as artisanal and agribusiness as bucolic, the virtual spaces of the Internet and VR as videogame romance—as "cyberspace"—now the toyetic and the ludic are the vanguard of new developments in data capitalism and its attention economies. Maybe the toyetic is, for now, so integral to the prevailing technocultural and economic order that it can't or doesn't

Figure 7.5
Automaton and simulacrum: clockwork-animated figure based on a collective group of characters ("LGMs" or little green men) from a CGI animated movie (*Toy Story*), in turn a nostalgic but nonspecific reference to 1950s American science fiction cinema. Photo: Dave Gibbons.

need to develop an imaginary relationship to it. Instead, it generates countless imaginative workings within its postdigital playgrounds and social spaces? We don't need the imaginary if we are fully living the imaginative. Sutton-Smith's ideoglyphs of today's "modern object reality" are not needed today, as children *directly* handle objects (virtual and actual) in the world.[13]

Simulacra

Finally, then, the fetishistic and illusory dimensions of the toy and the toyetic bring us to a concept that has proved persistently applicable to all of the toy types, behaviors, aesthetics, technologies, and systems discussed in this book: simulacra. I cannot offer a coherent summing up or definition of the simulacral and its implications for a toyetic perspective on technology and culture. The term is ambivalent and its instantiations in material culture and cultural theory diverse and contradictory. What I can state with confidence is its centrality to a toyetic perspective—that it deserves to be moved from the margins of inconsequential devices and amusements, and from recent apocalyptic diagnoses of late capitalist and media culture. Across ancient myth, children's play, fairground distractions, magic, performativity, frivolous consumption, and spectacular illusion can be tracked a diffuse but compelling logic that challenges Western thought's valorization of the authentic, the originary, and the true and its attendant realist cultural forms and critiques. The simulacral is culturally ubiquitous and immanent. Contemporary notions of simulation and simulacra assume a historically recent fall from grace, generally located as stemming from post–World War II consumer and media culture, accelerated by the virtualities of networked and digital culture.[14] Gilles Deleuze, however, traces the impulse to differentiate and legislate between true depictions and false or phantasmic copies back to ancient Greek philosophy.[15] For Deleuze, the simulacrum is not inferior, nor is it deceitful in and of itself. Rather, it has a positive and generative power "which negates both original and copy, both model and reproduction" in "a positive and joyous event."[16] This resonates with young children's imaginative play, in which objects, bodies, and behaviors become that which they are not, and questions of what is real and what is imaginary, what is original and what a representation, are more or less redundant.

The toy, and its toying, demonstrates at once the persistence of simulacra and their everyday reality. It also offers alternative ways of grasping the play of deceit and illusion. The child knows the toy is not an actual animal, but in the moment of play, it is more than enough that it functions *as if* it were an animal. It is not not an animal. Or, to take another not-animal, the hobbyhorse, as Gombrich describes it, is a substitute, but—crucially—not a substitute for anything existing. In this always-already simulacral register, like the kitten with a ball that becomes the mouse, the stick becomes the horse. Observation or experience of actual horse riding may provide a thematic or dramatic frame or prompt for hobbyhorse play, but the play itself is not constrained by it.[17] From the primitive "as if" gambit of the kitten and the hobbyhorse rider can be seen the construction or genealogy of a diffuse range of related ludic, imaginative, and epistemological attitudes. From Hero's fountains via stage magic to the CGI special effects of 1990s blockbuster films or virtual reality applications, the dynamic is the interplay of knowledge and belief: we know we are seeing an illusion, we know the seductive visible surface hides inner mechanisms, and we take pleasure in both being nearly tricked and in the spectacle and ingenuity of this deceit and its fabrication. The Chess Player epitomizes this dynamic: audiences knew it was a trick but were enthralled by its ingenuity and returned again and again to try to figure out how it was achieved. Where the Chess Player differs from other sideshow trickery and stage magic, I would suggest, however, is in its marshaling of a prevailing technological imaginary. As with spectacular developments in AI today, the attraction of the Chess Player and its automata forebears lies as well in their invitations to imaginative extrapolation. This device doesn't think, but it seems less unthinking than anything seen before, and . . . what if it *could* think?

This overarching toyetic imaginative regime, then, resists the fundamental binary oppositions of recent cultural theory, of nature and culture, and of knowledge and belief/fetishism, but it does not simply valorize or inscribe either instinct or magical thinking in post-Enlightenment rationality. As its presence in the play of animals demonstrates, it precedes and transcends both magical thinking and the rational and realist. The toy hints at a mode of relationality between artifact and source (and the mobilization of each) in which their separation is collapsed—like the transpositions of religious ritual, but everyday and without superstition, preternatural not supernatural.

On the one hand, then, the primary, benign deceit of the toy should keep reminding us that all human culture is fabrication, every cultural object, technology, and text is artificial, an artifact, manufactured or fabulated. On the other hand, attention to toys reminds us that every human life develops through this fabulous technoculture, whether the technologies are digital tablets or simple blocks of wood. Along the way, this book has, I hope, offered a few hints of the technical-imaginary phantasmagoria of children's play with objects, its moment-by-moment but incessant invention of the world.

Notes

Introduction

1. Iona Opie, *The People in the Playground* (Oxford: Oxford University Press, 1993).

2. See, for example, Shanly Dixon and Sandra Weber, "Playspaces, Childhood, and Videogames," in *Growing Up Online: Young People and Digital Technologies*, ed. Sandra Weber and Shanly Dixon (New York: Palgrave Macmillan, 2007), 15–34; and Seth Giddings, "'I'm the One Who Makes the LEGO Racers Go': Studying Virtual and Actual Play," in Weber and Dixon, *Growing Up Online*, 35–48.

3. Giovanna Mascheroni and Donell Holloway, eds., *The Internet of Toys: Practices, Affordances, and the Political Economy of Children's Smart Play* (Cham, Switzerland: Palgrave Macmillan, 2019).

4. Meredith A. Bak, "Building Blocks of the Imagination: Children, Creativity, and the Limits of Disney Infinity," *The Velvet Light Trap* 78 (2016): 59.

5. Donna Haraway, "A Manifesto for Cyborgs: Science, Technology, and Socialist-Feminism in the Late Twentieth Century," in *Feminism/Postmodernism*, ed. L. J. Nicholson (London: Routledge, 1991), 190–234.

6. As Miguel Sicart puts it, "Toys are defined by their cultural and technical dimensions: the toy as expression and the toy as thing." Miguel Sicart, *Play Matters* (Cambridge MA: MIT Press, 2014), 36.

7. Adrienne Mayor, *Gods and Robots: Myths, Machines, and Ancient Dreams of Technology* (Princeton, NJ: Princeton University Press, 2018). E. R. Truitt, *Medieval Robots: Magic, Mechanism, Nature and Art* (Philadelphia: University of Pennsylvania Press, 2015).

8. Rowan Hooper, "Wild Chimps Make Their Own 'Dolls,'" *New Scientist*, December 20, 2010.

9. For example, Sicart, *Play Matters*.

10. Michiel de Lange et al., eds., *Playful Identities: The Ludification of Digital Media Cultures* (Amsterdam: Amsterdam University Press, 2015); Steffen P. Walz and Sebastian Deterding, *The Gameful World: Approaches, Issues, Applications* (Cambridge MA: MIT Press, 2015); Eric Zimmerman and Heather Chaplin, "Manifesto: The 21st Century Will Be Defined by Games," *Kotaku*, 2013, https://kotaku.com/manifesto-the-21st-century-will-be-defined-by-games-1275355204.

11. https://www.playablecity.com/.

12. Jane MacGonigal, *Reality Is Broken: Why Games Make Us Better and How They Can Change the World* (London: Vintage, 2012).

13. Daniel Ashton and Seth Giddings, "At Work in the Toybox: Bedrooms, Playgrounds and Ideas of Play in Creative Cultural Work," *International Journal of Entrepreneurship and Innovation* 19, no. 2 (2018): 81–89.

14. D. W. Winnicott, *Playing and Reality* (London: Routledge, 2005 [1971]).

15. Stephen Kline, *Out of the Garden: Toys, TV, and Children's Culture in the Age of Marketing* (New York: Verso Books, 1993).

16. Brian Sutton-Smith, *Toys as Culture* (New York: Psychology Press, 1986).

17. For example, the International Toy Research Association: https://www.itratoy research.org/.

18. See, for example, Henry Giroux, *The Mouse that Roared: Disney and the End of Innocence* (Oxford: Rowman & Littlefield, 1999); Kline, *Out of the Garden*; Janet Wasko, *Understanding Disney: The Manufacture of Fantasy* (Malden, MA: Polity, 2001).

19. Such positions are rooted in persistent myths of the child as, on the one hand, a tabula rasa and, on the other unable, to distinguish fantasy and reality.

20. The observational work of Iona Opie is a key exception here, as is Sutton-Smith's long research career. In recent decades, digital games studies have conducted valuable work in this area—work that will be drawn on throughout this book.

21. Gregory Bateson, quoted in Brian Sutton-Smith, "Does Play Prepare the Future?" in *Toys, Play, and Child Development*, ed. Jeffrey Goldstein (Cambridge: Cambridge University Press, 1994), 143–144.

22. For a full explanation and rationale for my approach to ethnographic and ethological methods, see Seth Giddings, "Events and Collusions: A Glossary for the Microethnography of Videogames," *Games and Culture* 4, no. 2 (2009); *Gameworlds: Virtual Media and Children's Everyday Play* (New York: Bloomsbury, 2014), 55–66.

23. Lois Kuznets, *When Toys Come Alive: Narratives of Animation, Metamorphosis, and Development* (New Haven, CT: Yale University Press, 1994) has been a particularly valuable resource here.

Chapter 1

1. Karl Marx, *Grundrisse: Foundations of a Critique of Political Economy* (London: Penguin Classics, 1993 [1858]); Martin Heidegger, *The Question Concerning Technology and Other Essays* (New York: Garland, 1977 [1955]).

2. Bernard Suits, *The Grasshopper: Games, Life, and Utopia* (Peterborough: Broadview Press, 2005).

3. Antonia Fraser, *A History of Toys* (London: Weidenfeld & Nicolson, 1996), 25.

4. George Basalla, *The Evolution of Technology* (Cambridge: Cambridge University Press, 1988), 7–8.

5. Basalla, *Evolution of Technology*, 12.

6. Gordon F. Ekholm, "Wheeled Toys in Mexico," *American Antiquity* 11, no. 4 (1946): 226.

7. Ekholm, "Wheeled Toys," 227.

8. Martin Heidegger, 1927, in Paul Dourish, *Where the Action Is: The Foundations of Embodied Interaction* (Cambridge, MA: MIT Press, 2004), 108.

9. Dourish, *Where the Action Is*, 108–109.

10. Vilém Flusser, *The Shape of Things: A Philosophy of Design* (London: Reaktion Books, 1999).

11. For example, Fredric Jameson, *Postmodernism, Or the Cultural Logic of Late Capitalism* (London: Verso Books, 1991).

12. For example, Dick Hebdige, *Hiding in the Light: On Images and Things* (London: Routledge, 1988).

13. For example, Umberto Eco, *Travels in Hyperreality* (London: Mariner Books, 2014 [1986]).

14. Kevin Schut, "The Virtualisation of LEGO," in *LEGO Studies: Examining the Building Blocks of a Transmedial Phenomenon*, ed. Mark J. P. Wolf (New York: Routledge, 2014), 229.

15. Schut, "Virtualisation of LEGO," 229.

16. Sutton-Smith, *Toys as Culture*.

17. Susan Stewart, *On Longing: Narratives of the Miniature, the Gigantic, the Souvenir* (Baltimore: Johns Hopkins University Press, 1993).

18. Sutton-Smith, *Toys as Culture*, 249.

19. Giddings, *Gameworlds*, 37–41; Shirley R. Steinberg and Joe L. Kincheloe, *Kinder-Culture: The Corporate Construction of Childhood* (Boulder, CO: Westview Press, 2011).

20. Nicholas Taylor and Chris Ingraham, "Clickable Media in a Plastic World," in *LEGOfied: Building Blocks as Media*, ed. Nicholas Taylor and Chris Ingraham (New York: Bloomsbury, 2020), 1–19.

21. Katriina Heljakka, *Principles of Adult Play(fulness) in Contemporary Toy Cultures: From Wow to Flow to Glow* (Aalto, Finland: School of Arts, Design and Architecture, 2017).

22. Raymond Williams, *Television, Technology and Cultural Form* (New York: Schocken Books, 1975). See also Meredith Bak, *Playful Visions: Optical Toys and the Emergence of Children's Media Culture* (Cambridge, MA: MIT Press, 2020).

23. Bak, *Playful Visions*, 2020.

24. Sutton-Smith, *Toys as Culture*, 24.

25. Sutton-Smith, *Toys as Culture*, 21.

26. Winnicott, *Playing and Reality*.

27. See, for example, Roland Barthes's short chapter on plastic toys in *Mythologies* (London: Paladin Books, 1973 [1957]).

28. Claude Lévi-Strauss, *Tristes Tropiques* (London: Hutchinson, 1961), 155.

29. Lévi-Strauss, *Tristes Tropiques*, 155.

30. Roger Caillois, *Man, Play and Games* (Urbana: University of Illinois Press, 1962), 58.

31. Lévi-Strauss, *Tristes Tropiques*, 156.

32. In this, I am influenced by Gilles Deleuze's critique of Plato (and of Baudrillard). Gilles Deleuze, "Plato and the Simulacrum," *October* 27 (1983): 45–56. See also Seth Giddings, "Dionysiac Machines: Videogames and the Triumph of the Simulacra," *Convergence: The International Journal of Research into New Media Technologies* 13, no. 4 (2007): 417–431.

33. For example, Catherine Driscoll, "Girl-Doll: Barbie as Puberty Manual," in *Seven Going on Seventeen*, ed. Claudia Mitchell and Jacqueline Reid-Walsh (New York: Peter Lang, 2005), 217–33; and David Machin and Theo Van Leeuwen, "Toys as Discourse: Children's War Toys and the War on Terror," *Critical Discourse Studies* 6, no. 1 (2009): 51–63.

34. He was writing before the art movement of that name and so making a much broader point about art generated by ideas of things rather than their naturalistic depiction.

35. Fraser, *History of Toys*, 44.

36. Ernst H. Gombrich, *Meditations on a Hobby Horse* (Chicago: University of Chicago Press, 1985 [1951]), 7.

37. Gombrich, *Meditations on a Hobby Horse*, 7.

38. Gombrich, *Meditations on a Hobby Horse*, 2.

39. Gombrich, *Meditations on a Hobby Horse*, 4.

40. Fraser, *History of Toys*.

41. Fraser, *History of Toys*, 15.

42. Fraser, *History of Toys*, 24.

43. Marcel Mauss, "Techniques of the Body," *Economics and Society* 2, no. 1 (1973 [1935]): 70–88.

44. Furthermore, to assess the relationships between musical instruments and playful technoculture would require another book. Along with rattles, Fraser lists whistles, drums, cymbals, and flutes as popular medieval toys. See Fraser, *History of Toys*, 63. Fraser also notes a magical dimension to corals and rattles, with corals often shaped like a wolf's tooth to ward off evil spirits. See Fraser, *History of Toys*, 62.

45. Sicart, *Play Matters*, 38.

46. Caillois, *Man, Play and Games*. John and Elizabeth Newson group together as "hypnotic playthings" snow globes, spinning tops, and swings—objects that, as Dan Fleming puts it, "exert a sensory attraction that seems to precede the assignment of much meaning to the activity." See Dan Fleming, *Powerplay: Children, Toys and Popular Culture* (Manchester: Manchester University Press 1996), 67. As a category, this does not account for the range of toys and objects I want to include here, but it does suggest a fascinating correlation of bodily and sensory vertigo—a dynamic that would include bodily movement and visual attraction.

Chapter 2

1. Max von Boehn, *Dolls and Puppets* (Redditch, UK: Read Books, 2010 [1932]), 172.

2. Fraser, *History of Toys*, figure 84.

3. Von Boehn, *Dolls and Puppets*, 172.

4. Marquard Smith, *The Erotic Doll: A Modern Fetish* (New Haven, CT: Yale University Press, 2013), 10.

5. Von Boehn notes the ubiquity of the elementary or basic doll consisting "of a stick, with a thickening at the end as a head; it has preserved the essentials of the human shape—the upright form. When another stick is introduced, placed cross-wise on

the first, the line of shoulders is indicated and at once a great anatomical advance is attained." See von Boehn, *Dolls and Puppets*, 202.

6. Von Boehn, *Dolls and Puppets*, 103.

7. Von Boehn, *Dolls and Puppets*, 104.

8. Fraser, *History of Toys*, 50.

9. Kate Elderkin, "Jointed Dolls in Antiquity," *American Journal of Archaeology*, 34, no. 4 (1930): 456.

10. Smith, *The Erotic Doll*, 9.

11. Von Boehn, *Dolls and Puppets*, 111.

12. Von Boehn, *Dolls and Puppets*, 111.

13. Von Boehn, *Dolls and Puppets*, 110.

14. Fraser, *History of Toys*, 50.

15. Smith, *The Erotic Doll*, 9.

16. Von Boehn, *Dolls and Puppets*, 33.

17. Von Boehn, *Dolls and Puppets*, 33.

18. Von Boehn, *Dolls and Puppets*, 132.

19. Von Boehn, *Dolls and Puppets*, 78–79.

20. Von Boehn, *Dolls and Puppets*, 79.

21. Natalie Armitage, "European and African Figural Ritual Magic: The Beginnings of the Voodoo Doll Myth," in *The Materiality of Magic: An Artifactual Investigation into Ritual Practices and Popular Beliefs*, ed. Ceri Houlbrook and Natalie Armitage (Oxford: Oxbow Books, 2015), 85–101.

22. Von Boehn, *Dolls and Puppets*, 59.

23. Von Boehn notes: "At a charity bazaar held at London in 1901 there was exhibited an image of the Boer President Kruger which visitors were allowed to pierce thrice on payment of sixpence." See von Boehn, *Dolls and Puppets*, 61.

24. https://museumofwitchcraftandmagic.co.uk/exhibitions/2017-exhibition-poppets -pins-and-power-the-craft-of-cursing/.

25. See Louise Fenton, "A Tale of Two Poppets," *The Enquiring Eye: Journal of the Museum of Witchcraft and Magic* 3 (2020): 1–4, for a fascinating piece of detective work tracing the story behind two other museum poppets, fashioned from builder's putty and black tissue paper, back to a domestic drama in 1950s Surrey.

26. J. G. Frazer, *The Golden Bough* (Oxford: Oxford University Press, 2009).

27. Ernst Jentsch, in Hannah Field, *Playing with the Book: Victorian Movable Picture Books and the Child Reader* (Minneapolis: University of Minnesota Press, 2019), 157.

28. Smith, *The Erotic Doll.*

29. Marqard Smith, "Why Are Dolls So Creepy?" *BBC Culture* (blog), December 1, 2014. https://www.bbc.com/culture/article/20141201-why-are-dolls-so-creepy.

30. Ian Walker, *City Gorged with Dreams: Surrealism and Documentary Photography in Interwar Paris* (Manchester: Manchester University Press, 2002), 124–126.

31. Charles Baudelaire, "The Philosophy of Toys," in *Essays on Dolls*, ed. Idris Parry (London: Penguin/Syrens, 1994 [1853]), 14.

32. Baudelaire, "Philosophy of Toys," 15.

33. Charles Baudelaire, *The Poems in Prose*, Vol. II (London: Anvil Press, 1989), 83.

34. "Punch and Judy" in the English translation is a localization of the traditional British puppet show. In the poem, "punchinello" would refer to the singular seventeenth-century *commedia del'arte* character Punchinella and the "jumping jack" or Hampelmann type of puppet that often took his form. Baudelaire, *Poems in Prose*, 83.

35. Children's fascination with horror and violence has not been missed by toy manufacturers over the centuries. Von Boehn observed that "American children delight in playing at illness, death, and burial when they amuse themselves with their dolls," and that toy guillotines were popular toys in revolutionary France, and in the 1920s, Parisian shops sold *chemin de fer à catastrophes* set with dead and injured figures. See von Boehn, *Dolls and Puppets*, 216–217.

36. Helen S. Schwartz, "When Barbie Dated G. I. Joe: Analyzing the Toys of the Early Cold War Era," *Material History Review* 45 (1997): 50.

37. Erica Rand, *Barbie's Queer Accessories* (Durham, NC: Duke University Press, 1995), 3.

38. Kuznets, *When Toys Come Alive*, 95.

39. Giddings, *Gameworlds*; Frans Mäyrä, "Little Evils: Subversive Uses of Children's Games," in *The Dark Side of Game Play: Controversial Issues in Playful Environments*, ed. Torill Elvira Mortensen, Jonas Linderoth, and Ashlely M. L. Brown (New York: Routledge, 2014), https://homepages.tuni.fi/frans.mayra/Little_Evils.pdf; Brian Sutton-Smith, *The Ambiguity of Play* (Cambridge, MA: Harvard University Press, 1997).

40. Schwartz, "When Barbie Dated G. I. Joe," 50.

41. Beyond and before the Global North, the connotations of trickery seem less marked, but the doll figure is always a substitute, a proxy or copy—of a ritual object or a secular familial figure, always an animation of dead matter. To regard Barbie as

the epitome of postwar Western consumerism and a tool of sexual stratification would not be wrong, but her ancestry suggests that many of her features thus interpreted are not unique to late capitalist media culture.

42. Barbie memory, cited in Jacqueline Reid-Walsh and Claudia Mitchell, "'Just a Doll'? Liberating Accounts of Barbie-Play," *The Review of Education/Pedagogy/Cultural Studies* 22, no. 2 (2000): 175.

43. Karen E. Wohlwend and Kylie Peppler, "Designing with Pink Technologies and Barbie Transmedia," in *Young Children, Pedagogy and the Arts*, ed. Felicity McArdle and Gail Boldt (New York: Routledge, 2013), 129–145.

44. Elderkin, "Jointed Dolls," 462.

45. Elderkin, "Jointed Dolls," 464.

46. Elderkin, "Jointed Dolls," 464.

47. Von Boehn, *Dolls and Puppets*, 136.

48. Von Boehn, *Dolls and Puppets*, 153; Rebekah Willett, "Consuming Fashion and Producing Meaning through Online Paper Dolls," in *Growing Up Online: Young People and Digital Technologies*, ed. Sandra Weber and Shanly Dixon (New York: Palgrave Macmillan, 2007), 113–128.

49. Rand, *Barbie's Queer Accessories*, 23.

50. Kuznets, *When Toys Come Alive*, 96.

51. Ariane Fennetaux, "Transitional Pandoras: Dolls in the Long Eighteenth Century," in *Childhood by Design: Toys and the Material Culture of Childhood 1700–Present*, ed. Megan Brandow-Faller (New York: Bloomsbury, 2018), 47–66.

52. I'll return to this in the chapters on toy soldiers, construction toys, and cinema toys, but see Bak, *Playful Visions*; Giddings, *Gameworlds*; and Marina Warner, "Out of an Old Toy Chest," *Journal of Aesthetic Education*, 43, no. 2 (2009): 3–18.

53. Fennetaux, "Transitional Pandoras," 47–48.

54. There seem to be relatively more male rag dolls, sometimes produced in boy–girl pairs or families. The golliwog rag doll figure was popular in Britain well into the 1980s as a fictional character and as a brand logo and set of merchandise for Robertson's jam as well as a toy. The figure's characteristics are derived from racist caricature, including "minstrel" imagery, and as such, it has largely disappeared from commercial production and media, although Robertson's continued to distribute Golly badges into the twenty-first century.

55. Elderkin, "Jointed Dolls," 456.

56. Fraser, *History of Toys*, 12.

57. Elderkin, "Jointed Dolls," 457.

58. Kuznets, *When Toys Come Alive*, 16.

59. Carroll Pursell, *From Playgrounds to PlayStation: The Interaction of Technology and Play* (Baltimore: Johns Hopkins University, 2015), 6.

60. Pursell, *Playgrounds to PlayStation*, 6.

61. Pursell, *Playgrounds to PlayStation*, 8.

62. Elderkin, "Jointed Dolls," 455.

63. Elderkin, "Jointed Dolls," 456.

64. Fennetaux, "Transitional Pandoras," 49.

65. Pursell, *Playgrounds to PlayStation*, 6.

66. Fleming, *Powerplay*.

67. Megen de Bruin-Molé has studied recent *Star Wars* "adventure figures" produced by Hasbro, closer in scale to Barbie but with more complicated mechanics for dynamic play and targeted at a female audience. Megen de Bruin-Molé, "'Does It Come with a Spear?' Commodity Activism, Plastic Representation, and Transmedia Story Strategies in Disney's *Star Wars: Forces of Destiny*," *Film and Merchandise* 42, no. 2 (2018).

68. Heljakka, *Principles of Adult Play(fulness)*.

69. Heikki Tyni et al., "Hybrid Playful Experiences: Playing Between Material and Digital" (Tampere, Finland: Games Research Lab, University of Tampere, 2016), 73–74, https://trepo.tuni.fi/bitstream/handle/10024/98900/hybrid_playful_experiences_2016.pdf?sequence=1.

70. Jennifer Dawn Whitney, "'It's Barbie, Bitch!': Re-Reading the Doll Through Nicki Minaj and Harajuku Barbie," in *Doll Studies: The Many Meanings of Girls' Toys and Play*, ed. Miriam Forman-Brunell and Jennifer Dawn Whitney (New York: Peter Lang, 2015), 85–102. See also the song "Barbie Girl" by Aqua (1997) and its accompanying video for a playful exploration of the fake and the real.

71. Judith Butler, in Whitney, "It's Barbie, Bitch!" 98. The anthropomorphic and gendered artifact will be discussed further in chapter 5.

72. Kim Toffoletti, *Cyborgs and Barbie Dolls: Feminism, Popular Culture, and the Posthuman Body* (New York: I. B. Taurus, 2007).

73. Sara Grimes, *Digital Playgrounds: The Hidden Politics of Children's Online Play Spaces, Virtual Worlds, and Connected Games* (Toronto: University of Toronto Press, 2021).

74. For example, Jameson, *Postmodernism*; Laura Mulvey, *Fetishism and Curiosity* (London: BFI, 1996); Reid-Walsh and Mitchell, "'Just a Doll'?"; Smith, *The Erotic Doll*; "Why Are Dolls So Creepy?"

75. Detlef Mertens, "Playing at Modernity," in *Toys and the Modernist Tradition* (Montreal: Centre Canadien d'Architecture 1993), 12.

76. Baudelaire, "Philosophy of Toys," 15–16.

Chapter 3

1. Von Boehn, *Dolls and Puppets*, 34.

2. Fraser, *History of Toys*, 51.

3. Fleming notes that in Strasbourg in the mid-eighteenth century, a printer called Sieyfried produced a paper regiment of Louis XV's cavalry. These were called "French flats," although the term "flat" went on to refer to German nineteenth-century metal soldiers cut from sheets of tin, "overwhelming in numbers a longer-established tradition of carved wooden soldiers." Fleming, *Powerplay*, 85.

4. Kuznets, *When Toys Come Alive*, 79.

5. G. K. Chesterton, in Kuznets, *When Toys Come Alive*, 79–80.

6. Kuznets, *When Toys Come Alive*, 83.

7. Robert Barnard, and Louise Barnard, *A Brontë Encyclopedia* (Malden, MA: Blackwell, 2007), 172.

8. See, for example, the photography of Simon Brann Thorpe (2015), the song "Tin Soldiers" by Stiff Little Fingers (1980), or U. A. Fanthorpe's poem "The Constant Tin Soldier" (1986).

9. Kuznets, *When Toys Come Alive*, 16.

10. See, for instance, Tara Woodyer's work on Her Majesty's Armed Services, a recent Action Man–like toy line that served to domesticate the role of the British armed forces in contemporary geopolitics. Tara Woodyer and Sean Carter, "Domesticating the Geopolitical: Rethinking Popular Geopolitics through Play," *Geopolitics* 25, no. 5 (2020): 1050–1074.

11. There is probably a commercial dimension in operation here too: proprietorial fantasy storyworlds and characters can be copyrighted and transmedial, toyetic in the earlier sense of the term—in a way that historically accurate uniforms, weapons, and dramas cannot.

12. Gisela Wegener-Spöhring, "War Toys in the World of Fourth Graders: 1985 and 2002," in *Toys, Games, and Media*, ed. Jeffrey H. Goldstein, David Buckingham, and Gilles Brougère (Mahwah, NJ: Lawrence Erlbaum, 2004), 19–35.

13. For example, Martin Lister et al., *New Media: A Critical Introduction* (London: Routledge, 2009), 286–289.

14. Quoted in Fraser, *History of Toys*, 18.

15. Fraser, *History of Toys*, 56.

16. Fraser, *History of Toys*, 15.

17. Fraser, *History of Toys*, 74.

18. Fraser, *History of Toys*, 86.

19. Norman Joplin, *Toy Soldiers: The Collector's Guide to Identifying, Enjoying, and Acquiring New and Vintage Toy Soldiers* (London: Quintet, 1994), 8.

20. Joplin, *Toy Soldiers*, 15.

21. Fleming, *Powerplay*, 152.

22. For clarity, I use "Cowboys and Indians" as it was the contemporaneous term for these toys and related products for children, including dressing up sets and comic books. The toys' design and packaging reflect the racial stereotyping of both these 'groups' in popular cinema and literature, eliding national and ethnic diversity in and across each.

23. Unlike many other toys in the films, their diegetic role mapped closely to their symbolic form: they work as a vanguard squad surveilling the domestic terrain, complete with the language and gestures familiar from American war movies.

24. Joplin, *Toy Soldiers*, 34–35.

25. It is telling that one of Félix Guattari's main examples of his and Gilles Deleuze's concept of the machinic phylum is the Greek hoplite formation in which a technical arrangement of warriors, spears, and shields formed an effective and efficient war machine. Felix Guattari, "Balance Program for Desiring Machines," in *The New Media and Technocultures Reader*, ed. Seth Giddings (London: Routledge, 2011), 132.

26. Patrick Crogan, "Wargaming and Computer Games: Fun with the Future." In *Proceedings of the 2003 DiGRA International Conference: Level Up* (2003), 6, http://www.digra.org/wp-content/uploads/digital-library/05163.52183.pdf.

27. Jon Peterson, "A Game Out of All Proportions: How a Hobby Miniaturized War," in *Zones of Control: Perspectives on Wargaming*, ed. Pat Harrigan and Matthew G. Kirschenbaum (Cambridge, MA: MIT Press, 2016), 5.

28. Peterson, "A Game Out of All Proportions," 5; Crogan, *Gameplay Mode*, 3.

29. Peterson, "A Game Out of All Proportions," 7.

30. Crogan, "Wargaming and Computer Games," 3–4.

31. Crogan, "Wargaming and Computer Games," 4.

32. Peterson, "A Game Out of All Proportions," 7.

33. Peterson, "A Game Out of All Proportions," 3.

34. Crogan, "Wargaming and Computer Games," 3.

35. Crogan, "Wargaming and Computer Games," 4.

36. Crogan, "Wargaming and Computer Games," 3.

37. Peterson, "A Game Out of All Proportions," 6.

38. Peterson, "A Game Out of All Proportions," 8.

39. Peterson, "A Game Out of All Proportions," 8.

40. Peterson, "A Game Out of All Proportions," 9.

41. Quoted in Peterson, "A Game Out of All Proportions," 5.

42. Crogan, "Wargaming and Computer Games," 4.

43. Peterson, "A Game Out of All Proportions," 8.

44. Peterson, "A Game Out of All Proportions," 7.

45. Mikko Meriläinen, Jaakko Stenros, and Katriina Heljakka, "More than Wargaming: Exploring the Miniaturing Pastime," *Simulation and Gaming* (first published online June 2020). https://doi.org/10.1177/1046878120929052.

46. Peterson, "A Game Out of All Proportions," 10.

47. Peterson, "A Game Out of All Proportions," 10–11.

48. Peterson, "A Game Out of All Proportions," 3.

49. Peterson, "A Game Out of All Proportions," 12.

50. Celia Pearce, "Sims, Battlebots, Cellular Automata, God and Go: An Interview with Will Wright," *Games Studies* 2, no. 1 (2002). http://www.gamestudies.org/0102/pearce.

51. See also Adam Chapman on zombies in *Call of Duty* and Nazi robots in *Wolfenstein*. Adam Chapman, "Playing the Historical Fantastic: Zombies, Mecha-Nazis and Making Meaning about the Past through Metaphor," in *War Games: Memory, Militarism and the Subject of Play*, ed. Philip Hammond and Holger Pötzsch (New York: Bloomsbury, 2020), 95.

52. John A. Foley, "Combat Commander: Time to Throw Your Plan Away," in *Zones of Control: Perspectives on Wargaming*, ed. Pat Harrigan and Matthew G. Kirschenbaum (Cambridge, MA: MIT Press, 2016), 121.

53. Stewart, *On Longing*, 54.

54. Stewart, *On Longing*, 57. See also Johan Huizinga on the multiplication or augmentation of everyday time-space in play and games. Johan Huizinga, *Homo Ludens: A Study of the Play Element in Culture* (Boston, MA: Beacon Press, 1986 [1938]).

55. The British company Games Workshop published the first *40K* rulebook in 1987 as a science fiction–themed version of an earlier medieval fantasy game. Marcus Carter, Martin Gibbs, and Mitchell Harrop, "Drafting an Army: The Playful Pastime of Warhammer 40,000," *Games and Culture* 9, no. 2 (2014): 126. Games Workshop was established in 1978 as the UK distributor of *D&D* rulebooks and equipment and manufacturer and retailer of *Lord of the Rings* game figurines. Sarah Butler, "Warhammer Maker Games Workshop Hands Staff £5,000 Bonus after Lockdown Sales Surge," *The Guardian*, July 27, 2021, https://www.theguardian.com/business/2021/jul/27/warhammer-maker-games-workshop-hands-staff-5000-bonus-after-lockdown-sales-surge. *40K* is a dominant system, with a worldwide tabletop games sector that is predicted to be worth $12bn by 2023. Butler, "Warhammer Maker Games Workshop Hands Staff £5,000 Bonus." Games Workshop itself is a publicly listed company, with sales of £256.6 million in 2019. Sarah Butler, "How Games Workshop Grew to Be More Profitable than Google," *The Guardian*, July 31, 2021, https://www.theguardian.com/lifeandstyle/2021/jul/31/how-games-workshop-grew-to-become-more-profitable-than-google.

56. Carter et al., "Drafting an Army," 127.

57. https://warhammer40000.com/rules/.

58. Meriläinen et al., "More Than Wargaming," 2020.

59. Carter et al., "Drafting an Army," 127–128.

60. Patrick Crogan, *Gameplay Mode: War, Simulation, and Technology* (Minneapolis: University of Minnesota Press, 2011), 151.

61. Quoted by Patrick Crogan, "Wargaming and Computer Games," 6.

62. Crogan, "Wargaming and Computer Games," 6.

63. Peterson, "A Game Out of All Proportions," 18.

64. Henry Lowood, "War Engines: Wargames as Systems from the Tabletop to the Computer," in *Zones of Control: Perspectives on Wargaming*, ed. Pat Harrigan and Matthew G. Kirschenbaum (Cambridge MA: MIT Press, 2016), 86.

65. Peterson, "A Game Out of All Proportions," 26.

66. Crogan, "Wargaming and Computer Games," 7.

67. Crogan, "Wargaming and Computer Games," 6.

68. Peterson, "A Game Out of All Proportions," 23–24.

69. Peterson, "A Game Out of All Proportions," 29.

70. Peterson, "A Game Out of All Proportions," 3.

Chapter 4

1. Mertens, "Playing at Modernity," 7.

2. Norman Brosterman, "Potential Architecture: An Infinity of Buildings," in *Potential Architecture: Construction Toys from the CCA Collection* (Montreal: Centre Canadien d'Architecture, 1991), 7.

3. Fraser, *History of Toys*, 51.

4. Jose A. Muñoz Alvis, "Through a Technique of Building," *Icon* 23 (2017): 84.

5. Fraser, *History of Toys*, 90.

6. See also "Unbox: Cardboard Cinema" in chapter 6.

7. Maikke Lauwaert, *The Place of Play: Toys and Digital Cultures* (Amsterdam: Amsterdam University Press, 2009), 46.

8. Pursell, *From Playgrounds to PlayStation*, 17.

9. Fleming, *Powerplay*, 8–9.

10. Meccano was patented in the UK in 1901, originally named "Mechanics Made Easy," by Frank Hornby, who went on to establish the toy railway company and systems that bear his name. Hornby claimed he was inspired by watching a crane at work, being "struck by the simplicity of the idea, and it occurred to him that models could be easily made out of a small number of simple parts". Fraser, *History of Toys*, 194.

11. Brenda and Robert Vale trace a number of compelling aesthetic and formal similarities between toy systems and actual modernist buildings. Brenda Vale and Robert Vale, *Architecture on the Carpet: The Curious Tale of Construction Toys and the Genesis of Modern Buildings* (London: Thames & Hudson, 2013). See also Alice T. Friedman, "Model Homes and Dream Houses," in *Dream Houses, Toy Homes* (Montreal: Centre Canadien d'Architecture, 1995).

12. Quoted in Pursell, *From Playgrounds to PlayStation*, 17.

13. Fleming, *Powerplay*, 8–9.

14. Deborah Mulhearn, "Role Models," *The Guardian*, May 30, 2001, https://www.theguardian.com/society/2001/may/30/shopping.toys; Alvis, "Through a Technique of Building," 2017.

15. Warner, "Out of an Old Toy Chest," 8.

16. Walter Benjamin, in Mertens, "Playing at Modernity," 10.

17. Lauwaert, *The Place of Play*; Michelle Millar Fisher, "Work Becomes Play: Toy Design, Creative Play, and Unlearning in the Bauhaus Legacy," in *Childhood by Design: Toys and the Material Culture of Childhood, 1700–Present*, ed. Megan Brandow-Faller (New York: Bloomsbury, 2018), 153–172; Pursell, *From Playgrounds to PlayStation*.

18. Norman Brosterman claims Froebel's kindergarten movement, and the experience of many key figures in modernism as children in Froebelian kindergartens at the end of the nineteenth century, is at least as significant in this cultural, philosophical, and artistic revolution as Cezanne and African sculpture. Brosterman, "Potential Architecture." Marina Warner also cites the influence of Maria Montessori and Johannes Itten on modernist processes and ethos via play, the senses and experimentation. Warner, "Out of an Old Toy Chest," 9. See also Millar Fisher, "Work Becomes Play," for the early Bauhaus engagement with toy design.

19. Pursell, *From Playgrounds to Playstation*, 16.

20. Quoted in Colin Fanning, "Building Kids: LEGO and the Commodification of Creativity," in *Childhood by Design: Toys and the Material Culture of Childhood, 1700–Present*, ed. Megan Brandow-Faller (New York: Bloomsbury, 2018), 91.

21. Lauwaert, *The Place of Play*, 12–13.

22. See Gary Cross, *Kids' Stuff: Toys and the Changing World of American Childhood* (Cambridge, MA: Harvard University Press, 1997); Kline, *Out of the Garden*.

23. Colin Fanning argues, "By materializing and commodifying notions of individuality and originality . . . LEGO tethered the abstract quality of creativity to the concrete act of playful building," Fanning, "Building Kids," 89. Other accounts of the commodification of imagination in LEGO include: David Gauntlett, "The LEGO System as a Tool for Thinking, Creativity, and Changing the World," in *LEGO Studies: Examining the Building Blocks of a Transmedia Phenomenon*, ed. Mark J. P. Wolf (New York: Routledge, 2014), 189–205; Michael Lachney, "Building the LEGO Classroom," in *LEGO Studies: Examining the Building Blocks of a Transmedia Phenomenon*, ed. Mark J. P. Wolf (New York: Routledge, 2014), 166–188; and Lori Landay, "Myth Blocks: How LEGO Transmedia Configures and Remixes Mythic Structure in the Ninjago and Chima Themes," in *LEGO Studies: Examining the Building Blocks of a Transmedia Phenomenon*, ed. Mark J. P. Wolf (New York: Routledge, 2014), 55–80.

24. https://www.lego.com/en-gb/lego-group/.

25. Cross, *Kids' Stuff*, 220.

26. LEGO was not the first to develop this mode of connection. It is generally accepted that the idea was taken from Hilary Page's "Self-Locking Bricks" by Kiddicraft, itself influenced by earlier stud-and-socket mechanisms such as Belgian "Batima" pressed paper bricks (1905) and rubber British "Minibrix" (1935). Fanning, "Building Kids," 91.

27. Cross, *Kids' Stuff*, 220.

28. Lauwaert, *The Place of Play*, 59.

29. Cross, *Kids' Stuff*, 61.

30. Giddings, "Bright Bricks."

31. Kate Maddalena, "Palpable Pixels," in *LEGOfied: Building Blocks as Media*, ed. Nicholas Taylor and Chris Ingraham (New York: Bloomsbury, 2020), 24.

32. Jonathan Rey Lee, *Deconstructing LEGO: The Medium and Messages of LEGO Play* (Cham, Switzerland: Palgrave Macmillan, 2020), 28.

33. In Giddings, "Bright Bricks," 252.

34. See Lee, *Deconstructing LEGO*, 45–54. See also Jay David Bolter and Richard Grusin, *Remediation: Understanding New Media* (Cambridge, MA: MIT Press, 1999) for an application of McLuhan's model to digital culture.

35. Will Wright, quoted in IGN.com, "Top 100 Game Creators of All Time: 3. Will Wright," n.d. https://www.ign.com/top/game-creators/3.html.

36. Bart Simon and Darren Wershler, "Childhood's End (or, We Have Never Been Modern, Except in Minecraft)," *Cultural Politics* 14, no. 3 (2018): 293.

37. Simon and Wershler, "Childhood's End," 297.

38. Seth Giddings, "The History of Games Could Be a History of Technology," *ROM-Chip: A Journal of Game Histories* 1, no. 1 (2019). https://www.romchip.org/index.php/romchip-journal/article/view/74.

39. Gilles Brougère, "Toy Houses: A Socio-Anthropological Approach to Analysing Objects," *Visual Communication*, 5, no. 5 (2006): 16.

40. This notion of distributed imagination is inspired by Edwin Hutchin's concept of "distributed cognition." Edwin Hutchins, *Cognition in the Wild* (Cambridge, MA: MIT Press, 1995). I expand on it a little in Seth Giddings, "Pokémon Go and Distributed Imagination," *Mobile Media and Communication* 5, no. 1 (2017): 59–62.

41. Fanning, "Building Kids"; Gauntlett, "The LEGO System as a Tool for Thinking," 2014.

42. Anthony Dunne and Fiona Raby, *Speculative Everything: Design, Fiction, and Social Dreaming* (Cambridge, MA: MIT Press, 2013).

43. Alvis, "Through a Technique of Building," 85.

44. See Maikke Lauwaert, "Challenge Everything? Construction Play in Will Wright's SIMCITY," *Games and Culture* 2, no. 3 (2007): 194–212, https://doi.org/10.1177/1555412007306205, for an incisive critique of this notion of "borderless playgrounds"

and a compelling genealogy of the toyetic relationships between construction sets and contemporaneous ideas about urban growth and planning. Note too that simulation games are often referred to as "sandbox" games, the reference here is to an enclosed environment for playing with toys—and shaping the environment itself—the game as a space for toys and toying.

45. Maddalena, "Palpable Pixels," 24.

46. Maddalena, "Palpable Pixels," 24.

47. Taylor and Ingraham, *LEGOfied*, 12.

48. Jonathan Rey Lee talks of LEGO brick building following the instruction book as "a *procedural rhetoric* that encourages most mechanical builders to become fluent in the underlying principles of LEGO design." Lee, *Deconstructing LEGO*, 28. This invokes Ian Bogost's concept of the cultural manifestations, in videogames, of computer affordances and processes. Ian Bogost, *Persuasive Games: The Expressive Power of Videogames* (Cambridge MA: MIT Press, 2010).

Chapter 5

1. Derek Price, quoted in Daniel Tiffany, *Toy Medium: Materialism and Modern Lyric* (Berkeley: University of California Press, 2000), 40.

2. Lister et al., *New Media*, 352.

3. Note that for Aristotle, as self-moving bodies, humans counted as automata (an inclusion that resonates with early-modern science and Leibniz's categorization of all living things as "natural automata"), but here, "self-movement" includes the dimension of free will or intention. Thus, ordinary citizens were self-moving, but slaves were not, as their movements and behavior were directed by their owners.

4. Truitt, *Medieval Robots*.

5. Kuznets, *When Toys Come Alive*; Lister et al., *New Media*; David Tomas, "Feedback and Cybernetics: Reimagining the Body in the Age of the Cyborg," in *The New Media and Technocultures Reader*, ed. Seth Giddings (London: Routledge, 2011); Cathryn Vasseleu, "A Is for Animatics (Automata, Androids, and Animals)," in *Living With Cyberspace*, ed. John Armitage and Joanne Roberts (London: Continuum, 2002); Gaby Wood, *Living Dolls: A Magical History of the Quest for Mechanical Life* (London: Faber & Faber, 2002).

6. Lister et al., *New Media*, 345.

7. Lister et al., *New Media*; Mayor, *Gods and Robots*; Jessica Riskin, "The Defecating Duck, or the Ambiguous Origins of Artificial Life," *Critical Inquiry* 29 no. 4 (2003): 599–633; *The Restless Clock: A History of the Centuries-Long Argument Over What Makes Living Things Tick* (Chicago: University of Chicago Press, 2016); Barbara Stafford, *Artful*

Science: Enlightenment Entertainment and the Eclipse of Visual Education (Cambridge, MA: MIT Press, 1999); Barbara Stafford and Frances Turpek, *Devices of Wonder: From the World in a Box to Images on a Screen* (Los Angeles: Getty Research Institute, 2001); Tiffany, *Toy Medium*; Tomas, "Feedback and Cybernetics"; Truitt, *Medieval Robots*; Vasseleu, "A Is for Animatics"; Adelheid Voskuhl, *Androids in the Enlightenment: Mechanics, Artisans, and Cultures of the Self* (Chicago: University of Chicago Press, 2013); Wood, *Living Dolls*.

8. However, some of the mechanical techniques developed through automaton design find their way into the cheapest toys—for instance, the gadgets and punchinellos that Baudelaire buys on the street, and, later, clockwork.

9. Lister et al., *New Media*, 352.

10. Norbert Weiner, *Cybernetics, or Control and Communication in the Animal and Machine* (Cambridge, MA: MIT Press, 2019 [1961]), 56.

11. Mayor, *Gods and Robots*, 7–32.

12. Mayor, *Gods and Robots*, 2. The different origins and material construction of Talos and Galatea have echoes in the material and gendered distinctions between the doll and the toy soldier.

13. Lister et al., *New Media*; Tomas, "Feedback and Cybernetics"; Vasseleu, "A Is for Animatics."

14. Lister et al., *New Media*, 348.

15. Lister et al., *New Media*, 357.

16. Tiffany, *Toy Medium*, 52.

17. Wood, *Living Dolls*, 58.

18. The tour included other automata built by Maelzel, including musicians and a panorama. Maelzel also gave the Turk the ability to say check—*échec*—via bellows. Maelzel met P. T. Barnum in the US, and the two collaborated. Wood, *Living Dolls*, 71.

19. For example, Lister et al., *New Media*, 351.

20. Von Boehn, *Dolls and Puppets*, 263.

21. The mechanism was subsequently influential in its own right—for example, in the development of prosthetic limbs. As Wood puts it, "the automaton helped to design the human." Wood, *Living Dolls*, 68.

22. Wood, *Living Dolls*, 64.

23. Wood, *Living Dolls*, 61.

24. Wood, *Living Dolls*, 65.

25. Wood, *Living Dolls*, 73.

26. Wood, *Living Dolls*, 77.

27. The Jacquet-Droz family were watchmakers, and the firm continues today. Along with its range of luxury watches, it produces an elegant little clockwork device that can be similarly programmed to write out its owner's signature. https://www.jaquet -droz.com/en/watches/automata/signing-machine-j899-000-064.

28. Tiffany, *Toy Medium*, 37.

29. Von Boehn, *Dolls and Puppets*, 3.

30. While they were banished from English churches in the Reformation, they remained a feature in France up to the seventeenth century. Von Boehn, *Dolls and Puppets*, 253.

31. Truitt, *Medieval Robots*. See also Truitt's account of the remarkable, theme park– like, fourteenth-century chateau at Hesdin, France.

32. Wax figures have a long simulacral history of their own. Von Boehn discusses the extensive use of wax effigies as funerary statues in the Middle Ages, for instance.

33. Von Boehn, *Dolls and Puppets*, 262.

34. Wood, *Living Dolls*. See also Meredith A. Bak, "Between Technology and Toy: The Talking Doll as Abject Artifact," in *Abjection Incorporated: Mediating the Politics of Pleasure and Violence*, ed. Maggie Hennefeld and Nicholas Sammond (Durham, NC: Duke University Press, 2020), 164–184; Catherine Driscoll, "The Doll-Machine: Dolls, Modernism, Experience," in *Doll Studies: The Many Meanings of Girls' Toys and Play*, ed. Miriam Forman Brunell and Jennifer Dawn Whitney (New York: Peter Lang, 2015), 185–204; Fennetaux, "Transitional Pandoras," 47–66; Kuznets, *When Toys Come Alive*; Mulvey, *Fetishism and Curiosity*; Harold Segel, *Pinocchio's Progeny: Puppets, Marionettes, Automatons, and Robots in Modernist and Avant-Garde Drama* (Baltimore: Johns Hopkins University Press, 1995); Smith, *The Erotic Doll*; Tiffany, *Toy Medium*; Tomas, "Feedback and Cybernetics."

35. Kate Devlin, *Turned On: Science, Sex, and Robots* (London: Bloomsbury, 2018).

36. Stafford and Terpak, *Devices of Wonder*, 268.

37. Wood, *Living Dolls*, 37.

38. The children and virtual robot were gathered at a workshop run at an inner-city primary school in Bristol, UK. The research was supported by a prototype funding award from REACT, a knowledge exchange hub for the creative economy funded by the Arts and Humanities Research Council (UK). The start-up robotics company, Reach Robotics, was developing a robot-based computer game platform, in which physical robots would be controlled by an app. This stage of the research looked to explore

the balance between technology and user experience, focusing on the everyday and popular contexts of play with technology. This Unbox is adapted from Seth Giddings, "Toying with the Singularity: AI, Automata, and Imagination in Play with Robots and Virtual Pets," in The Internet of Toys: Practices, Affordances, and the Political Economy of Children's Smart Play, ed. Giovanna Mascheroni and Donell Holloway (New York: Palgrave Macmillan 2019), 67–88. Used with permission, Springer Nature.

39. Alan Winfield, *Robotics: A Very Short Introduction* (Oxford: Oxford University Press, 2012).

40. See also Reem Hilu, "Girl Talk and Girl Tech," *Velvet Light Trap: A Critical Journal of Film and Television* 78 (2016): 4–23.

41. Tom Gunning, "The Cinema of Attraction: Early Film, the Spectator and the Avant Garde," *Wide Angle* 8, no. 3 (1986): 63–70.

42. Winfield, *Robotics*.

43. Sherry Turkle, "Cyborg Babies and Cy-Dough-Plasm: Ideas About Self and Life in the Culture of Simulation," in *Cyborg Babies: From Techno-Sex to Techno-Tots*, ed. Robbie Davis-Floyd and Joseph Dumit (New York: Routledge, 1998), 317.

44. Sherry Turkle, *Life on the Screen: Identity in the Age of the Internet* (London: Weidenfeld & Nicolson, 1996), 170.

45. David Kritt, "Loving a Virtual Pet: Steps Towards the Technological Erosion of Emotion," *Journal of American and Comparative Literatures* 23, no. 4 (1999): 81–87.

46. Linda Renée Bloch and Dafna Lemish, "Disposable Love: The Rise and Fall of a Virtual Pet," *New Media and Society* 1, no. 3 (1999): 295.

47. Anne Allison, *Millennial Monsters: Japanese Toys and the Global Imagination* (Berkeley: University of California Press, 2006), 164.

48. Allison, *Millennial Monsters*, 179.

49. Thomas Apperley and Nichole Heber, "Capitalizing on Emotions: Digital Pets and the Natural User Interface," in *Game Love: Essays on Play and Affection*, ed. Jessica Enevold and Esther Macallum-Stewart (Jefferson, NC: McFarland, 2015), 149–161.

50. Minna Ruckenstein, "Toying with the World: Children, Virtual Pets and the Value of Mobility," *Childhood* 17, no. 4 (2010): 501. https://doi.org/10.1177/090756 8209352812.

51. Ruckenstein, "Toying with the World," 506.

52. Jackie Marsh, "The Internet of Toys: A Posthuman and Multimodal Analysis of Connected Play," *Teachers College Record* 119, no. 2 (2017). https://eprints.whiterose .ac.uk/113557/.

53. Marsh, "The Internet of Toys."

54. Johnson, "Artificial Intelligence," 16.

55. Emma Reay, "Cute, Cuddly and Completely Crushable: Plushies as Avatars in Video Games," *Journal of Gaming and Virtual Worlds* 13, no. 2 (2021): 139.

56. David Sudnow, *Pilgrim in the Microworld* (London: Heinemann, 1983).

57. William Gibson, *Neuromancer* (London: Gollancz, 1984).

58. Disney 1984.

59. Viewpoint and virtual camera angles figure here too, however, with top-down virtual camera angles in, say, the first *The Sims* game or early real-time strategy games, evoking the miniature.

60. But see Maciej Musiał's book for a thorough exploration of the relationships between magical thinking and automata. Maciej Musiał, *Enchanting Robots: Intimacy, Magic, and Technology* (Palgrave Macmillan, 2019).

61. See Lister et al., *New Media*, 150–157.

Chapter 6

1. Iona Opie, Peter Opie, and Brian Alderson, *The Treasures of Childhood: Books, Toys and Games from the Opie Collection* (New York: Arcade, 1989), 143.

2. I am using the term "theatrical cinema" to refer specifically to mainstream, commercial, or state-supported feature-film production primarily for theater-based projection.

3. Giroux, *The Mouse that Roared*; Kline, *Out of the Garden*; Wasko, *Understanding Disney*. Note, though, Dan Fleming's book, *Powerplay*, is an important exception to this, as is the more recent work by Bak, "Building Blocks of the Imagination."

4. For LEGO, see Roy T. Cook and Sondra Bacharach, eds., *LEGO and Philosophy: Constructing Reality Brick by Brick* (Minneapolis: University of Minnesota Press, 2015); Joyce Goggin, "'How Do Those Danish Bastards Sleep at Night?' Fan Labor and the Power of Cuteness," *Games and Culture* 13, no. 7 (2018): 747–764; Rebecca C. Hains and Sharon R. Mazzarella, eds., *Cultural Studies of LEGO: More Just Bricks* (Cham, Switzerland: Palgrave Macmillan, 2019); Matt Hills, "LEGO Dimensions Meets Dr Who: Transbranding and New Dimensions of Transmedia Storytelling?" *Icono* 14, no. 1 (2015): 8–29; Nicholas Taylor and Chris Ingraham, eds., *LEGOfied: Building Blocks as Media* (New York: Bloomsbury, 2020); and Mark J. P. Wolf, ed., *LEGO Studies: Examining the Building Blocks of a Transmedia Phenomenon* (New York: Routledge, 2014). See also de Bruin-Molé, "'Does It Come with a Spear?'" discussed in chapter 2.

5. Bak, *Playful Visions*; Nicola Dulac and André Gaudreault, "Circularity and Repetition at the Heart of the Attraction: Optical Toys and the Emergence of a New Cultural Series," in *A Companion to Early Cinema*, ed. André Gaudreault, Nicolas Dulac, and Santiago Hidalgo (Chichester, UK: John Wiley, 2012), 227–244; Thomas Elsaesser,

"Early Film History and Multi-Media: An Archaeology of Possible Futures," in *New Media Old Media: A History and Theory Reader*, ed. Wendy Hui Kyong Chun and Thomas Keenan (New York: Routledge, 2006), 13–25; Tom Gunning, "An Aesthetic of Astonishment: Early Film and the (in)Credulous Spectator," in *The Cinema of Attractions Reloaded*, ed. Wanda Strauven (Amsterdam: University of Amsterdam Press, 2006), 114–133; Erkki Huhtamo and Jussi Parikka, eds. *Media Archaeology: Approaches, Applications, and Implications* (Berkeley: University of California Press, 2011); Wanda Strauven, "Early Cinema's Touch(able) Screens: From Uncle Josh to Ali Barbouyou," *NECSUS*, 2012, https://necsus-ejms.org/early-cinemas-touchable-screens-from-uncle-josh-to-ali-barbouyou/; Wanda Strauven, *Touchscreen Archaeology: Tracing Histories of Hands-On Media Practices* (Lüneberg: meson press, 2021); Nicholas J. Wade, "Philosophical Instruments and Toys: Optical Devices Extending the Art of Seeing," *Journal of the History of Neurosciences* 13, no. 1 (2004): 102–124; Christopher Williams, *Cinema: The Beginnings and the Future* (London: University of Westminster Press, 1996).

6. David Forgacs, "Disney Animation and the Business of Childhood," *Screen* 33, no. 3 (1992): 361–364.

7. Von Boehn, *Dolls and Puppets*, 295.

8. Fleming, *Powerplay*, 83–84.

9. Stig Hjarvard, "From Bricks to Bytes: The Mediatization of a Global Toy Industry," in *European Culture and the Media*, ed. Ib Bondebjerg and Peter Golding (Bristol: Intellect Press, 2004), 43–64.

10. Fraser, *History of Toys*.

11. For a detailed study, see Kline, *Out of the Garden*.

12. Of course, not all children live in households with the space or resources for extensive toy play. But given the relatively inexpensive nature of many toys today, this scenario is more prevalent than at any earlier historical moment.

13. Meredith A. Bak, "The Ludic Archive: The Work of Playing with Optical Toys," *The Moving Image*, 16, no. 1 (2016): 13.

14. Mulvey, *Fetishism and Curiosity*.

15. See, for instance, Baudelaire's description of a phenakistoscope that articulates preternatural wonder and technical and perceptual investigation, unencumbered by the knowledge of cinema to come. Baudelaire, "Philosophy of Toys," 21–22.

16. Jean-Louis Comolli, "Machines of the Visible," in *The Cinematic Apparatus*, ed. Teresa de Lauretis and Stephen Heath (London: Palgrave Macmillan, 1980), 121.

17. Comolli, "Machines of the Visible," 140.

18. Comolli, "Machines of the Visible," 123.

19. Jussi Parikka, *What Is Media Archaeology?* (Cambridge: Polity Press, 2012), 10.

20. The game is based on the 1976 remake, not the 1933 original. Paramount, dir. John Guillermin.

21. *Ben Hur*, MGM, dir. William Wyler, 1959.

22. The notion of board and tabletop games as a simulational media form is developed in more depth in chapter 3. In 2005, the Lionhead videogame developers released a Hollywood-themed simulation game, *The Movies*.

23. Von Boehn, *Dolls and Puppets*, 156.

24. Von Boehn, *Dolls and Puppets*, 293.

25. See chapter 4.

26. Jacqueline Reid-Walsh, "'Everything in the Picture Book Was Alive': Hans Christian Andersen's Strategy of Textual Animation in His Fairy Tales and the Interactive Child Reader," in *Hans Christian Andersen Between Children's Literature and Adult Literature*, ed. Johan de Myllius, Aage Jørgenson, and Viggo Hørnagen Pedersen (Odense: University Press of Southern Denmark, 2007), 284.

27. Field, *Playing with the Book*, 153–181.

28. Disney's multiplane camera technique, which added depth effects to the previously shallow pictorial space of cel animation (see *Snow White and the Seven Dwarves*, 1938), uses very similar visual, perceptual, and technical principles to the peep show and toy theatre. See Mark Langer, "The Disney-Fleischer Method: Product Differentiation and Technological Innovation," *Screen* 33, no. 4 (1992): 343–360.

29. Olive Cook, *Movement in Two Dimensions: A Study of the Animated and Projected Pictures which Preceded the Invention of Cinematography* (London: Hutchinson, 1963).

30. A visitor to the gift shop of any science museum or visitor center today will find kaleidoscopes and kits to make thaumatropes and zoetropes alongside more recent technological toys such as robots, chemistry sets, dinosaurs, and space-themed toys and clothing.

31. Comolli, "Machines of the Visible."

32. Before CGI animation, simply, the fewer the drawings needed, the lower the cost in production. For instance, Japanese *anime*, but also the static backgrounds of American cel animation, from Disney feature films to Hanna-Barbera TV cartoons.

33. Erkki Huhtamo, "Toward a History of Peep Practice," in *A Companion to Early Cinema*, ed. André Gaudreault and Nicolas Dulac (Chichester, UK: John Wiley, 2012), 32–51. See also Laurent Mannoni, Werner Nekes, and Marina Warner, *Eyes, Lies and Illusions* (London: Hayward Gallery, 2004); and Stafford, *Artful Science*.

34. Fraser, *History of Toys*, 78.

35. Fraser, *History of Toys*, 82.

36. Huhtamo, "Peep Practice," 35.

37. The museum catalogue lists it as of US origin, but it is undated. I would guess from the style of the cartoon imagery and the depiction of an orchestra under the screen that is from the silent era and 1920s.

38. Phenomenology-inspired film studies has produced rich conceptualizations of the tactile attributes of theatrical cinema and the relationships between the visual and the haptic in cinema spectatorship. See Laura U. Marks, *Touch: Sensory Theory and Multisensory Media* (Minneapolis: University of Minnesota Press, 2002); Vivian Sobchack, *Carnal Thoughts: Embodiment and Moving Image Culture* (Berkeley: University of California Press, 2004).

39. Parikka, *What Is Media Archaeology?* 28.

40. Parikka, *What Is Media Archaeology?* 28.

41. Teresa de Lauretis and Stephen Heath, eds., *The Cinematic Apparatus* (London: Palgrave Macmillan, 1980).

42. Wanda Strauven, "The (Noisy) Praxis of Media Archaeology," in *At the Borders of (Film) History: Temporality, Archaeology, Theories*, ed. Alberto Bertrame, Giuseppe Fidotta, and Andrea Mariani (Udine, Italy: University of Udine, 2014), 33–42. See also Strauven, *Touchscreen Archaeology.*

43. Wanda Strauven, "The Observer's Dilemma: To Touch or Not to Touch," in *Media Archaeology: Approaches, Applications, and Implications*, ed. Erkki Huhtamo and Jussi Parikka (Berkeley: University of California Press, 2011), 148–163; Strauven, *Touchscreen Archaeology.*

44. Strauven, "Observer's Dilemma," 152.

45. Dulac and Gaureault, quoted in Strauven, "Observer's Dilemma," 153.

46. Strauven also connects her archaeology of mediated tactility to contemporary "hacking" and "making" cultures as a postdigital reemphasis on the hands-on manipulation, experimentation, and construction. "Making" in this sense is a markedly toyetic process, not the fabrication of instrumental objects but toylike gadgets (or actual toys), sharing a spirit as well as terminology with the computer hackers of the 1950s and 1960s.

Chapter 7

1. As such, they are distinct (conceptually and heuristically but not materially) from other models of syncretic relationality, notably the "network" in actor-network theory, media environments/ecologies, or Deleuze and Guattari's notion of the machinic.

2. Sara Grimes, *Digital Playgrounds.*

3. There is extensive scholarly work on digital games, networked play, and new playful platforms through social media and mobile games and apps. See, for example, Victoria Carrington and Clare Dowdall, "'This Is a Job for Hazmat Guy!' Global Media Culture and Children's Everyday Lives," in *The International Handbook of Research on Children's Literacy*, ed. Kathy Hall, Teresa Cremin, Barbara Comber, and Luis C. Moll (Oxford: John Wiley, 2013), 96–109; Grimes, *Digital Playgrounds*; Matt Hills, "LEGO Dimensions Meets Doctor Who: 8–29; Larissa Hjorth et al., *Exploring Minecraft: Ethnographies of Play and Creativity* (New York: Palgrave Macmillan, 2020); Mascheroni and Holloway, *The Internet of Toys*; Bjorn Nansen, *Young Children and Mobile Media: Producing Digital Dexterity* (Cham, Switzerland: Palgrave Macmillan, 2020); Thomas Poell, David Nieborg, and Brooke Erin Duffy, *Platforms and Cultural Production* (London: Polity Press, 2021); Tyni et al., "Hybrid Playful Experiences."

4. Theo Van Leeuwen, "The World According to Playmobil," *Semiotica* 173, no. 1–4 (2009): 299–315.

5. Benjamin Nicoll and Bjorn Nansen, "Mimetic Production in YouTube Toy Unboxing Videos," *Social Media and Society* (2018): 1–12. https://doi.org/10.1177/25305118790761.

6. For example, the American Ryan Kaji began presenting toy unboxing videos when he was four years old. An early video of his, of the opening of a large egg containing numerous toys, has more than a billion views. In 2018, he was the highest earning YouTube influencer, earning more than GBP17 million from his own TV show and partnerships with toy manufacturers. Charlie Jones, "Should Children Watch Toy Unboxing Videos?" *BBC News*, 2018, https://www.bbc.co.uk/news/uk-england-beds-bucks-herts-49975644#.

7. Stewart, *On Longing*.

8. Grimes, *Digital Playgrounds*; Maikke Lauwaert, "Playing Outside the Box: On LEGO Toys and the Changing World of Construction Play," *History and Technology* 24, no. 3 (2008): 221–237.

9. For example, Roland Barthes on wooden toys, in *Mythologies*.

10. Zimmerman and Chaplin, "Manifesto"; de Lange et al., *Playful Identities*; Tyni and Sotamaa, "Material Culture," 28.

11. Ashton and Giddings. "At Work in the Toybox."

12. Grimes, *Digital Playgrounds*, 265.

13. Quoted in Fleming, *Powerplay*, 32.

14. However, note that Jean Baudrillard places the emergence of simulacral culture in Europe in the Renaissance period, with the waning of the fixed universe

of medieval Christianity and the rise of fashion in clothing and architecture. Jean Baudrillard, *Symbolic Exchange and Death* (London: Sage, 2016).

15. "Simulacra are like false claimants, built on a dissimilitude, implying a perversion, an essential turning away. It is in this sense that Plato divided the domain of the image idols in two: on the one hand, the iconic copies (likenesses); on the other, the phantasmic simulacra (semblances). It is a question of ensuring the triumph of the copies over the simulacra, of repressing the simulacra." Deleuze, "Plato and the Simulacrum," 47–48.

16. Deleuze, "Plato and the Simulacrum," 53. See also Giddings, "Dionysiac Machines," for an exploration of videogame simulacra via this argument.

17. Gombrich, *Meditations on a Hobby Horse*, 2.

Bibliography

Allison, Anne. "Cuteness as Japan's Millennial Product." In *Pikachu's Global Adventure: The Rise and Fall of Pokémon*, edited by Joseph Tobin, 34–52. Durham, NC: Duke University Press, 2004.

Allison, Anne. *Millennial Monsters: Japanese Toys and the Global Imagination*. Berkeley: University of California Press, 2006.

Alvis, Jose A. Muñoz. "Through a Technique of Building." *Icon* 23 (2017): 83–112.

Apperley, Thomas, and Nichole Heber. "Capitalizing on Emotions: Digital Pets and the Natural User Interface." In *Game Love: Essays on Play and Affection*, edited by Jessica Enevold and Esther Macallum-Stewart, 149–161. Jefferson, NC: McFarland, 2015.

Apperley, Thomas, Bjorn Nansen, and Darshana Jayemanne. "Postdigital Play and the Aesthetics of Recruitment," 2015. http://www.digra.org/digital-library/publications/postdigital-play-and-the-aesthetics-of-recruitment/.

Armitage, Natalie. "European and African Figural Ritual Magic: The Beginnings of the Voodoo Doll Myth." In *The Materiality of Magic: An Artifactual Investigation into Ritual Practices and Popular Beliefs*, edited by Ceri Houlbrook and Natalie Armitage, 85–101. Oxford: Oxbow Books, 2015.

Ashton, Daniel, and Seth Giddings. "At Work in the Toybox: Bedrooms, Playgrounds and Ideas of Play in Creative Cultural Work." *International Journal of Entrepreneurship and Innovation* 19, no. 2 (2018): 81–89.

Attfield, Judy. "Barbie and Action Man: Adult Toys for Girls and Boys, 1959–93." In *The Gendered Object*, edited by Pat Kirkham, 80–89. Manchester: Manchester University Press, 1996.

Bak, Meredith A. "Between Technology and Toy: The Talking Doll as Abject Artifact." In *Abjection Incorporated: Mediating the Politics of Pleasure and Violence*, edited by Maggie Hennefeld and Nicholas Sammond, 164–184. Durham, NC: Duke University Press, 2020.

Bak, Meredith A. "Building Blocks of the Imagination: Children, Creativity, and the Limits of Disney Infinity." *The Velvet Light Trap* 78 (2016): 53.

Bak, Meredith A. *Playful Visions: Optical Toys and the Emergence of Children's Media Culture*. Cambridge, MA: MIT Press, 2020.

Bak, Meredith A. "The Ludic Archive: The Work of Playing with Optical Toys." *The Moving Image* 16, no. 1 (2016): 1–16.

Barnard, Robert, and Louise Barnard. *A Brontë Encyclopedia*. Malden, MA: Blackwell, 2007.

Barthes, Roland. *Mythologies*. London: Paladin Books, 1973 [1957].

Bartlett, Marigold. "So, What Exactly Is Roblox?" *Medium* (blog), March 18, 2021. https://ghosttowngoldie.medium.com/so-what-exactly-is-roblox-3bfcdf2d6a2.

Basalla, George. *The Evolution of Technology*. Cambridge: Cambridge University Press, 1988.

Bateson, Gregory. *Steps to an Ecology of Mind: A Revolutionary Approach to Man's Understanding of Himself*. New York: Ballantine Books, 1972.

Baudelaire, Charles. *Baudelaire: The Poems in Prose*, Vol. II. London: Anvil Press, 1989.

Baudelaire, Charles. "The Philosophy of Toys." In *Essays on Dolls*, edited by Idris Parry, 13–30. London: Penguin/Syrens, 1994 [1853].

Baudrillard, Jean. *Simulations*. New York: Semiotext(e), 1983.

Baudrillard, Jean. *Symbolic Exchange and Death*. London: Sage, 2016.

Benjamin, Walter. *Selected Writings/Walter Benjamin*. Edited by Michael W. Jennings, Howard Eiland, and Gary Smith. Cambridge, MA: Harvard University Press, 1999.

Benjamin, Walter. *Walter Benjamin: Selected Writings, Volume 2: Part 1: 1927–1930*. Cambridge, MA: Belknap Press of Harvard University Press, 2005.

Bloch, Linda Renée, and Dafna Lemish. "Disposable Love: The Rise and Fall of a Virtual Pet." *New Media and Society* 1, no. 3 (1999): 283–303.

Boehn, Max von. *Dolls and Puppets*. Redditch, UK: Read Books, 2010 [1932].

Bogost, Ian. *Persuasive Games: The Expressive Power of Videogames*. Cambridge, MA: MIT Press, 2007.

Bolter, Jay David, and Richard Grusin. *Remediation: Understanding New Media*. Cambridge, MA: MIT Press, 1999.

Brandow-Faller, Megan, ed. *Childhood by Design: Toys and the Material Culture of Childhood*. New York: Bloomsbury, 2018.

Brosterman, Norman. "Potential Architecture: An Infinity of Buildings." In *Potential Architecture: Construction Toys from the CCA Collection*, 7–14. Montreal: Centre Canadien d'Architecture, 1991.

Brougère, Gilles. "Toy Houses: A Socio-Anthropological Approach to Analysing Objects." *Visual Communication* 5, no. 5 (2006): 5–24.

Bruin-Molé, Megen de. "'Does It Come with a Spear?' Commodity Activism, Plastic Representation, and Transmedia Story Strategies in Disney's *Star Wars: Forces of Destiny.*" *Film and Merchandise* 42, no. 2 (2018).

Bruner, Jerome S., Alison Jolly, and Kathy Sylva, eds. *Play: Its Role in Development and Evolution.* London: Pelican, 1976.

Butler, Sarah. "How Games Workshop Grew to Be More Profitable than Google." *The Guardian*, July 31, 2021. https://www.theguardian.com/lifeandstyle/2021/jul/31/how-games-workshop-grew-to-become-more-profitable-than-google.

Butler, Sarah. "Warhammer Maker Games Workshop Hands Staff £5,000 Bonus after Lockdown Sales Surge." *The Guardian*, July 27, 2021. https://www.theguardian.com/business/2021/jul/27/warhammer-maker-games-workshop-hands-staff-5000-bonus-after-lockdown-sales-surge.

Caillois, Roger. *Man, Play and Games.* Urbana: University of Illinois Press, 2001 [1962].

Carrington, Victoria, and Clare Dowdall. "'This Is a Job for Hazmat Guy!': Global Media Cultures and Children's Everyday Lives." In *International Handbook of Research on Children's Literacy, Learning, and Culture*, edited by Kathy Hall, Teresa Cremin, Barbara Comber, and Luis C. Moll, 96–109. Oxford: John Wiley, 2013.

Carter, Marcus, Martin Gibbs, and Mitchell Harrop. "Drafting an Army: The Playful Pastime of Warhammer 40,000." *Games and Culture* 9, no. 2 (2014): 122–147.

Carter, Marcus, Mitchell Harrop, and Martin Gibbs. "The Roll of the Dice in Warhammer 40,000." *Transactions of the Digital Games Research Association* 1, no. 3 (2014). http://todigra.org/index.php/todigra/article/view/20.

Carter, Marcus, and Jane Mavoa. "Why Is Kids' Video Game Roblox Worth $38 Billion and What Do Parents Need to Know?" *The Conversation*, March 17, 2021. https://theconversation.com/why-is-kids-video-game-roblox-worth-38-billion-and-what-do-parents-need-to-know-157133.

Chapman, Adam. "Playing the Historical Fantastic: Zombies, Mecha-Nazis and Making Meaning about the Past through Metaphor." In *War Games: Memory, Militarism and the Subject of Play*, edited by Philip Hammond and Holger Pötzsch, 91–111. New York: Bloomsbury, 2020.

Comolli, Jean-Louis. "Machines of the Visible." In *The Cinematic Apparatus*, edited by Teresa de Lauretis and Stephen Heath, 121–142. London: Palgrave Macmillan, 1980.

Cook, Olive. *Movement in Two Dimensions: A Study of the Animated and Projected Pictures which Preceded the Invention of Cinematography*. London: Hutchinson, 1963.

Cook, Roy T., and Sondra Bacharach, eds. *LEGO and Philosophy: Constructing Reality Brick by Brick*. Minneapolis: University of Minnesota Press, 2017.

Crogan, Patrick. *Gameplay Mode: War, Simulation, and Technology*. Minneapolis: University of Minnesota Press, 2011.

Crogan, Patrick. "Wargaming and Computer Games: Fun with the Future." In *Proceedings of the 2003 DiGRA International Conference: Level Up*, 2003. http://www.digra.org/wp-content/uploads/digital-library/05163.52183.pdf.

Cross, Gary. *Kids' Stuff: Toys and the Changing World of American Childhood*. Cambridge, MA: Harvard University Press, 1997.

Deleuze, Gilles. "Plato and the Simulacrum." *October* 27 (1983): 45–56.

Devlin, Kate. *Turned On: Science, Sex and Robots*. London: Bloomsbury, 2018.

Dixon, Shanly, and Sandra Weber. "Playspaces, Childhood, and Videogames." In *Growing Up Online: Young People and Digital Technologies*, edited by Sandra Weber and Shanly Dixon, 15–34. New York: Palgrave Macmillan, 2007.

Dourish, Paul. *Where the Action Is: The Foundations of Embodied Interaction*. 1st ed. Cambridge, MA: MIT Press, 2004.

Driscoll, Catherine. "Girl-Doll: Barbie as Puberty Manual." In *Seven Going on Seventeen*, edited by Claudia Mitchell and Jacqueline Reid-Walsh, 217–233. New York: Peter Lang, 2005.

Driscoll, Catherine. "The Doll-Machine: Dolls, Modernism, Experience." In *Dolls Studies: The Many Meanings of Girls' Toys and Play*, edited by Miriam Forman-Brunell and Jennifer Dawn Whitney, 185–204. New York: Peter Lang, 2015.

Dulac, Nicolas, and André Gaudreault. "Circularity and Repetition at the Heart of the Attraction: Optical Toys and the Emergence of a New Cultural Series." In *A Companion to Early Cinema*, edited by André Gaudreault, Nicolas Dulac, and Santiago Hidalgo, 227–244. Chichester, UK: John Wiley, 2012.

Dunne, Anthony, and Fiona Raby. *Speculative Everything: Design, Fiction, and Social Dreaming*. Cambridge, MA: MIT Press, 2013.

Eco, Umberto. *Travels in Hyperreality*. London: Mariner Books, 2014 [1986].

Ekholm, Gordon F. "Wheeled Toys in Mexico." *American Antiquity* 11, no. 4 (1946): 222–228.

Elderkin, Kate. "Jointed Dolls in Antiquity." *American Journal of Archaeology* 34, no. 4 (1930): 455–479.

Elsaesser, Thomas. "Early Film History and Multi-Media: An Archaeology of Possible Futures?" In *New Media Old Media: A History and Theory Reader*, edited by Wendy Hui Kyong Chun and Thomas Keenan, 13–25. New York: Routledge, 2006.

Fanning, Colin. "Building Kids: LEGO and the Commodification of Creativity." In *Childhood by Design: Toys and the Material Culture of Childhood, 1700–Present*, edited by Megan Brandow-Faller, 89–109. New York: Bloomsbury, 2018.

Fennetaux, Ariane. "Transitional Pandoras: Dolls in the Long Eighteenth Century." In *Childhood by Design: Toys and the Material Culture of Childhood, 1700–Present*, edited by Megan Brandow-Faller, 47–66. New York: Bloomsbury, 2018.

Fenton, Louise. "A Tale of Two Poppets." *The Enquiring Eye: Journal of the Museum of Witchcraft and Magic* 3 (2020): 1–4.

Field, Hannah. *Playing with the Book: Victorian Movable Picture Books and the Child Reader*. Minneapolis: University of Minnesota Press, 2019.

Fizek, Sonia. "Interpassivity and the Joy of Delegated Play in Idle Games." *Transactions of the Digital Games Research Association* 3, no. 3 (2018). http://todigra.org/index.php/todigra/article/view/81.

Fleming, Dan. *Powerplay: Children, Toys and Popular Culture*. Manchester: Manchester University Press, 1996.

Flusser, Vilém. *The Shape of Things: A Philosophy of Design*. London: Reaktion Books, 1999.

Foley, John A. "Combat Commander: Time to Throw Your Plan Away." In *Zones of Control: Perspectives on Wargaming*, edited by Pat Harrigan and Matthew G. Kirschenbaum, 121–132. Cambridge, MA: MIT Press, 2016.

Forgacs, David. "Disney Animation and the Business of Childhood." *Screen* 33, no. 4 (1992): 361–374.

Forman-Brunell, Miriam, and Jennifer Dawn Whitney, eds. *Doll Studies: The Many Meanings of Girls' Toys and Play*. New York: Peter Lang, 2015.

Fraser, Antonia. *A History of Toys*. London: Weidenfeld & Nicolson, 1966.

Frazer, J. G. *The Golden Bough*. Oxford: Oxford University Press, 2009.

Freud, Sigmund. *The Uncanny*. London: Penguin Books, 2003.

Friedman, Alice T. "Model Homes and Dream Houses." In *Dream Houses, Toy Homes*, 7–28. Montreal: Centre Canadien d'Architecture, 1995.

Gauntlett, David. "The LEGO System as a Tool for Thinking, Creativity, and Changing the World." In *LEGO Studies: Examining the Building Blocks of a Transmedia Phenomenon*, edited by Mark J. P. Wolf, 189–205. New York: Routledge, 2014.

Gibson, William. *Neuromancer*. London: Gollancz, 1984.

Giddings, Seth. "Accursed Play: The Economic Imaginary of Early Game Studies." *Games and Culture: A Journal of Interactive Media* 13, no. 7 (2018): 765–783.

Giddings, Seth. "Bright Bricks, Dark Play: On the Impossibility of Studying LEGO." In *LEGO Studies: Examining the Building Blocks of a Transmedia Phenomenon*, edited by Mark J. P. Wolf, 241–267. New York: Routledge, 2014.

Giddings, Seth. "Dionysiac Machines: Videogames and the Triumph of the Simulacra." *Convergence: The International Journal of Research into New Media Technologies* 13, no. 4 (2007): 417–431.

Giddings, Seth. "Events and Collusions: A Glossary for the Microethnography of Videogames." *Games and Culture* 4, no. 2 (2009): 144–157.

Giddings, Seth. *Gameworlds: Virtual Media and Children's Everyday Play*. New York: Bloomsbury, 2014.

Giddings, Seth. ""I'm the One Who Makes the LEGO Racers Go": Studying Virtual and Actual Play." In *Growing Up Online: Young People and Digital Technologies*, edited by Sandra Weber and Shanly Dixon, 35–48. New York: Palgrave Macmillan, 2007.

Giddings, Seth. "Playing with Nonhumans: Digital Games as Technocultural Form." In *Worlds in Play: International Perspectives on Digital Games Research*, edited by Suzanne de Castell and Jen Jenson, 115–128. New York: Peter Lang, 2007.

Giddings, Seth. "Pokémon Go and Distributed Imagination." *Mobile Media and Communication* 5, no. 1 (2017): 59–62.

Giddings, Seth. "The History of Games Could Be a History of Technology." *ROMchip: A Journal of Game Histories* 1, no. 1 (2019). https://www.romchip.org/index.php /romchip-journal/article/view/74.

Giddings, Seth, ed. *The New Media and Technocultures Reader*. London: Routledge, 2011.

Giroux, Henry. *The Mouse that Roared: Disney and the End of Innocence*. Oxford: Rowman & Littlefield, 1999.

Goggin, Joyce. ""How Do Those Danish Bastards Sleep at Night?" Fan Labor and the Power of Cuteness." *Games and Culture* 13, no. 7 (2018): 747–764.

Goldstein, Jeffrey, ed. *Toys, Play, and Child Development*. New York: Cambridge University Press, 1994.

Goldstein, Jeffrey, David Buckingham, and Gilles Brougère, eds. *Toys, Games, and Media*. Mahwah, NJ: Lawrence Erlbaum, 2004.

Gombrich, Ernst H. *Meditations on a Hobby Horse*. Chicago: University of Chicago Press, 1985 [1951].

Grimes, Sarah. *Digital Playgrounds: The Hidden Politics of Children's Online Play Spaces, Virtual Worlds, and Connected Games*. Toronto: University of Toronto Press, 2021.

Grimes, Sarah. "I'm a Barbie Girl, in a BarbieGirls World." *Escapist Magazine*, 2008, 165 edition. https://www.escapistmagazine.com/im-a-barbie-girl-in-a-barbiegirls-world/.

Guattari, Félix. "Balance Program for Desiring Machines." In *The New Media and Technocultures Reader*, edited by Seth Giddings, 129–138. London: Routledge, 2011.

Gunning, Tom. "An Aesthetic of Astonishment: Early Film and the (in)Credulous Spectator." In *The Cinema of Attractions Reloaded*, edited by Wanda Strauven, 114–133. Amsterdam: University of Amsterdam Press, 2006.

Gunning, Tom. "The Cinema of Attraction: Early Film, the Spectator and the Avant Garde." *Wide Angle* 8, no. 3 (1986): 63–70.

Hains, Rebecca C., and Sharon R. Mazzarella, eds. *Cultural Studies of LEGO: More than Just Bricks*. Cham, Switzerland: Palgrave Macmillan, 2019.

Hammond, Philip, and Holger Pötzsch, eds. *War Games: Memory, Militarism and the Subject of Play*. New York: Bloomsbury, 2021.

Haraway, Donna J. "A Manifesto for Cyborgs: Science, Technology, and Socialist-Feminism in the Late Twentieth Century." In *Feminism/Postmodernism*, edited by L. J. Nicholson, 190–234. London: Routledge, 1991.

Harrigan, Pat, and Matthew G. Kirschenbaum, eds. *Zones of Control: Perspectives on Wargaming*. Cambridge, MA: MIT Press, 2016.

Hebdige, Dick. *Hiding in the Light: On Images and Things*. London: Routledge, 1988.

Heidegger, Martin. *The Question Concerning Technology and Other Essays*. New York: Garland, 1977 [1955].

Heljakka, Katriina. *Principles of Adult Play(fulness) in Contemporary Toy Cultures: From Wow to Flow to Glow*. Aalto, Finland: School of Arts, Design and Architecture, 2017.

Hills, Matt. "LEGO Dimensions Meets Doctor Who: Transbranding and New Dimensions of Transmedia Storytelling?" *Icono* 14, no. 1 (2015): 8–29.

Hilu, Reem. "Girl Talk and Girl Tech." *Velvet Light Trap: A Critical Journal of Film and Television* 78 (2016): 4–23.

Hjarvard, Stig. "From Bricks to Bytes: The Mediatization of a Global Toy Industry." In *European Culture and the Media*, edited by Ib Bondebjerg and Peter Golding, 43–64. Bristol: Intellect Press, 2004.

Hjorth, Larissa, and Ingrid Richardson. *Ambient Play*. Cambridge, MA: MIT Press, 2020.

Hjorth, Larissa, Ingrid Richardson, Hugh Davies, and William Balmford. *Exploring Minecraft: Ethnographies of Play and Creativity*. New York: Palgrave Macmillan, 2020.

Hooper, Rowan. "Wild Chimps Make Their Own 'Dolls.'" *New Scientist*, December 20, 2010.

Houlbrook, Ceri, and Natalie Armitage, eds. *The Materiality of Magic: An Artefactual Investigation into Ritual Practices and Popular Beliefs*. Oxford: Oxbow Books, 2015.

Huhtamo, Erkki. "An Archaeology of Mobile Media." *Exhibition Catalogue?*, 2004.

Huhtamo, Erkki. "From Kaleidoscopomaniac to Cybernerd." In *The New Media and Technocultures Reader*, edited by Seth Giddings, 62–69. London: Routledge, 2011.

Huhtamo, Erkki. "Toward a History of Peep Practice." In *A Companion to Early Cinema*, edited by André Gaudreault and Nicolas Dulac, 32–51. Chichester, UK: John Wiley, 2012.

Huhtamo, Erkki, and Jussi Parikka, eds. *Media Archaeology: Approaches, Applications, and Implications*. Berkeley: University of California Press, 2011.

Huizinga, Johan. *Homo Ludens: A Study of the Play Element in Culture*. Boston, MA: Beacon Press, 1986 [1938].

Hutchins, Edwin. *Cognition in the Wild*. Cambridge, MA: MIT Press, 1995.

IGN.com. "Top 100 Game Creators of All Time: Will Wright." *IGN* (blog), n.d. https://www.ign.com/top/game-creators/3.html.

Jameson, Fredric. *Postmodernism, or the Cultural Logic of Late Capitalism*. London: Verso Books, 1991.

Jentsch, Ernst. "On the Psychology of the Uncanny (1906)." *Angelaki* 2, no. 1 (1997): 7–16.

Jones, Charlie. "Should Children Watch Toy Unboxing Videos?" *BBC News*, 2018. https://www.bbc.co.uk/news/uk-england-beds-bucks-herts-49975644#.

Joplin, Norman. *Toy Soldiers: The Collector's Guide to Identifying, Enjoying, and Acquiring New and Vintage Toy Soldiers*. London: Quintet, 1994.

Keene, Melanie. "Noah's Ark-Aeology and Nineteenth Century Children." In *Pasts at Play: Childhood Encounters with History in British Culture, 1750–1914*, edited by Rachel Bryant Davies and Barbara Gribling, 25–47. Manchester: Manchester University Press, 2021.

Kerrison, Ruby. "News from the Archives: Noah's Ark—A Toy with Contemporary Relevance." *Winterbourne* (blog), 2020. https://www.winterbourne.org.uk/blog/2020/03/01/news-from-the-archives-noahs-ark-a-toy-with-contemporary-relevance/.

Kinder, Marsha. *Playing with Power in Movies, Television, and Video Games: From Muppet Babies to Teenage Mutant Ninja Turtles*. Berkeley: University of California Press, 1991.

Kirkham, Pat, ed. *The Gendered Object*. Manchester: Manchester University Press, 1996.

Kline, Stephen. *Out of the Garden: Toys, TV, and Children's Culture in the Age of Marketing*. New York: Verso Books, 1993.

Kline, Stephen, Nick Dyer-Witheford, and Greig de Peuter. *Digital Play: The Interaction of Technology, Culture, and Marketing*. Montreal: McGill-Queen's University Press, 2003.

Kritt, David. "Loving a Virtual Pet: Steps toward the Technological Erosion of Emotion." *Journal of American and Comparative Literatures* 23, no. 4 (2000): 81–87.

Kuznets, Lois. *When Toys Come Alive: Narratives of Animation, Metamorphosis, and Development*. New Haven, CT: Yale University Press, 1994.

Lachney, Michael. "Building the LEGO Classroom." In *LEGO Studies: Examining the Building Blocks of a Transmedia Phenomenon*, edited by Mark J. P. Wolf, 166–188. New York: Routledge, 2014.

Landay, Lori. "Myth Blocks: How LEGO Transmedia Configures and Remixes Mythic Structure in the Ninjago and Chima Themes." In *LEGO Studies: Examining the Building Blocks of a Transmedia Phenomenon*, edited by Mark J. P. Wolf, 55–80. New York: Routledge, 2014.

Lange, Michiel de, Joost Raessens, Valerie Frissen, Sybille Lammes, and Jos de Mul, eds. *Playful Identities: The Ludification of Digital Media Cultures*. Amsterdam: Amsterdam University Press, 2015.

Langer, Mark. "The Disney-Fleischer Method: Product Differentiation and Technological Innovation." *Screen* 33, no. 4 (1992): 343–360.

Lauretis, Teresa de, and Stephen Heath, eds. *The Cinematic Apparatus*. London: Palgrave Macmillan, 1980.

Lauwaert, Maaike. "Challenge Everything? Construction Play in Will Wright's SIMCITY." *Games and Culture* 2, no. 3 (2007): 194–212. https://doi.org/10.1177/1555412007306205.

Lauwaert, Maaike. "Playing Outside the Box: On LEGO Toys and the Changing World of Construction Play." *History and Technology* 24, no. 3 (2008): 221–237.

Lauwaert, Maaike. *The Place of Play: Toys and Digital Cultures*. Amsterdam: Amsterdam University Press, 2009.

Lee, Jonathan Rey. *Deconstructing LEGO: The Medium and Messages of LEGO Play*. Cham, Switzerland: Palgrave Macmillan, 2020.

Leslie, Esther, and Ursula Marx, eds. *Walter Benjamin's Archive: Images, Texts, Signs*. London: Verso Books, 2007.

Lévi-Strauss, Claude. *Tristes Tropiques*. London: Hutchinson, 1961.

Lister, Martin, Jon Dovey, Seth Giddings, Iain Grant, and Kieran Kelly. *New Media: A Critical Introduction*. London: Routledge, 2009.

Lowood, Henry. "War Engines: Wargames as Systems from the Tabletop to the Computer." In *Zones of Control: Perspectives on Wargaming*, edited by Pat Harrigan and Matthew G. Kirschenbaum, 83–106. Cambridge, MA: MIT Press, 2016.

MacGonigal, Jane. *Reality Is Broken: Why Games Make Us Better and How They Can Change the World*. London: Vintage, 2012.

Machin, David, and Theo Van Leeuwen. "Toys as Discourse: Children's War Toys and the War on Terror." *Critical Discourse Studies* 6, no. 1 (2009): 51–63.

Maddalena, Kate. "Palpable Pixels." In *LEGOfied: Building Blocks as Media*, edited by Nicholas Taylor and Chris Ingraham, 23–39. New York: Bloomsbury, 2020.

Mannoni, Laurent, Werner Nekes, and Marina Warner. *Eyes, Lies and Illusions*. London: Hayward Gallery, 2004.

Marks, Laura U. *Touch: Sensory Theory and Multisensory Media*. Minneapolis: University of Minnesota Press, 2002.

Marsh, Jackie. "The Internet of Toys: A Posthuman and Multimodal Analysis of Connected Play." *Teachers College Record* 119, no. 2 (2017). https://eprints.whiterose.ac.uk/113557/.

Marx, Karl. *Grundrisse: Foundations of the Critique of Political Economy*. London: Penguin Classics, 1993 [1858].

Mascheroni, Giovanna, and Donell Holloway, eds. *The Internet of Toys: Practices, Affordances, and the Political Economy of Children's Smart Play*. Cham, Switzerland: Palgrave Macmillan, 2019.

Mauss, Marcel. "Techniques of the Body." *Economics and Society* 2, no. 1 (1973 [1935]): 70–88.

Mayor, Adrienne. *Gods and Robots: Myths, Machines, and Ancient Dreams of Technology*. Princeton, NJ: Princeton University Press, 2018.

Mäyrä, Frans. "Little Evils: Subversive Uses of Children's Games." In *The Dark Side of Game Play: Controversial Issues in Playful Environments*, edited by Torill Elvira Mortensen, Jonas Linderoth, and Ashley M. L. Brown, 82–99. New York: Routledge, 2015. https://homepages.tuni.fi/frans.mayra/Little_Evils.pdf.

Meriläinen, Mikko, Jaakko Stenros, and Katriina Heljakka. "More than Wargaming: Exploring the Miniaturing Pastime." *Simulation and Gaming*, first published online June 2020.

Mertens, Detlef. "Playing at Modernity." In *Toys and the Modernist Tradition*, 7–16. Montreal: Centre Canadien d'Architecture, 1993.

Millar Fisher, Michelle. "Work Becomes Play: Toy Design, Creative Play, and Unlearning in the Bauhaus Legacy." In *Childhood by Design: Toys and the Material Culture of Childhood, 1700–Present*, edited by Megan Brandow-Faller, 153–172. New York: Bloomsbury, 2018.

Mulhearn, Deborah. "Role Models." *The Guardian*, May 30, 2001. https://www.theguardian.com/society/2001/may/30/shopping.toys.

Mulvey, Laura. *Fetishism and Curiosity*. London: BFI, 1996.

Musiał, Maciej. *Enchanting Robots: Intimacy, Magic, and Technology*. Cham, Switzerland: Palgrave Macmillan, 2019.

Nansen, Bjorn. *Young Children and Mobile Media: Producing Digital Dexterity*. Cham, Switzerland: Palgrave Macmillan, 2020.

Nansen, Bjorn, Thomas Apperley, and Benjamin Nicholl. "Postdigitality in Children's Crossmedia Play: A Case Study of Nintendo's Amiibo Figurines." In *The Internet of Toys: Practices, Affordances and the Political Economy of Children's Play*, edited by Giovanna Mascheroni and Donell Holloway, 89–108. Cham, Switzerland: Palgrave Macmillan, 2019.

Neely Hall, A. *Home-Made Toys for Girls and Boys*. Boston, MA: Lothrop, Lee & Shepard, 1915. https://www.gutenberg.org/files/41669/41669-h/41669-h.htm.

Nicoll, Benjamin, and Bjorn Nansen. "Mimetic Production in YouTube Toy Unboxing Videos." *Social Media and Society* (2018): 1–12. https://doi.org/10.1177/25305118790761.

Opie, Iona. *The People in the Playground*. Oxford: Oxford University Press, 1993.

Opie, Iona, and Peter Opie. *Children's Games with Things*. Oxford: Oxford University Press, 1997.

Opie, Iona, Peter Opie, and Brian Alderson. *The Treasures of Childhood: Books, Toys and Games from the Opie Collection*. New York: Arcade, 1989.

Parikka, Jussi. *What Is Media Archaeology?* Cambridge: Polity Press, 2012.

Parry, Idris, ed. *Essays on Dolls*. London: Syrens/Penguin, 1994.

Pearce, Celia. "Sims, Battlebots, Cellular Automata, God and Go: A Conversation with Will Wright." *Game Studies* 2, no. 1 (2002). http://www.gamestudies.org/0102/pearce.

Peterson, Jon. "A Game Out of All Proportions: How a Hobby Miniaturized War." In *Zones of Control: Perspectives on Wargaming*, edited by Pat Harrigan and Matthew G. Kirschenbaum, 3–32. Cambridge MA: MIT Press, 2016.

Poell, Thomas, David Nieborg, and Brooke Erin Duffy. *Platforms and Cultural Production*. London: Polity Press, 2021.

Pursell, Carroll. *From Playgrounds to PlayStation: The Interaction of Technology and Play*. Baltimore: Johns Hopkins University Press, 2015.

Rand, Erica. *Barbie's Queer Accessories*. Durham, NC: Duke University Press, 1995.

Reay, Emma. "Cute, Cuddly and Completely Crushable: Plushies as Avatars in Video Games." *Journal of Gaming and Virtual Worlds* 13, no. 2 (2021): 131–149.

Reid-Walsh, Jacqueline. "'Everything in the Picture Book Was Alive': Hans Christian Andersen's Strategy of Textual Animation in His Fairy Tales and the Interactive Child Reader." In *Hans Christian Andersen Between Children's Literature and Adult Literature*, edited by Johan de Myllius, Aage Jørgenson, and Viggo Hørnagen Pedersen, 275–289. Odense: University Press of Southern Denmark, 2007.

Reid-Walsh, Jacqueline. *Interactive Books: Playful Media before Pop-Ups*. New York: Routledge, 2018.

Reid-Walsh, Jacqueline, and Claudia Mitchell. "'Just a Doll?' Liberating Accounts of Barbie-Play." *The Review of Education/Pedagogy/Cultural Studies* 22, no. 2 (2000): 175–190.

Riskin, Jessica. "The Defecating Duck, or the Ambiguous Origins of Artificial Life." *Critical Inquiry* 29, no. 4 (2003): 599–633.

Riskin, Jessica. *The Restless Clock: A History of the Centuries-Long Argument over What Makes Living Things Tick*. Chicago: University of Chicago Press, 2016.

Ruckenstein, Minna. "Toying with the World: Children, Virtual Pets and the Value of Mobility." *Childhood* 17, no. 4 (2010): 500–513. https://doi.org/10.1177/0907568209352812.

Schut, Kevin. "The Virtualisation of LEGO." In *LEGO Studies: Examining the Building Blocks of a Transmedial Phenomenon*, edited by Mark J. P. Wolf, 227–240. New York: Routledge, 2014.

Schwarcz, H. Joseph. "Machine Animism in Modern Children's Literature." *Library Quarterly* 37, no. 1 (1967): 78–95.

Schwartz, Helen S. "When Barbie Dated G. I. Joe: Analyzing the Toys of the Early Cold War Era." *Material History Review* 45 (1997): 38–50.

Segel, Harold B. *Pinocchio's Progeny: Puppets, Marionettes, Automatons, and Robots in Modernist and Avant-Garde Drama*. Baltimore: Johns Hopkins University Press, 1995.

Sicart, Miguel. *Play Matters*. Cambridge, MA: MIT Press, 2014.

Simon, Bart, and Darren Wershler. "Childhood's End (or, We Have Never Been Modern, Except in Minecraft)." *Cultural Politics* 14, no. 3 (2018): 289–303.

Smith, Marquard. *The Erotic Doll: A Modern Fetish*. New Haven, CT: Yale University Press, 2013.

Smith, Marquard. "Why Are Dolls So Creepy?" *BBC Culture* (blog), December 1, 2014. https://www.bbc.com/culture/article/20141201-why-are-dolls-so-creepy.

Smithson, Peter. "Toy Towns . . . Cradles of Authenticity." In *Toy Town*, 7–14. Montreal: Centre Canadien d'Architecture, 1997.

Sobchack, Vivian. *Carnal Thoughts: Embodiment and Moving Image Culture*. Berkeley: University of California Press, 2004.

Stafford, Barbara Maria. *Artful Science: Enlightenment Entertainment and the Eclipse of Visual Education*. Cambridge, MA: MIT Press, 1999.

Stafford, Barbara Maria, and Frances Terpak. *Devices of Wonder: From the World in a Box to Images on a Screen*. Los Angeles: Getty Research Institute, 2001.

Steinberg, Shirley R., and Joe L. Kincheloe, eds. *Kinder-Culture: The Corporate Construction of Childhood*. Boulder, CO: Westview Press, 2011.

Stewart, Susan. *On Longing: Narratives of the Miniature, the Gigantic, the Souvenir*. Baltimore: Johns Hopkins University Press, 1993.

Strauven, Wanda. "Early Cinema's Touch(able) Screens: From Uncle Josh to Ali Barbouyou." *NECSUS*, 2012. https://necsus-ejms.org/early-cinemas-touchable-screens-from-uncle-josh-to-ali-barbouyou/.

Strauven, Wanda. "The (Noisy) Praxis of Media Archaeology." In *At the Borders of (Film) History: Temporality, Archaeology, Theories*, edited by Alberto Bertrame, Giuseppe Fidotta, and Andrea Mariani, 33–42. Udine, Italy: University of Udine, 2014.

Strauven, Wanda. "The Observer's Dilemma: To Touch or Not to Touch." In *Media Archaeology: Approaches, Applications, and Implications*, edited by Erkki Huhtamo and Jussi Parikka, 148–163. Berkeley: University of California Press, 2011.

Strauven, Wanda. *Touchscreen Archaeology: Tracing Histories of Hands-on Media Practices*. Lüneberg, Germany: meson press, 2021.

Sudnow, David. *Pilgrim in the Microworld*. London: Heinemann, 1983.

Suits, Bernard. *The Grasshopper: Games, Life, and Utopia*. Peterborough, UK: Broadview Press, 2005.

Sutton-Smith, Brian. *The Ambiguity of Play*. Cambridge, MA: Harvard University Press, 1997.

Sutton-Smith, Brian. "Does Play Prepare the Future?" In *Toys, Play, and Child Development*, edited by Jeffrey Goldstein, 143–144. Cambridge: Cambridge University Press, 1994.

Sutton-Smith, Brian. *Toys as Culture*. New York: Psychology Press, 1986.

Sweney, Mark. "Roblox Shares Surge 60% on First Day of Trading amid Lockdown Gaming Boom." *The Guardian*, March 10, 2021.

Taylor, Nicholas, and Chris Ingraham. "Clickable Media in a Plastic World." In *LEGOfied: Building Blocks as Media*, edited by Nicholas Taylor and Chris Ingraham, 1–19. New York: Bloomsbury, 2020.

Taylor, Nicholas, and Chris Ingraham, eds. *LEGOfied: Building Blocks as Media*. New York: Bloomsbury, 2020.

Thorpe, Simon Brann. *Toy Soldiers*. Stockport: Dewi Lewis, 2015.

Tiffany, Daniel. *Toy Medium: Materialism and Modern Lyric*. Berkeley: University of California Press, 2000.

Toffoletti, Kim. *Cyborgs and Barbie Dolls: Feminism, Popular Culture, and the Posthuman Body*. New York: I. B. Taurus, 2007.

Tomas, David. "Feedback and Cybernetics: Reimaging the Body in the Age of the Cyborg." In *The New Media and Technocultures Reader*, edited by Seth Giddings, 164–176. London: Routledge, 2011.

Truitt, E. R. *Medieval Robots: Magic, Mechanism, Nature and Art*. Philadelphia: University of Pennsylvania Press, 2015.

Truitt, E. R. "Preternatural Machines: Medieval Technology, Indistinguishable from Magic." *Aeon*, March 30, 2015. https://aeon.co/essays/medieval-technology-indistin guishable-from-magic.

Turing, Alan. "Computing Machinery and Intelligence." *Mind* 59 (1950): 433–460.

Turkle, Sherry. "Cyborg Babies and Cy-Dough-Plasm: Ideas About Self and Life in the Culture of Simulation." In *Cyborg Babies: From Techno-Sex to Techno-Tots*, edited by Robbie Davis-Floyd and Joseph Dumit, 317–329. New York: Routledge, 1998.

Turkle, Sherry. *Life on the Screen: Identity in the Age of the Internet*. London: Weidenfeld & Nicolson, 1996.

Turkle, Sherry. *The Second Self: Computers and the Human Spirit*. London: Granada, 1984.

Tyni, Heikki, Annakaisa Kultima, Kati Alha, Ville Kankainen, and Frans Mäyrä. "Hybrid Playful Experiences: Playing between Material and Digital." TRIM Research Reports. Tampere, Finland: Game Research Lab, University of Tampere, 2016. https://trepo.tuni .fi/bitstream/handle/10024/98900/hybrid_playful_experiences_2016.pdf?sequence=1.

Tyni, Heikki, Frans Mäyrä, and Annakaisa Kultima. "Dimensions of Hybrid in Playful Products." In *Proceedings of International Conference on Making Sense of Converging*

Media (AcademicMindTrek '13), 237–244. New York: Association for Computing Machinery. https://doi.org/10.1145/2523429.2523489.

Vale, Brenda, and Robert Vale. *Architecture on the Carpet: The Curious Tale of Construction Toys and the Genesis of Modern Buildings*. London: Thames & Hudson, 2013.

Van Leeuwen, Theo. "The World According to Playmobil." *Semiotica* 173, no. 1–4 (2009): 299–315.

Varney, Wendy. "Love in Toytown." *M/C Journal: A Journal of Media and Culture* 5, no. 6 (2002). http://journal.media-culture.org.au/0211/loveintotytown.php.

Vasseleu, Cathryn. "A Is for Animatics (Automata, Androids, and Animals)." In *Living with Cyberspace*, edited by John Armitage and Joanne Roberts, 83–91. London: Continuum, 2002.

Voskuhl, Adelheid. *Androids in the Enlightenment: Mechanics, Artisans, and Cultures of the Self*. Chicago: University of Chicago Press, 2013.

Wade, Nicholas J. "Philosophical Instruments and Toys: Optical Devices Extending the Art of Seeing." *Journal of the History of the Neurosciences* 13, no. 1 (2004): 102–124.

Walker, Ian. *City Gorged with Dreams: Surrealism and Documentary Photography in Interwar Paris*. Manchester: Manchester University Press, 2002.

Walter, Natasha. *Living Dolls: The Return of Sexism*. London: Hachette, 2010.

Walz, Steffen P., and Sebastian Deterding. *The Gameful World: Approaches, Issues, Applications*. Cambridge MA: MIT Press, 2015.

Warner, Marina. "Out of an Old Toy Chest." *Journal of Aesthetic Education* 43, no. 2 (2009): 3–18.

Wasko, Janet. "Children's Virtual Worlds: The Latest Commercialization of Children's Culture." In *Childhood and Consumer Culture*, edited by David Buckingham and Vebjørg Tingstad, 113–129. London: Palgrave Macmillan, 2010.

Wasko, Janet. *Understanding Disney: The Manufacture of Fantasy*. Malden, MA: Polity, 2001.

Weber, Sandra, and Dixon, eds. *Growing Up Online: Young People and Digital Technologies*. New York: Palgrave Macmillan, 2007.

Wegener-Spöhring, Gisela. "War Toys and Aggressive Play Scenes." In *Toys, Play, and Child Development*, edited by Jeffrey H. Goldstein, 85–109. Cambridge: Cambridge University Press, 1994.

Wegener-Spöhring, Gisela. "War Toys in the World of Fourth Graders: 1985 and 2002." In *Toys, Games, and Media*, edited by Jeffrey H. Goldstein, David Buckingham, and Gilles Brougère, 19–35. Mahwah, NJ: Lawrence Erlbaum, 2004.

Weiner, Norbert. *Cybernetics, or Control and Communication in the Animal and Machine.* Cambridge, MA: MIT Press, 2019 [1961].

Weiner, Norbert. "The First and Second Industrial Revolution (1950)." In *The New Media and Technocultures Reader*, edited by Seth Giddings, 8–18. London: Routledge, 2011.

Wells, H. G. *Little Wars and Floor Games (A Companion Piece to Little Wars).* Cirencester, UK: Echo Library, 2005.

Whitney, Jennifer Dawn. "'It's Barbie, Bitch!': Re-Reading the Doll through Nicki Minaj and Harajuku Barbie." In *Doll Studies: The Many Meanings of Girls' Toys and Play*, edited by Miriam Forman-Brunell and Jennifer Dawn Whitney, 85–102. New York: Peter Lang, 2015.

Willett, Rebekah. "Consuming Fashion and Producing Meaning through Online Paper Dolls." In *Growing Up Online: Young People and Digital Technologies*, edited by Sandra Weber and Shanly Dixon, 113–128. New York: Palgrave Macmillan, 2007.

Williams, Christopher, ed. *Cinema: The Beginnings and the Future.* London: University of Westminster Press, 1996.

Williams, Raymond. *Television, Technology and Cultural Form.* New York: Schocken Books, 1975.

Wilson, Andrew. *The Bomb and the Computer: Wargaming from Ancient Chinese Mapboard to Atomic Computer.* New York: Delacorte Press, 2014.

Winfield, Alan. *Robotics: A Very Short Introduction.* Oxford: Oxford University Press, 2012.

Winnicott, D. W. *Playing and Reality.* London: Routledge, 2005.

Wohlwend, Karen E., and Kylie Peppler. "Designing with Pink Technologies and Barbie Transmedia." In *Young Children, Pedagogy and the Arts*, edited by Felicity McArdle and Gail Boldt, 129–145. New York: Routledge, 2013.

Wolf, Mark J. P., ed. *LEGO Studies: Examining the Building Blocks of a Transmedial Phenomenon.* New York: Routledge, 2014.

Wood, Gaby. *Living Dolls: A Magical History of the Quest for Mechanical Life.* London: Faber & Faber, 2002.

Woodyer, Tara, and Sean Carter. "Domesticating the Geopolitical: Rethinking Popular Geopolitics through Play." *Geopolitics* 25, no. 5 (2020): 1050–1074.

Zimmerman, Eric, and Heather Chaplin. "Manifesto: The 21st Century Will Be Defined by Games." *Kotaku* (blog), 2013. https://kotaku.com/manifesto-the-21st-century-will -be-defined-by-games-1275355204.

Index